STET Again!

More Tricks of the Trade for Publications People

It was a dark and stormy night...

...outside the library of
Darlene Leverett

EEI PRESS

EEI Press
66 Canal Center Plaza, Suite 200
Alexandria, VA 22314-5507
Phone: 703-683-0683, Fax: 703-683-4915
books@eei-alex.com
http://www.eei-alex.com

EEI Press publishes other books on editorial topics. For a free catalog, call 800-683-8380. EEI Press books are available at quantity discounts for sales promotions, premiums, fund raising, and educational use. Please call or write to the address above for pricing information.

Library of Congress Cataloging-in-Publication Data

Stet again!: more tricks of the trade for publications people: selections from the Editorial eye.
        p.   cm.
    Includes index.
    ISBN 0-935012-20-6
    1. Editing.   I. Editorial eye.
PN162.S744   1996
808'.027--dc20   96-34410
                                                                        CIP

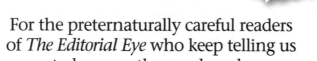

For the preternaturally careful readers
of *The Editorial Eye* who keep telling us
to keep up the good work.
You, too.

There are two ways of spreading light: to be
The candle or the mirror that reflects it.
—*Edith Wharton*

Acknowledgments

Stet Again! was entirely produced by the versatile EEI Communications Design, Editorial, and Production Services staff who create all EEI Press books. The editor is grateful to them:

> Davie Smith created the cover design and directed the art.
> Jennifer Whittington designed pages and was desktop publisher/production editor.
> Jean Spencer assembled and coded articles for the first draft.
> Jayne Sutton managed book production and also is one of the authors.
> Robin Cormier critiqued an early draft and also wrote many articles.
> Janis Hubbard and Martha Sencindiver prepared the index.
> The book was checked at different stages by several EEI proofreaders, notably Jeanne Nicholls, Lynn Burke, and Patricia Moran. Quality control specialist Patricia Caudill read the final draft and also is one of the authors.

Specs
This book was created in QuarkXPress 3.32, Adobe Photoshop 3.0, Macromedia FreeHand 5.5, and DeltaGraph Pro 3.5 on a PowerMac 8100/100. The fonts are Stone Serif for body text and Stone Sans and ITC Machine for display type. The paper is 60 # Woodlawn Opaque and the cover is 10 pt. Warrenflo with an aqueous dull coating. *Stet Again!* was printed by United Book Press, Inc., of Baltimore, MD.

The Editorial Eye Hall of Fame

Over the past eight years, it's been the editor's joy to work with these dedicated, irrepressible EEI contributing editors and writers, art directors, desktop publishing specialists, photographers, and editorial board members. They have all taken more than one turn at enriching *The Editorial Eye*, the newsletter for which the pieces in this book were originally written:

Ellie Abrams	Sherrel Hissong	Connie Moy	Elaine Sullivan
Diana Adams	Keith Ivey	Jane Rea	Andrea Sutcliffe
Patricia Caudill	Eleanor Johnson	Sharon Rogers	Jayne Sutton
Judy Cleary	Claire Kincaid	Carla Shaw	Priscilla Taylor
Robin Cormier	Amy Lenihan	Davie Smith	Jeanne Todd
Elisabeth Dahl	Lee Mickle	Sally Smith	Craig Tyler
Rick Darby	Dana Mitchell	Dianne Snyder	Diane Ullius
Cathy Dettmar	Ann Molpus	Jean Spencer	Jen Whittington
Steven Fleshman	June Morse	Mary Stoughton	Candee Wilson

Contents

The Craft of Editing   61

Usage and Grammar **127**

6

Publications Management and Trends 277

Preface

This is a new volume of *The Editorial Eye*'s "Greatest Hits"—a selection of original pieces from the subscription newsletter for professional writers, editors, designers, publications managers, and journalists. The previous edition (*Stet!*) concentrated on traditional editorial work as we knew it before 1990. That was then, this is now. Hence, *Stet Again!*

Many of the "rules" of the publications process have changed. The one thing we can count on is that technology won't stand still (though we might wish it would as it invades our comfort zone). It's making offers we can't refuse. Since there's no turning back, sources of continuing education are essential—that's what *The Eye* is here for. We know that the demand for talented writers, editors, designers, and publications managers isn't going to go away, but we'll have to do some homework if we want to keep our professional reflexes spry in the next millennium. The trick is to hold on to guidelines that still work well while adapting to new media and hybridized tasks.

Virtually anyone can be a "publisher," a "document" may never be produced on paper, "readability" is a term that applies to multimedia and World Wide Web screens, and "literacy" is knowing how to talk back to computers. Precisely because publishing is overrun with new definitions, *The Eye* honors the mission established by founding editor Laura Horowitz in 1978: to help define publishing excellence and offer resources for upholding it.

In that light, we selected some of the more thought-provoking, enduring articles and practical problem-solving features that *The Eye* published between 1990 and 1996. We've barely touched on evolving issues of electronic copyright, cross-training, and Web publishing. This book will probably look quaint in the year 2000; so what else is new? Consider *Stet Again!* a film-in-camera snapshot of a backlit moving target.

The authors are all veterans of real-world publishing skirmishes (biographical notes are on page 343). The other *Eye* contributors listed on page iv are witness to the truly collaborative nature of our newsletter publishing venture. Finally, on page iv we acknowledge the talented EEI people who created this book, in which we hope readers will find an indication of what's going on in our field these days and an inkling of what's to come.

—Linda B. Jorgensen
Editor

The Art
of Writing

Infected Prose

Bugs by the thousands are itching to infest our writing,
and antivirus software can't save us

Within every editor there's a sort of Howard Hughes on the lookout for infectious bugs—in our case, the bugs that threaten communication rather than the bloodstream. Like microbes, they fill the atmosphere; not just the catch phrases, sitcom babble, PC talk, and other such invasive pests, but the mechanical bugs—the errors, oversights, and breakdowns that lie in wait. All compete for a shot at our editorial well-being.

Of the mechanical group, computer viruses are among the latest to rattle our leukocytes. Just one infected disk, the fear-mongers warn us, and all our lovingly crafted and encoded pages collapse into a twitching heap of hacker graffiti.

For a while I tried an antivirus protection program because everyone in intimate contact with my disks jumped back and yelled, "Man, you got the *Stoned* virus!" My protection software, however, was the type that set off Gestapo sirens whenever it was on to something—and it was always on to something, no matter how innocent a disk I sneaked up the back stairs and into an A drive. So I removed the protection and have lived uneventfully with *Stoned*, which, as I understand it, will do no worse than inject a lively message into my text on an otherwise leaden afternoon.

Microbe-hunting among words

Oh, the energy we devote to such techno-problems as computer viruses! Applied to language, that energy could light up a whole readership; applied to software, it barely turns an eyeball. What about grammar checkers, designed to attack infestations of jargon and clichés? Mouthwashes in a plague. The big challenge is to *produce* writing—expressive writing—in control of its microbes. No software does it. No Twelve-Step Program to Bug-Free Prose comes forth, and, if it did, we'd need to cleanse it of its own infestations.

In trying to be expressive, many writers simply pick up expressions, including the facile pop phrases that tickled us at first but now lack originality and force. It's not easy to shake these cocci once they've entered the left cerebral hemisphere. Just try writing a page of text or even thinking for five minutes without echoing some of the goofy noises that assail us until we believe them to be the building blocks of communication. Lately I find myself driving through town babbling, "Mother of all intersections.... It's the right turn, baby, uh-huh!" Bugs are everywhere. Slogans.

Signs. Blurbs. Jingles. Talking T-shirts. Jockese. One-liners. I open a news-paper and like, a blown-up quote from Jennifer Capriati flies out and into my language: "When I look back on 1992, I'm kind of like, 'wow, what a waste.'"

Everywhere people are issuing statements, media bytes, that release more bugs. Managers are walking about swollen with head-of-state bom-bast: "...prolonged deliberations...deepest gravity...I have today ordered the...." E-mail is flying over the Internet, trailing clouds of cyberspeak and FTPing itself into my communications.

Corporate communiqués are klunking against my eardrums: "...identi-fy, develop, and implement training plan for internal and external oppor-tunities for career enhancement." Everyone is calling everything "great"—that endemic adjective, worming its way through our worm-eaten vocabularies. From the *New York Times,* May 4, 1993: "'Julio was a great brother, a great partner, and a great human being,' Ernest Gallo said in a statement. 'His passing is a great personal loss....'"

Good bugs, bad bugs

No one wants sterile, bug-free prose. Certain microorganisms and other bugs benefit human life, and terms that crawl in from the subcultures fer-tilize standard English. Resisting them categorically would be like Howard Hughes' dreading doorknobs and shunning fresh air. But how to distin-guish the good bugs from the bad? Always, the measures include audience tastes, timing (freshness), mix (balance), context (juxtaposition), and the symbolic values of the invading term. On the subject of borrowed jargon, Bruce O. Boston (*The Editorial Eye,* April 1992) describes another criterion, suggested by I.A. Richards: Does the communication gain *precision* from the borrowed language?

Leave in the bugs
that do more good than harm

Take the verb *morph,* identified in a recent *Editorial Eye* article as a sub-cultural contender for standard English. *To morph* is still a contagious in-vader to be watched carefully in its context. In "the task force morphed into a committee to tackle the job," the word seems an out-of-place irri-tant displacing the more accurate if less dynamic *reorganized.* But if I were writing for an audience of cyberpunks or if the context called for a verb denoting fluid, cartoonlike progression into a vastly different form, I might risk the word, even if it's joltingly out of tone with the subject. The jolt might boost the energy of the piece: "The task force morphed into Silly Putty at the first sign of opposition."

A bit of advice. On your first drafts or first rewrites, open the windows and let everything fly in. Too much initial screening invites creative block. Then, with the teeming mix of good and bad before you, pluck out anything that weakens your message. But leave the bugs that flourish in their new context, doing more good than harm. Your readers will appreciate the effort, which is considerable. Your manager, however, may fail to see the bubonic horrors in the drivel of the day—a notion that inspired the following specimen of infected prose:

TO: Editorial staff

FROM: Management

RE: Your worst nightmare

Management has this day declared complete and all-out war against originality in the editorial department. We are closing in on the needed resources to move forward on this challenge and are well positioned to harness the on-board leadership to see it through.

An in-your-face petulance has lately prevailed in the at-risk editorial offices, where right-sizing and a freeze on new hires has enabled the achievement of fiscal objectives. Central to the game plan is a body check on time-consuming originality. Paradigms for the full spectrum of editorial expression are now in stock and ready to roll. Outsourcing has already knocked the roof off runaway staff writing. Shall this management stand idly by while out-of-control wannabes put a negative spin on responsible leadership? NOT.

We have long labored to build a multiculturally abled, gender-neutral corps of staff persons. Shall we be marginalized by the shrill voices of a creative few? I don't think so. Excellent. Way! We stand at the threshold of an historic era. We are context-sensitive. Our tray tables are up, our seat backs are in the upright position. It's not about money. It's about staying power. And we intend to keep going and going and going....

Can you achieve potable prose on the first revision? No. Maybe by the fifth or sixth you've got a paragraph that won't make you ill when you read it in print. But fifth and sixth revisions are a luxury of creative writers, not usually an option for editors under the gun who may spend half the week doping out software. Such editors can only sharpen their juggling act, balancing audience needs, employer goals, tight deadlines, electronic exigencies, and a thirst for spring-fresh language.

Howard's end. Long before he hid from sight and let his fingernails grow, Howard Hughes juggled his divergent enterprises with an agility that confounded his enemies. The world's microbes, however, proved more than even he could take on, contributing to his demise. So, too, will the language bugs outlive us all, mutating and multiplying at astonishing rates. We must persevere in screening out the worst of them, if only to keep alive the language that stimulates hearts and minds. The trick is not to go buggy doing it.

—Arthur Plotnik

specialty/speciality

Several dictionaries say that both spellings are acceptable and that the words are synonyms, but most editors consider *specialty* to be the correct spelling for American audiences. *Speciality* is the preferred spelling in British English, though copywriters seem attracted to it, perhaps because it sounds like the French *specialité*.

But for those who want more than this simple rule of thumb, *American Heritage Dictionary*, third editon (*AHD*), gives first meanings to *speciality*—"a distinguishing mark or feature"—and the plural *specialities*—"special points of consideration, particulars"—that do not overlap with *specialty* at all. The third definition ends up by agreeing that *speciality* is British usage for *specialty*.

Specialty itself is treated quite separately. *AHD* refers us to *forte* (not *speciality*) as a synonym for it in the sense of "a special pursuit, occupation, aptitude, or skill." Other definitions relating to distinctiveness or superiority are offered along with *specialty*'s legal sense of "a special contract or agreement, especially a deed kept under seal."

In short, it's unlikely that *speciality* is the best choice in most contexts outside of Britain, no matter what your spell checker says. Now you know why.

When Less Is More:
Avoiding Repetitious Writing

When you're picking your battles, pick the one for tight prose

I recently had a call from a client to whom I had just returned an edited manuscript. She began, somewhat diffidently, "I have a question. Around the office we've been reviewing your work, and several of us re-member being taught in eighth-grade English class and even in college that you should never begin a sentence with *because*."

I answered, "And I'll bet you also remember being taught not to begin sentences with *and* or *but,* too."

"That's right," was the response. I could have gone on to the perils of split infinitives and other bugaboos. I do not intend to blame the English teachers of the world for what people choose to remember from their in-struction. But wouldn't it be great if those in a position to influence stu-dents' thought and writing—perhaps for a lifetime—concentrated on more important issues?

My candidates for being worthier of close attention are **repetition** and **verbosity** in writing, for I believe "less is more." It's more important to avoid these excesses than to buff antiquated points of grammar.

Pat Golbitz, a senior editor at William Morrow, said in *Editors on Editing,* second edition (HarperCollins, 1985), "Almost every manuscript im-proves with judicious cutting. It is the nature of many artists to be exces-sive...and the job of an editor is to keep the book within its natural bounds."

Also on this subject, writer Irwin Shaw once said, "The editors I had at *The New Yorker* quietly helped me in peculiar, small ways. One thing they taught me was the value of cutting out the last paragraph of stories, some-thing I pass down as a tip to all writers. The last paragraph in which you tell what the story is about is almost always best left out" (quoted in *The Writer's Chapbook*, ed. by George Plimpton, Viking, 1989).

Of course, good writers can break all the rules for effect, as E.B. White did in his essay "Dusk in Fierce Pajamas" (*Poems and Sketches of E.B. White,* Harper & Row, 1981), a satire on the gushy descriptions of celebrity settings in *Harper's Bazaar* and *Vogue,* which he was reduced to reading when he was a patient "ravaged by pinkeye." He begins, "It is dusk. (It is almost always dusk in the fashion magazines.)" Most subse-quent paragraphs begin, "It is dusk...," and some end that way too, until the last paragraph, which begins

All over the world it is dusk!... It is really dusk in my own apartment. I am down on my knees in front of an airbound radiator, trying to fix it by sticking pins in the vent. Dusk in these fierce pajamas....

Never cut the last paragraph of a writer such as E.B. White. But for most of the rest of us, quite a lot else is "best left out."

Writers also need to remember that a manuscript is substantially different from a speech. In a written text, unlike a speech, you usually do not need to tell your audience first what you're *going* to tell them, and you rarely need to summarize at the end what you've already *told* them. In fact, your audience will be impatient if you forget that any reader who feels the need can easily review the written word.

Here are a few other suggestions for avoiding repetitive writing:

- Don't say the same thing in two ways: "About one-third (34 percent)...."

- Don't say the same thing in several places. Look throughout a paragraph or manuscript for whole sentences that repeat what's already been said.

- Don't use "about" or "approximately" with "estimated": "The police estimated the crowd at about 400,000." And, of course, don't use "about" or "approximately" with a number that is exact: "about 11,483."

- Avoid vague, trendy words and terms. Here are some that spring to mind:

  ➤ "a more limited level of service" (more limited service); "raising levels of overall academic achievement" (raising overall academic achievement); "local-level government" (local government); and "traffic levels" (traffic)

  ➤ "in the area of education" (in education); "a problem area" (a problem); "in the American history field" (in American history)

  ➤ "an indictment involving six counts" (a six-count indictment)

  ➤ "including but not limited to" (including)

  ➤ "They shared their experiences in common." (They discussed their experiences.)

  ➤ "on the other hand" (but, however, conversely)

  ➤ "my sense is" (I think)

In short, if people developed the habit of making every word count, they would avoid finding themselves quoted on the front page of the *Washington Post* with a comment like this about a county supervisor's repeated absences from board meetings: "It's unfortunate that his attendance pattern is such that he's often not there."

—*Priscilla S. Taylor*

Breaking the Wordiness Habit

Remember what used to happen when we were assigned a 500-word writing assignment in English class? After diligently outlining, drafting, revising, and rewriting, we came to the end of what we had to say and we were still 73 words short and out of time. What did we do? We added "filler": *Beginnings* became *early beginnings, in Ohio* became *in the state of Ohio*, and *approximate* became *make an approximation of*. Unfortunately, the habit of wordiness can be hard to break. Can you cut the following fillers down to size?

1. in this day and age
2. it is incumbent on me
3. six in number
4. following after
5. 2 o'clock in the afternoon
6. for the price of $50
7. to the fullest possible extent
8. advance warning
9. in my personal opinion
10. enclosed herewith
11. merge together
12. bring to a conclusion
13. new innovation
14. past history
15. contained on
16. make an assumption that
17. it is recommended that consideration be given to
18. until such time as
19. on the occasion of
20. pursuant to our agreement
21. in view of the fact that, due to the fact that
22. of considerable magnitude
23. within the realm of possibility
24. oval in shape
25. refer back
26. for the purpose of explaining
27. in the not-too-distant future
28. one and the same
29. extend an invitation
30. give authorization for

ANSWERS

1. today or now
2. I must
3. six
4. after
5. 2:00 p.m.
6. for $50
7. fully
8. warning
9. in my opinion or I think
10. enclosed
11. merge
12. conclude
13. innovation
14. history
15. on
16. assume that
17. please consider
18. when, until
19. on, for, when
20. as we agreed
21. because, since
22. large
23. possible
24. oval
25. refer
26. to explain
27. soon, next week, tomorrow, or a specific date
28. the same
29. invite
30. authorize

—Ellie Abrams

percent/percentage

"**A** five (usually spelled out) percentage point difference" and "a 5 percent difference" are two completely different numbers. A difference that amounts to 5 percent of the total is "a 5 percent difference." But the difference between, say, 15 and 20 percent is expressed as "a five percentage point difference."

Remember that a quantity can be increased by any percentage but decreased by no more than 100 percent. To say that "The number of defective part claims has been reduced by 150 percent" is to claim the impossible.

Eight Problems of Logic in Writing

Persuasive writing avoids these rhetorical flaws

Few things ruin a piece of good writing quicker than a bad argument. The theme may be as clear as distilled water. The words may fit the topic, and the sentences may flow like warm honey. The rhetorical flourishes may all be subtle, and the tone seductive. But if the writer falls into the many logical errors to which all argument is prone, the whole effort is jeopardized.

Here we look at eight logic problems in writing: faulty generalization, false dilemmas, the *post hoc ergo propter hoc* argument, the *ad hominem* argument, question begging, the improper appeal to authority, imperfect or false analogies, and the *non sequitur*. Examples and editorial strategies are suggested for each.

Faulty generalization. This is perhaps the most common error in argument construction. Broad generalizations about difficult and controversial topics seldom stand scrutiny; hence, one useful rule of thumb for editors is: *The stronger the generalization, the more bells should go off in the editor's mind.*

Fortunately, faulty generalizations give off powerful signals. Often they are preceded by absolute words like *all, always, anyone, every(one)(thing), only, never,* and *none.* Frequently they are flagged by superlatives: *best, greatest, most, least.* The recommended editorial treatment is to qualify the absolutes and superlatives.

> ***Example and strategy:*** "*Hamlet* is the best play ever written in English" can be easily changed to "Many scholars agree that *Hamlet* is one of the best plays..." once the author agrees.

False dilemma. This error usually takes the form of presenting two (or three) alternatives as if they were mutually exclusive, when they are really just the obvious options or the ones the writer finds easiest to manipulate. The words and phrases that commonly signal false dilemmas are these: *either...or; the only alternative/possibility/choice is; since X is obviously false/has not worked, Y is clearly true/our only choice.* The recommended treatment is to break open the dilemma by broadening the statement or, where called for, the entire argument.

> ***Example and strategy:*** "Either the courts or the individual conscience is entitled to speak on abortion, but not both." Here, the editor must point out the logical problems created by the implication that there are only two possible camps to be in. It is well within the realm of logic for both conscience *and* courts to speak, for example. Or the dilemma can be broken open by querying the role of the church and other moral leaders.

Post hoc ergo propter hoc. This error is among the most common fallacies of thinking and therefore of writing. The Latin phrase means "after this, therefore on account of this." The error lies in assuming that establishing a chronological relationship automatically establishes a causal one. Some of the key signals to look for, of course, are words that highlight conclusory statements: *therefore, thus, consequently, as a result, accordingly, on account of.* But not all *post hoc* errors are that easy to spot.

> ***Example and strategy:*** "The period following the U.S. hydrogen bomb tests in the South Pacific was marked by uncharacteristic and dramatic weather changes, directly related to the tests." As the statisticians say, "Correlation is not causality." In the absence of strong evidence to bolster the writer's implication, the statement draws a hidden and unwarranted conclusion and therefore should be qualified, perhaps by inserting some phrase like "leading many meteorological experts to conclude that the changes were..." before the word "directly," followed by the evidence itself.

Argument *ad hominem*. This logic error substitutes discrediting one's opponent for discrediting the opponent's arguments. The fallacy is sometimes difficult to identify, primarily because the individual involved may be relevant to the issue. For example, the 1947 conviction of James Michael Curley for mail fraud while in office became an issue in his 1949 campaign for reelection as mayor of Boston. But in most cases, the *ad hominem* argument should not be allowed to stand.

> ***Example and strategy:*** "Karl Marx's poor performance as a provider for his own family is reason enough to doubt the validity of his social and economic theories." Marx's ability to earn a living may or may not have anything to do with the validity of his theories, which are quite large in scale. The editor must ask the author either to present historical and economic facts discrediting the theories, independent of Marx's performance as a provider, or show that Marx's application of his theories in his own household caused his family economic hardship.

Question begging. Question begging comes in two main forms. One is a form of circular or tautological reasoning. Setting out to make a point, the writer posits the conclusion the reader is expected to make, then supports or "proves" it by some restatement or assertion of the original point. The conclusion gives rise to the reason, which supports the conclusion.

> ***Example and strategy:*** "The study of history gives excellent insights into human nature because one can learn much about personal character by learning about the events and circumstances of the past." Here, the reason provided for the proposition in the first half of the sentence is simply the proposition's restatement in slightly different words in the second half. The editor needs to flag the error with *"Tautol."* or *"Circ. Arg.,"* improve the sentence simply by breaking off the last half of it, and follow up by asking the author to give a concrete example.

A second form of question begging is the smuggled assumption. In this case the writer hides an assumption in the statement of a proposition and proceeds to prove or support the proposition by drawing on the hidden assumption.

Example and strategy: "Capital punishment is forbidden in Sweden and its homicide rate is lower than ours. We should therefore abolish capital punishment." The hidden assumption is that the relationship between the absence of capital punishment and Sweden's low homicide rate is a *causal* one. What should be proven—that we should abolish capital punishment—is supported by this assumption. A useful editorial strategy is to state the question that is, in fact, begged by the offending sentence: *"Does lack of capital punishment **cause** low murder rate? Are there other factors?"*

Improper appeals to authority. Appeals to authority are common in all writing: "As Churchill once said...," "Four out of five doctors agree...," "According to the *AMA Journal*...," "Research shows...." But appeals to authority have different weights, and not all authorities are trustworthy beyond their fields of expertise. Henry Kissinger's statements about Russian cuisine are less authoritative than his statements about Soviet foreign policy.

Nor is the evidence provided by polls necessarily authoritative.

Example and strategy: "Forty-seven percent of New York viewers characterized William Hurt's performance in *The Accidental Tourist* as his best ever." The editor could pencil in any or all of the following questions in the margin: *"What New York viewers?" "What are their qualifications for judging acting?" "What was the size of the sample?"* Other questions editors can put to appeals to authority include: *"Is this authority competent in this field?" "Is the authority providing evidence, reasoned analysis, or merely opinion to support the argument?" "Is the authority known to have a specific bias?" "Is the authority's statement up-to-date?"*

Imperfect or false analogy. Reasoning by analogy attempts to make a case by comparing something known with something not known or not as well known. The potential for error lies in an unwarranted leap of logic: The writer jumps from the fact that two partners in the analogy share one or more characteristics to the assumption that the second partner in the analogy shares an *additional* characteristic of the first, which characteristic is relevant to the matter at hand. The logical argument of the false analogy has this syllogistic form:

X and Y share characteristics *a, b,* and *c.*

X has the further characteristic *z.*

Therefore, Y must share characteristic *z.*

Example and strategy: "Education cannot possibly prepare a couple for parenthood. Trying to educate them for such a task is like trying to teach them to swim without putting them in the water; it can't be done." Here the argument assumes a set of shared characteristics between parenthood and swimming—overcoming fears, learning new skills, adapting to a new environment, adopting new behavior patterns, and so forth. But, the editor can point out, swimming and parenthood are also very different from each other. A terse *"Analogy doesn't work. Swimming skills physical; parenting skills psychosocial"* should wake the author up.

The great value of analogical argument lies in the insight revealed by the unexpected juxtaposition of two elements. But all analogies break down when pressed too far. The trick the editor must learn is to find where the line is and not let the writer cross it.

Non sequiturs. A *non sequitur* is a conclusion or inference that "does not follow" from the premises offered. Some examples of *non sequiturs* are

Delton drinks too much. He probably beats his kids, too.

Phogbound is a politician. Can we trust him?

Elyse has perfect Sunday school attendance; I'll bet she's well behaved at home.

Non sequiturs are similar to false analogies in that both depend on the transfer of imputed characteristics from one context to another to make the point. But *non sequiturs* are more fallacious forms of reasoning than false analogies because the relationships on which they depend are usually more tenuous. There may be a certain "reasonableness" to *non sequiturs*; for example, Elyse's perfect Sunday school attendance may lead us to think she's a "nice little girl," but there may be another, better reason that explains her behavior (perhaps her parents make her go); she may be a perfect hellion at home. The editor can simply query: *"Perfect attendance = good behavior @ home?"*

Logic is crucial to sound argument and persuasion, and thus to clear writing. It is, as Jean de la Bruyère has said, "the art of making truth prevail." But logic can also be overdone. Some of our most profound experiences—love of country, romantic passion, religious awe, aesthetic joy—defy logic, and these too must be expressed. The beginning editor will thus slowly learn the lesson taught by Pascal, which experienced editors already know, that "the last function of reason is to know the infinity of things that surpass it."

—*Bruce O. Boston*

Verbless Sentences:
Fresh or Just Fragments?

A little of this technique goes a long way, but give it a try

Are sentence fragments ever acceptable in formal writing? Are they worth the calculated risk that someone may think they have been used in ignorance? Worth the risk of annoying people who dislike them? H.W. Fowler, in *Modern English Usage* (Oxford University Press, 1965), said, "The verbless sentence is a device for enlivening the written word by approximating it to the spoken." According to Fowler, verbless sentences can serve six purposes:

- transitional *(So far so good.)*
- afterthought *(Well, almost.)*
- dramatic effect *(We will face difficulties as we always have. As a united nation.)*
- commentary *(Brilliant!)*
- pictorial *(It is an entire streetful of shops. Complete with side arcades. And a restaurant. And two snack bars. All piled on top of one another.)*
- aggressive *(The particular dynamics of the publishing group which this book concerns springs, of course, from the rumbustious school of journalism it nurtured. Defying the conventions.)*

Many verbless sentences, of course, cannot be so neatly characterized and are rather "the product of the author's conviction that the more staccato the style, the livelier the effect." But longer fragments can be effective mixed with short ones. A good example can be found in the fiction of Pulitzer winner E. Annie Proulx. From *The Shipping News*—

> At last the end of the world, a wild place that seemed poised on the lip of the abyss. No human sign, nothing, no ship, no plane, no animal, no bird, no bobbing trap marker nor buoy. As though he stood alone on the planet.

Granted, this style is a bit evocative for most nonfiction and probably all business writing, and it's infuriating when overdone. But it's worth a try now and then to leaven an otherwise boring piece. Say, one on verbless sentences. Fowler concludes,

> Since the verbless sentence is freely employed by some good writers (as well as extravagantly by many less good ones), it must be classed as modern English usage. That grammarians may deny it the right to be called a sentence has nothing to do with its merits.... Used sparingly and with discrimination, the device can no doubt be an effective medium of emphasis, intimacy, and rhetoric.

—Linda B. Jorgensen

When Writers Have Trouble Getting Started

It's easier to break through a block
when you know what you're up against

How do *you* get started on a piece of writing? Wait for inspiration to strike? Wait for the deadline to force your hand? Wait for the perfect first sentence to appear? Water the begonias?

Getting started does not have to be a hit-or-miss enterprise or an exercise in procrastination. Speaking as a professional writer who has tried all of the above, I have wasted days searching for a magic combination to start the flow of words. What follows are insights I've wrested from my bouts with the problem, from working with fellow sufferers, and from the research of others (notably Linda Flower of Carnegie-Mellon University) into the writing process itself.

What are writers made of?

All writers (defined here as anyone called upon to write) are inhabited by three selves: a **creator**, a **critic**, and a **scribe**. The first two are natural rivals who spend much of the time contradicting each other's dictates to the third.

I think of the creative self as a demon in the classical Greek sense—a zealous rather than an evil spirit. *My* demon is willful, unpredictable, and equally capable of inspired and dreadful prose; it works best when left alone. My critical self is an editor with a mean perfectionist streak whose sole mission is to point out the demon's weaknesses and sins. My scribe is a drudge who deserves to be paid much more for putting up with the other two.

The writing process is a struggle

The writing process is essentially a tug-of-war between the demon's impulse to try out new ideas and shape them into something different and the editor's impulse to criticize, cross out, amend, and perfect. The writer's progress depends in good part on keeping the two impulses from working at cross-purposes.

Ideally, the demon commands the conceptual part of the process (brainstorming, planning, writing a first draft) while the editor governs the critical part (editing, proofreading), and there's a companionable overlap at the middle (the revision stage). But the ideal mix does not come easily. Here are some problems all writers face sooner or later.

16

The overactive editor. If the editor intrudes on the demon's domain, the writer ends up trying to be creative and critical at the same time. For most writers, that's a disastrous way to work.

Typically the battle goes something like this. The writer begins with a proposition: *All men are created equal.*

"Wait a minute," says the editor. "Are you sexist or something?"

The demon amends the sentence: *All men and women are created equal.*

"What about hermaphrodites and children under 18?"

The demon amends the amendment: *All people, regardless of race, religion, sex, or age, are created equal.*

"Are you writing this for the Equal Employment Opportunity Commission?"

The demon hits the delete—hard: *All people are created equal.*

"Do you really mean *equal*? What about Siamese twins with one heart and two brains...?"

The demon snarls, changes the period to a comma, and an hour later finishes the sentence. *All people are created equal, but some are more equal than others.*

"Better footnote that so you're not accused of plagiarizing Orwell. And by the way, are you sure it's correct to use *equal* in the adjectival rather than the adverbial form?"

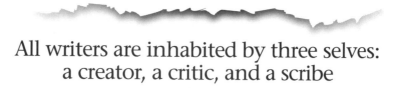

All writers are inhabited by three selves: a creator, a critic, and a scribe

This interior war plays out to a greater or lesser degree in the head of every writer. For those like me, who also work as editors, it's a particularly pernicious problem that, if not resolved quickly, saps creative energy and self-confidence, as well as wastes time.

To pacify my editor I use a strategy that Flower calls "satisficing," a term borrowed from economists, who use it for "the process of resolving a problem as satisfactorily as possible." Flower uses the term to mean accepting a less than perfect expression or idea for the moment rather than searching for the very best one.

My creative and critical selves strike a bargain, agreeing to bracket rough spots but leave revision for later. This frees my creative self to get on with the writing but also assures my critic that all those questionable formulations and embarrassingly bad bits of prose will ultimately get their editorial comeuppance.

The slothful demon. Satisficing, however, will not help the writer whose problems are more conceptual than editorial. Here the culprit is the demon, who has failed to do one or more of the tasks necessary to writing a first draft: (1) generating ideas, (2) developing a logical framework for them, and (3) defining the purpose.

1. Words in search of ideas. Writers who have an idea—a single idea—often begin writing with a burst of energy; they expect to discover more ideas and figure out what to do with them while they're writing. For most writers, that's like expecting first-time visitors to Washington, DC, to find their way around without a map. The obvious solution is to go back a step and take time out to brainstorm. Asking yourself specific questions about the topic is a good way to stimulate ideas. So is discussing the topic with someone else.

2. Ideas in search of a framework. Writers who start out with plenty of ideas can still have trouble getting started if they haven't thought them through. The most effective tool for developing and organizing ideas is a nonlinear outline. For most shorter writing projects, I use one of two schemas. The **issue tree**, a form favored by Flower, is a tree whose trunk is the topic (or proposition) to be examined and whose branches present the writer's main ideas about that topic. A similar schema is the **spokewheel**, where the hub is the topic and the spokes are the main ideas.

Both schemas offer three advantages over the standard linear outline: They make it easier to visualize the relationships among parallel issues and to spot logical inconsistencies and overlapping or missing material; they help the writer generate ideas; and they leave the order of presentation for the writer to decide later.

3. Ideas in search of a purpose. The process of doing an outline can also help a writer decide the purpose of a piece of writing—without that, it's hard to make progress. Sometimes new ideas emerge in the course of writing and the purpose changes; still, in getting started it helps to have a clear purpose in mind and to define it in terms of the reader: *I want single parents to understand how the change in tax laws will affect them.*

Procrastination. Finally, what of the writer who starts by watering the begonias? When does ritual (something writers do to compose themselves for the task ahead) become procrastination?

I use a form of satisfice to keep my rituals from getting out of hand. I allow myself to do them but set strict limits—only the begonias, not the other plants, and no pruning, only watering. If I still feel like avoiding the writing task, I tell myself that I won't begin the actual writing, I'll simply make some notes—no big deal. With any luck, these will soon gather momentum and lead to a draft.

A first draft is a first draft is a...

After all, the beginning is only a beginning. Why should we agonize over something that probably won't survive intact beyond the first draft? A better draft is yet to come, and we can get there from here if we shift mental gears and become (to borrow from Shakespeare) "like greyhounds in the slips/Straining upon the start."

—*Dianne Snyder*

while/whereas

Since the early 20th century, some grammarians have preferred that *while* be used exclusively in a temporal sense ("during the time that," "as long as") to avoid ambiguity. *Webster's Dictionary of English Usage* says that other uses of *while* are "standard and established" and that it often sounds less stilted than *whereas* to mean "despite the fact that" or "while on the contrary." Statements such as the following are clear and extremely common: "I hate snow, while you love it." And to say "I've had enough of this snow, whereas you revel in it," though correct, seems overly formal. Rote replacement by editors of *while* with *whereas* is unnecessary.

Roy Copperud (*American Usage and Style: The Consensus*) and others, however, advise against interchanging the conjunctions when meaning could be misconstrued. "I made soup while you were cross-country skiing" is correct when "at the same time" is meant, but with *whereas* substituted, the connotation is quite different: "I've been slaving away over a hot stove whereas you've been off having fun" becomes the message. While *The Editorial Eye* resists fusty formulations, we endorse *whereas* where it works better.

Handpicked Descriptive Words

Evocative writing is exacting work

Writing a good description is fun, but it's delicate work. In a passage from his recent *New Yorker* essay about contemporary artist Edward Kienholz, Lawrence Weschler offers a model of description that succeeds: It's agile and effective while seeming breezy and effortless. This passage follows the statement that Kienholz acknowledges the connection between eating meat and sacrificing animals. Weschler continues:

> Not that Ed was a namby-pamby vegetarian, or anything like that—he wolfed veal, for instance, with considerable gusto—but he was one for taking responsibility, for not evading the sinewy interconnectedness of the world, in meat, as in all things.

We recognize vivid writing when we come across it, and we know the bad stuff, too—it makes us squirm instinctively. Here are some types of descriptions the world can do without.

Wrong words. Remember Richard Sheridan's character Mrs. Malaprop from *The Rivals*—the woman who proclaimed another character "the pineapple of politeness"? Master of the misapplied word—and a good comic character—Mrs. Malaprop taught many high school readers of this play a valuable lesson: Take care in choosing your words. Don't just stick them jauntily into sentences for effect. I recently read a description of a new building development in which a writer stated that his company would need to "incubate new construction workers for the site." *Incubate?* Downy, egg-bound construction workers hatching on the job site? The more modest *train* would have been more appropriate.

Dictionary words. Academic words—words you wouldn't expect in conversational writing—tend to clog the flow of a sentence. Take an example from a travel writer's description of Vietnam: "Not far from bustling Hanoi, with its flocks of construction cranes and packs of buzzing motor scooters, is a lovely sanctuary that offers a respite from the exciting but cacophonous Vietnamese capital." While much of this description is fine, offering up sounds and visual images, *cacophonous* goes too far. Why? For one thing, it's redundant—the buzzing motor scooters and flocking construction cranes earlier in the sentence have established their own cacophony. Besides that, *cacophonous* is a mouthful that comes at the end of an already-long sentence. "A respite from the noise of the Vietnamese capital" would have sufficed.

Thesaurus words. Be careful not to take as literal truth what a thesaurus says are synonyms, particularly when choosing verbs. Because a verb is the natural heart of a sentence, the connotations it introduces will be especially noticeable.

Think how forceful "he wolfed veal" seemed in Weschler's paragraph. It succeeds not just because it's direct and simple (unlike the dictionary words *ingested* and *consumed*), but because the image fits the tone, the thesis, of the whole piece. It joins "considerable gusto" and "sinewy interconnectedness" in portraying an artist who is passionate, even carnal. We sense that the writer has given a well-formed, accurate rendering of Kienholz's spirit because the images themselves mirror his intensity. If we had read that Kienholz ate veal with "some degree of enthusiasm," we would have made a completely different kind of association.

Handpicking words, turning them over carefully, uncovers the connotations behind their dictionary definitions. This work can't be done mechanically; it's labor intensive. But it offers generous rewards. It's a pleasure not to be missed.

—*Elisabeth Dahl*

Getting Print-worthy Quotes from Interviews

People say surprising things when they feel comfortable

As writers who specialize in publications for and about companies and organizations, we conduct some 200 telephone interviews annually. These are not journalistic, "60 Minutes"-type interviews. We interview people with expertise to get quotes for projects such as annual reports, testimonials, and speeches.

Sometimes the people we interview are employees of the client we're working for; they cooperate because they have no choice! Most often, however, the interview subjects are busy executives and professionals who stand to gain little more than some decidedly limited exposure by patiently answering our questions.

We've developed some interviewing techniques that are quite effective in getting the last drop of information from the know-it-all who has no interest in being a tell-it-all. At one time or another most of us have secretly wished we could just make quotes up, but that would be missing the point: authenticity. People can say surprising and thoughtful things—the words just need a little help getting out.

- **Schedule an appointment for the interview.** Then call to do the interview. We began this practice just for our own convenience, realizing that there's no reason to spend time formulating questions for someone we may not be able to reach. But we found over time that setting appointments boosted our success rate in getting interviews by about 30 percent, perhaps because people will agree to anything to postpone being put on the spot just then. (But there's always someone who says, "I'm leaving on vacation tomorrow, so let's talk now." To seize these opportunities, we keep close at hand a list of basic, all-purpose questions that are appropriate for many contexts.)

  An alternative is to fax a "request for interview" memo before calling to set an appointment. In this fax introduce yourself, state your purpose, estimate the time involved, and provide sample questions. The fax gives you the chance to say more about what's in it for the person to be interviewed. In the management newsletter we write, for example, each article quotes only one expert. We mention this in our fax so our subjects know they don't have to share the spotlight with others or risk unfavorable comparison.

- **Start the interview with low-key questions.** You may be tempted to get right to the heart of the matter immediately, perhaps by challenging an expert's most controversial opinions or asking a consultant for his or her best advice right away. But even people who are experienced at being interviewed need a chance to warm up and become focused. A possible opener: "How did you first become interested in [this topic]?" People get to talk about themselves for a moment and, even if you don't actually use what they give you, the interchange smoothes the way for the first real content question.

- **Ask short, open-ended questions—then clam up.** An example of how well this advice works is the program "Booknotes" on the C-SPAN cable channel. Each week, host Brian Lamb, who interviews a book author, asks questions that are masterpieces of restraint. Recently, he simply asked someone, "Where's home?" The author responded that he'd lived in New York City for 40 years but would always consider the small town in Ohio where he was reared his real home. If Lamb had asked an even slightly more specific question like "Where did you grow up?" the response elicited would probably not have been as interesting—or phrased in a way that revealed something about the author's values.

- **Don't rush in with words to fill dead air.** It's a trait endemic in middle-class American society: the fear of a pause in the conversation. Mystery novelist Tony Hillerman's fictional Navajo detective, Joe Leaphorn, knows about the "white abhorrence for conversational silences. Sometimes the resulting uneasiness caused [white] witnesses to blurt out more than they intended to say." People do feel responsible for saying *something*—and often what pops into the air, unguarded, is the truth. We've never gotten a confession by out-pausing someone, but we've often gotten our lead quote.

- **Always ask "What one thing...?"** Make this question a standard part of every interview. For example, "You're known across the country for your expertise in human resources management. What one thing do you most often see applicants doing wrong?" The opening flattery, coupled with the open-ended opportunity to expound, can produce some intriguing answers.

- **Don't cut off the interview process too early.** You may have "enough" quotes from someone to fill the space they're intended for, but often the real gold comes 15 to 30 minutes into an individual conversation. And even if you have lots of bright quotes from one person, keep going until you have more than enough material from more than one person. A surplus gives you more flexibility in where and how you'll use them and extras in case any subjects withdraw. For an annual report, we asked each customer for comments on the same items: cleanliness, pricing, display, and so forth. Overkill? No. Insurance.

- **Challenge interviewees—but stay on their side.** You may want to ask for an opinion about a controversial matter or challenge a possible flaw in the thinking behind the answers you're getting. But you don't want to make anyone feel defensive or irritated. A ploy that works for us is to ascribe the contrary ideas to others: "Some say that's not possible" or "I've read claims that your study was flawed. How do you respond to such critics?"

- **Cheat on closing.** When you reach the question that's third or fourth from the bottom of your list, say, "One last thing: What do you think about...." You get double duty from this tactic. People, all too likely to be restive by now, stop worrying about the time because it's almost up. And people may noticeably relax and become more open because a stressful situation has been weathered. Not once have we ever been subsequently challenged with "You said that was the last question."

- **Make it clear what the payback is.** As you're winding things down, be careful to get the interviewee's name, title, address, and the like exactly right. Mention that the person will be identified in your publication as a reminder that his or her remarks are understood to be for attribution—make it sound like a good thing: "I want to make sure I give you credit."

  Ask for the preferred business bio line, for example, "a management consultant who specializes in identifying challenging and satisfying new positions for dissatisfied star performers." Countless interviewees have thanked us for allowing such "free advertising" tags to be used, so do so if you have the option.

- **Send complimentary copies of the finished piece.** Many interview subjects have told us that this follow-up is often promised but seldom delivered. Make sure you offer this tangible form of thanks. There's something in it for you, too, even when the project is long finished. Some day, someone you interviewed may be perfect for another project.

  We interviewed one consultant for a management newsletter article. Later, he turned out to be the perfect expert to interview for the feature section of another client's annual report. And he was willing to cooperate with us again because we had shared the results of the previous interview with him.

Many of our clients have been shocked to learn that not every name they give us will result in a productive interview. In our experience, no matter the type of project, out of every ten names you're given as possible interview subjects, two or three will seem to have vanished from the planet, another two or three will decline or won't return your phone calls, and one or two won't say anything worth using. That usually leaves about 40 percent of the original list. The more specific and defined your purpose for interviewing, the more names you need (because not all quotes will be germane or print-worthy). When one company asked us to approach community leaders for favorable quotes for its annual report, only one-third of those identified as sources made it into the printed piece.

Hazards to getting the quotes you need lie everywhere along the production path. Once we interviewed retirees to be featured in an organization's annual report. We got wonderful quotes from one gentleman; later in the process, our client learned that he had brought numerous lawsuits against the organization during his employment. Another retiree who was identified as Hispanic—an important consideration for the diversity of those quoted—in fact had her roots in Spain. Sadly, one retiree died before the report was finished; the client accepted our suggestion to keep the interview in, prefaced with a brief memorial statement.

An executive we interviewed for a corporate newsletter defected to the company's chief competitor right about press time. For another client's annual report, we got a quote with glowing praise from the chairman of a major retail chain. He approved for printing not only the version of his remarks but also a full two-page layout, only to withdraw permission to quote him in any way at the last minute. The client was left with an embarrassing hole in the copy and an expensive production problem.

The moral of these war stories is, of course, to line up three or more names for every one quotable interviewee you need. Once you have a live prospect (and we do mean live), follow the steps we've outlined for a successful telephone interview. At least the odds will be in your favor!

—*Susan Bury and David Stauffer*

Writing Spoken Comments

Here are a few ethical considerations

Can writers clean up spoken comments for print? The answer depends on your editorial policy, but the rules for quoting oral statements differ from those for published material. Speech is "thinking out loud" and almost always needs editing; how much is a matter of editorial judgment. (Note: People won't call to complain about sounding too good in your piece.)

Use common sense when deciding how much idiomatic expression to keep. A little colorful vocabulary or quirky syntax can humanize copy, but too much may make the speaker look foolish. (Dialect and substandard English are hard to read and often annoy readers as well.) Take care not to put uncharacteristic words in someone else's mouth or to change the meaning.

- Get approval in advance to print attributed comments. Sooner is better than later, when quoted material is a substantial part of final copy, to clear up any misunderstanding.

- Double-check all direct quotes if you've taped the interview. Transcribing from tape is tricky.

- Edit a quote if necessary to save your interviewee from being embarrassed in print by the awkward or colloquial English most of us use in conversation.

- Preserve individual style that reveals character and spices up the content, but avoid quotes that border on caricature or stereotype.

- Help an interviewee who skips around, backtracks, or repeats statements in the course of an interview by imposing a logical sequence on the quotes you select for print. Paraphrase as necessary for transition, but be sure to use ellipsis when you leave out a substantial part of an answer. If you impose logical order, don't create misleading transitions or gaps that misrepresent the original answers.

- Remember that extensive paraphrasing in an article defeats the purpose of doing an interview: to get lively voices, warmth, and approachable tone, and different perspectives into print. Keep your scene-setting observations to a minimum.

Finally, the Q & A print format seems simple but really works well only for short profiles or for a group interview limited to a clear core of ideas.

—Linda B. Jorgensen

Misplaced Modifiers

A **misplaced modifier** is a word, phrase, or clause that is placed incorrectly in the sentence, thus distorting the meaning. Move the misplaced modifier next to the word it actually modifies.

1. The teacher said that my son only did his homework on Wednesdays.

2. The coordinator of the adult education program told us eventually the institution would purchase new computers for the lab.

3. While adjusting his new field glasses, a red-headed woodpecker landed on a nearby branch.

4. On recalculating the tax return totals, the discrepancy between my accountant's results and the IRS's results became apparent.

5. When four years old, Kate's father was transferred to San Francisco to direct the marketing division.

6. He suggested that our 12-year-old start mowing the lawn last night.

7. Madeline showed the available flowers to the customer in the refrigerated showcase.

8. While the bank teller stood still grasping the money tightly the robber darted forward.

ANSWERS

A misplaced modifier can be ambiguous or downright funny.

- A **squinting modifier** is a word, phrase, or clause that may logically refer to either a preceding or following word and so is ambiguous. First establish which word is being modified, then move the modifier.

- A **limiting modifier** is a word that should immediately precede the word, phrase, or clause that it refers to. Examples of limiting modifiers are *almost, exactly, hardly, just, merely, only, scarcely,* and *simply.* A common error is to place these modifiers before the verb, regardless of the word being modified.

- A **dangling modifier** is a phrase or an elliptical clause (a clause in which some essential words are omitted) that is placed next to a word it cannot sensibly modify. Dangling modifiers are usually found at the beginning of sentences, and often the word that should be modified by the dangler has been dropped. Change the dangling phrase to a clause or move the word that should be modified to immediately follow the modifier.

1. The limiting modifier *only* is misplaced. The sentence really means that except for Wednesdays my son was unprepared.

> The teacher said that my son did his homework **only** on Wednesdays.

2. The word *eventually* is squinting. Does it modify *told* or *purchase?* There are three possible correct positions for *eventually* in this sentence depending on meaning.

> The coordinator of the adult education program **eventually** told us....

> **Eventually** the coordinator of the adult education program told us....

> The coordinator of the adult education program told us the institution would **eventually** purchase new computers....

3. An introductory verbal phrase is understood to modify the nearest noun or pronoun. This sentence says the woodpecker was looking through the field glasses (the true subject has been left out).

> While adjusting his new field glasses, he saw a red-headed woodpecker land on a nearby branch.

4. As this sentence stands, the discrepancy recalculated the totals. Changing the introductory phrase to a clause is one solution.

> When I recalculated the tax return totals, the discrepancy between my accountant's results and the IRS's results became apparent.

5. This sentence says that a four-year-old is the director of marketing—a child prodigy perhaps?

> When Kate was four years old, her father was transferred to San Francisco to direct the marketing division.

6. This sentence implies that the youngster should start mowing the previous evening—a physical impossibility. What the writer probably meant was that the suggestion was made last night.

> Last night he suggested that our 12-year-old start mowing the lawn.

7. The customer must have been a bit chilly. The flowers are of course in the refrigerated showcase.

> Madeline showed the customer the available flowers in the refrigerated showcase.

8. The question is, "Who has the money?" In one case, commas will solve the problem. In the other, the phrase should be moved.

> While the bank teller stood still, grasping the money tightly, the robber darted forward.

> While the bank teller stood still, the robber darted forward grasping the money tightly.

—*Ellie Abrams*

Writing 'Behind the Scenes': The Art of Ghostwriting

Finding the right voice can be as difficult as ventriloquism

In many organizations large and small, senior executives and managers rely on others to draft their speeches, articles, press releases, letters, and so forth. Although each of these products calls for a different type of research and writing, all of them require the writer to communicate in someone else's voice.

The hard part is making it look easy

In any organization, staff writers are among the hardest-working and the least-recognized employees. Figuring out what somebody else should be saying is the art of ghostwriting. Getting a chance to write for a living is what makes learning to balance the contradictions of the job worthwhile. Here's a behind-the-scenes look at some of the challenges ghostwriters encounter.

- First, face the fact that you're going to have to adapt your tone and diction to fit someone else's preferred writing or natural speaking style. People who write for someone else often err on the side of formality, but putting overly casual words in someone else's mouth can produce a result that's just as awkward.

- Good writing for other people has to take into account their strengths, weaknesses, and preferences—for anecdotes or facts, or historical references or statistics, to give just a few examples. A friend who works for a Cabinet-level official has observed that her boss has a passionate, powerful style when he speaks from the heart, as when he responds to questions at a press conference or mingles with guests at an informal luncheon. But when he speaks at a larger, more formal event, his delivery lacks genuine emotion. The challenge here, then, is to construct a speech that builds on his penchant for the vernacular, the personal, and the humorous.

- Finding the right voice can be as difficult as ventriloquism, except for the fact that the person you're doing it for can talk back. As with any writing assignment, the more information you have, the better. Before you begin writing, it helps to discuss in detail the purpose and scope of the writing and its desired effect on the audience. At the very least, ask for direction after your first draft so you'll know whether you're on the right track, not only with the message, but also with the tone and style.

- Conflicting schedules can make it difficult to sit down and work close-ly with your employer or client, and the two of you may have little di-rect daily contact. Writers often prepare testimony and statements for elected officials and corporate managers who are in a different city and whom they've never met. Or senior staff may provide writers with in-formation. Slightly better than having nothing at all to rely on are comments from second- or thirdhand sources. Your judgment always comes into play: You need a true eye for context and a sharp ear for what will ring true.

- A writer may not get useful criticism or reinforcement after the writing has been completed. Even if you work closely with your employer in preparing a presentation, in many organizations there is no time for re-flection afterward. You most likely will not get a chance to sit down after the event for a postmortem because by the time a publication is printed or a speech is delivered, new deadlines are approaching. Per-haps the most telling feedback is simply whether you're asked to write for that person again.

- Even if you've picked the appropriate writing style, you may disagree about the substance of some of the material you're asked to draft. Do you have opinions that could make it difficult to write for someone who's taking a position you disagree with? Writers are selected for their skills, not their personal opinions, but if you have the luxury of passing on such an assignment, perhaps you should let someone who feels more neutral take it.

Giving credit where it's due—to someone else

You must accept that someone else will get credit for your work; don't for-get why it's called ghostwriting. Although speechwriters know that their scripts will come to life only in someone else's voice—literally and pub-licly—sometimes writers come to regard a printed piece as "theirs." Even among writers who say, "I care about producing good writing—not about getting recognition for it," most have experienced at least a brief tug-of-war between professionalism and personal pride. Having an ego is a part of being a writer.

Firing-line accountability and, at best, reflected glory: That sounds about right as a motto for ghostwriters. But the ability to help others com-municate well can be useful in any field, and some of us actually prefer to be the person behind the curtain. Seeing a piece in print, with or without your name on it, is a big reward for the effort involved in researching, writing, and refining a piece.

—Mark R. Miller

Five Nonfiction Writing Ailments

Editors won't buy work that doesn't give readers something fresh

I have a private practice as a doctor—a "book doctor," that is. The editor as book doctor—or prequel editor, someone who works on the manuscript before the acquisition editor buys it—is a comparatively new editorial mutation. Book doctors are really freelance editors who are highly skilled at analyzing the problems in a manuscript—and at suggesting solutions in an in-depth report that should serve to guide an author in rethinking and revising a manuscript. A book doctor may also offer line editing, revising, rewriting, and collaborative writing services.

Book doctoring has evolved as a specialty in response to two facts of life: the fierce competition faced by writers in the worlds of magazine and book publishing and the heavy, often onerous workloads carried by house editors, many of whom lack the experience or time to edit a manuscript after it has been accepted by a publisher. Editors often begin their careers as first readers without formal editorial training and then learn on the job, but there are fewer and fewer mentors around with the time or patience to teach the fine points of line editing.

Understandably, then, acquisition editors who are pressured to find manuscripts tend to avoid taking on projects that appear to require a great deal of work. Enter the book doctor, to whom many writers turn for manuscript editing before their work has been acquired and whom editors consult afterward. In 40 years of being an acquisition, developmental, and line editor, as well as a book doctor, I've seen almost every manuscript problem imaginable. Here are five of the most common mistakes I see nonfiction writers make.

Mistake 1. *Failing to make a map or outline* of the piece you want to write *before* you start writing. Doing at least a free-form outline will enable your central ideas to develop to their fullest and help you make associations in a natural, convincing manner. If you wanted to drive to a distant place you had never seen, you would map your journey to avoid getting lost. The consequences of poor planning are abrupt transitions that give the piece a jerky, hard-to-follow quality, confusing organization that prevents the reader from following the development of concepts, and repetition that weakens the power and impact of your thesis.

Mistake 2. *Failing to tailor the vocabulary* to your audience. Many writers who know a subject well but want to write for a wide readership suffer from what I call "the curse of expertise." They are so steeped in their field that they write naturally in the jargon of the field and not in lay language—fine for one's peers, but alienating to a general audience. If I'm working with a lawyer, physician, psychiatrist, psychologist, architect, management consultant, or any other professional, I ask the writer if he or she is writing for "Mr. Gross" or "Dr. Gross." You may want to impress your peers with jargon that says you are in every way their equal, but be careful: Too much jargon can put even experts to sleep.

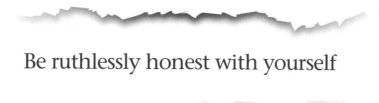

Be ruthlessly honest with yourself

For a lay audience, make your prose as conversational as possible. One way to check for a relaxed style is to read your piece into a tape recorder and listen to how the sentences flow (or don't flow). This self-editing technique is especially effective if you have used dialogue or direct quotes from an interview.

Mistake 3. *Failing to use the right ratio of theoretical to anecdotal material.* As a corollary of the previous advice to choose the right vocabulary for the audience, I suggest explaining the theory or point of view you want to write about early on in the piece. State it simply and then use the rest of the article or chapter to dramatize, with case histories or anecdotal material, how the reader's everyday life is affected by the information. Conversely, if you are writing for experts, I suggest focusing most of the manuscript on a detailed explication of your material and augmenting it with a few examples that show the application of the theory. I recommend the following ratios: For a lay audience, use 20 percent theory and 80 percent dramatized application; for an expert peer group, 80 percent theory and 20 percent dramatized application.

Mistake 4. *Failing to research the field* to see if a topic has been overworked. It's important to establish that your approach to a subject and your discussion of it make a real contribution to the body of knowledge about a subject. Will readers gain a new or more thorough understanding? Be ruthlessly honest with yourself. Check the bookstores, libraries, and databases of books and articles in print (including *Books in Print*) to see what's out there. If you can't make a real contribution to the field, don't even bother to do an outline, much less a proposal, for your manuscript. Why? Because if your work doesn't give the reader something valuable— that means up-to-date, fresh, and informative—an editor won't buy it.

To make an editor more receptive to the theme of your manuscript, clearly identify in your letter the niche, overlooked by others, that your work will fill. For example, cite the three or four most recent articles or books on the subject and explain how your work differs from them.

Mistake 5. *Failing to write to the very best of your ability* before submitting your work to an editor. This mistake may not be as obvious as the others; it may not even be apparent to the editor who reads your work. But no amount of doctoring can make up for a writer's decision to settle for second-best just to get something shipped off.

A writer is an athlete who exercises the imagination. A serious writer must treat every writing assignment as a challenge to achieve a "personal best." To do less is to betray one's art and craft and to risk damage to one's career and, ultimately, to one's self-respect. In its way, a writer's life is as fierce as any Olympic competitor's. Take care with your writing to the extent of polishing the format of the manuscript: It should be in dark type in a font large enough to read without squinting, double-spaced, on clean paper, with a crisp and pertinent cover letter. First impressions count, so make the manuscript editor-friendly to look at. Then observe a Writer's First Commandment: "Thou shalt not be boring."

—Gerald Gross

Six Elements of Good Technical Writing

Here's a checklist for clearing up 'techspeak'

Just as chemical elements make up many different compounds, six elementary attributes can be used to construct good technical writing—whether an instruction manual, a technical article, or a product data sheet.

1. Accuracy. How can you convince a reader that you are an expert on your subject if your facts are incorrect? Since most technical writing tends to be instructive in some way, accuracy is critical. A technical mistake can make your results impossible for your reader to duplicate. For instance, if a test kit is supposed to be stored at –20° C and you write *Store components at 20° C*, the reagents in the kit will be ruined. I've worked with technical writers who think that because a mistake is a so-called "typo," it's not their responsibility. Wrong! This is the type of error that many editors would not necessarily catch or check—they would assume, as well they should, that *you* know the correct temperature for storing your kit. If your writing has a lot of careless errors, you will lose your credibility with knowledgeable readers and, eventually, with your editors.

2. Consistency. Here's how lack of it can confuse readers. In a manual I edited recently, a procedure recommended the use of a medium called *Sf-900 II SFM*. Later in the manual, related procedures referred to the medium as *SF-900 II* and *Sf-900*. Cell culturists use *Sf* as an abbreviation to mean an insect line and *SF* to mean "serum free." Also, *Sf-900 II SFM* means a "second-generation medium" (the improved version). By leaving out the generation number in some cases, the scientist made the reader guess whether the first-generation medium (the original version) should be used or not.

3. Clarity. Much technical writing tends to be complicated. Often, however, the complications arise from the writing itself rather than the subject matter. A procedure should be described with such precision that a reader can easily and accurately replicate it. Don't bury your results under abstract nouns, puzzling pronoun antecedents, and passive verbs. I recently edited a manual in which one step of a procedure read, *Heat the mixture to 65° C, then chill for 2 minutes.* Heat for how long? And what is the exact temperature for "chilling"? The corrected version of this sentence read, *Heat the mixture to 65° C for 10 minutes, then chill on ice for 2 minutes.*

4. Conciseness. All readers appreciate tightly written copy because it's easier to understand and gets to the point quickly; the mere sight of a long manual or article can be intimidating. Wordy procedural steps and explanations tend to result when writers want to be considered intelligent and knowledgeable but aren't sure they will be. Which of these examples do you prefer?

> An insatiable need to know that which it did not understand led to the inevitable demise of the *felis catus*.
>
> Curiosity killed the cat.

Though this chestnut is facetious, the technical literature is filled with examples of filling up the page rather than informing the reader. Using the active voice and imperative forms will help trim the word count. Instead of writing *The program shall be tested,* write *Test the program.* Instead of writing *Latex gloves should be worn by the user,* write *Wear latex gloves.* The "you" understood with the imperative involves the reader more directly as well.

5. Persuasiveness. A primary goal for a technical writer is to tell readers about a better way to do something. But as one who works with scientific information, you should be aware of the law of inertia: People and things keep moving on the same path unless there is a compelling reason to change direction. You must persuade readers that your ideas are better if you expect them to adopt your method. Explain how your results relate to your readers' work and can improve their performance. Here is an example from an overview of a manual I edited:

> The RACE procedure has been used to amplify and clone rare mRNAs and may be applied to existing cDNA libraries. Products of the RACE reaction can also be directly sequenced without any intermediate cloning steps, or the products may be used to prepare probes.

6. Liveliness. Technical writing has a reputation for being dry and, in fact, much of it is. But if you bore your readers, they may never finish your article. You want readers to be moved to try your method. Lively copy can be achieved by using short sentences, a relaxed style, and in some cases, even humor. While *Avoid using recycled glassware unless it has been specifically rendered RNase-free* accomplishes its warning, it is overly formal. To say *Being eco-minded can be harmful to your experiment. Recycled glassware is not always RNase-free* is friendlier and less of a mouthful.

If you want to write outstanding technical pieces, you shouldn't try to sound like everyone else. These six elements will help you write technical articles, manuals, and data sheets that keep a reader's attention long enough to make your case.

—James Rada, Jr.

Five Rules for Writing User-Friendly Technical Manuals

Readers are often left out of the 'tech doc' picture

While creating user-friendly manuals would seem to be an obvious step in product development, it is one that is frequently forgotten. This oversight does not mean that the authors don't know their products. Although technical writers may know what chemicals to pipette into what test tube, they often draw a blank when they try to put what they know on paper.

Writing manuals is a time-consuming process that you can make easier or harder on yourself. If you approach the task with enthusiasm, it will carry over into your writing and help you write a manual that won't put readers to sleep or set their teeth on edge with frustration. Look at manual writing as tying all your product development efforts together in a friendly way that makes the product that much more attractive to a user. Your readers will appreciate your hard work, and they'll show it by continuing to buy your product.

Here are five rules for making documentation as painless as possible for both you and your readers.

1. Keep your language simple. This basic rule for all types of writing is consistently ignored. Keep in mind that you are writing to offer information to someone else, not to impress the user with how much technical knowledge *you* have. Having someone unfamiliar with the product try to follow the procedures (called by some research scientists *protocols*) that you've written in an early draft of the manual is a good way to see how well you are communicating. If this reader can't follow the procedures, you need to rewrite them. Here are two ways to keep the writing clear and simple:

- **Use the second person wherever possible.** Some clients may insist that second person is too informal, but tell them it's the quickest way to get readers' attention and the surest way to move them from A to B.

- **Avoid passive voice and smothered verbs.** They make sentences longer and insulate the meaning from the reader. (See the example in rule 2.)

2. Tell readers why they should read the manual. At the beginning, you should always have some sort of introductory paragraph or overview that answers the question, "What's in this for me?" An overview not only tells the reader what to expect from the manual, but it also serves as a map for you as you write—telling you what you need to say to accomplish the objectives you set.

Here's the opening line in the overview of a manual I recently edited:

> The EXPRESSAMPTM System for *In Vitro* Expression of PCR Products is designed to permit the preparation of PCR products that can rapidly be transcribed, translated, and cloned.

Don't talk down to your readers

This sentence, despite the long kit name, does say what the product will do for the reader. There's a problem, though: The statement contains two passive constructions (*is designed, can be transcribed...*) and a smothered verb (*preparation*). The publisher and the user are invisible and it is less than clear exactly what the user can do. This rewrite is better:

> The EXPRESSAMPTM System...allows you to prepare PCR products for rapid transcribing, translating, and cloning.

3. Assume that your readers are novices. This is important from the very beginning. Don't take the chance that you will be writing over someone's head. Readers who are experts will most likely skip over the overview; those who read it are often unfamiliar with the product.

Also, the easiest way to lose a reader is by using acronyms that haven't been spelled out. While this doesn't include such basic scientific terms as *DNA* and *RNA*, it does include the more advanced acronyms. How do you decide what's "advanced"? Consider the audience. For example, a cell culturist knows that *IVD* stands for *in vitro diagnostic*, but a molecular biologist may not.

Conversely, don't talk down to your readers. Nothing insults them more than realizing that the writer thinks of them as idiots. Here's an example I caught in the first draft of a manual I edited:

> The milky-white plaques are small, of low contrast, and easily missed by novice BEVS practitioners.

Most professionals do not particularly enjoy being called novices, and writers who make such offhand references can seem condescending. This sentence was easily fixed by deleting "by novice BEVS practitioners."

4. Be thorough in the methods section of the manual. This is the critical section. Assume that your reader has never performed the procedure before. The ease with which a reader can use the procedures you outline will make or break the product. Don't risk a dissatisfied customer because you wrongly assumed that the intermediate step between 1 and 2 was too obvious to mention. There are two important offshoots of this rule.

- **Omitting information confuses readers.** The information needed to perform the step in the following example was left out because the writer was so familiar with the product that he took for granted that the user would know what the relative centrifugal force should be.

    Centrifuge the appropriate volume of suspension culture for the number of cells necessary for the experiment.

    What's the centrifugal force? For how long do you centrifuge the sample? Here's a better—more specific, that is—way to say this:

    Use the appropriate volume of suspension culture for the number of cells necessary for the experiment. Centrifuge the culture at 12,000 x g for 5 minutes.

- **Make sure you place steps in the right order.** If the reader is performing the experiment or process step-by-step, placing the steps out of order could cause an experiment or procedure to fail. Placing two actions out of order in the same step could also cause failure. Here is an example of a common error I run into when I am editing manuals:

    Discard the supernatant and keep the pellet.

    If directions are followed as written, the reader will not be able to keep the pellet because it will have been discarded with the supernatant. Though a writer may find it hard to believe that someone would read only half a step, perform it, then read the second half of the step and try to perform it, believe me, it happens every day. Technical services departments are always getting calls for help in cases like this.

5. Tell your reader all the ways the final product can be used. Don't be afraid to brag about the many uses for your product. More uses mean a larger audience of possible users and more perceived value for your product. Besides, no one knows your product as well as you do, so if you don't tell your readers how to use it, who will?

—*James Rada, Jr.*

Scare Tactics

Do you superstitiously avoid certain words?

Are there words that you're afraid to use? I'm not referring to naughty words or the ever-evolving list of politically incorrect terms. I'm thinking of words that, although used by most people every day without a second thought, frighten many writers and editors.

Like heads the list. It seems that ever since someone pointed out the grammatical faux pas in the slogan "Winston tastes good, like a cigarette should," wordsmiths have shied away from this innocuous preposition. The substitutes of choice are usually *such as* or simply *as*, but the change is often unnecessary and sometimes silly. The following sentences are acceptable uses of "like."

> In a softer market like that of the early 1990s, many owners have become more realistic.
>
> She looks like her sister.
>
> Like martins, bluebirds feed on insects.
>
> Or: Birds like martins and bluebirds feed on insects.

(While grammatically correct, these sentences may be factually in error. I'm no ornithologist!)

While we're at it: Does the wording of the preceding disclaimer bother you? *While* has that effect on many editors. Strict constructionists let "while" stand in its temporal sense: "While I'm out, please bathe the cat," but disdain it as a synonym for *whereas* and *although*: "While it's possible to bathe the cat, it certainly isn't easy." Copperud's *American Usage: The Consensus* supports the idea that such uses of *while* often lead to ambiguity, but treats its cousin *since* quite differently: "It is a delusion that *since* may be used only as an adverb in a temporal sense." ("Since you admit that it is possible to bathe the cat, I expect you to do it.")

Over may be underused. Copperud's *Consensus* puts the case succinctly: "It is a superstition endemic to newspapers that there is something wrong with *over* in the sense *more than*. The superstition has spread beyond the newspaper world; many copy editors routinely kill the word." The *Associated Press Stylebook* reflects the "superstition" in its somewhat waffling entry:

> *Over* can, at times, be used with number: *She is over 30. I paid over $200 for this suit.* But *more than* may be better: *Their salaries went up more than $20 a week.* Let your ear be your guide.

The *New York Times Manual of Style and Usage* shuns superstition by standing above the fray: It has no entry for *over*.

Where would we be without the last word on this short shunned list? The use of *where* to indicate location would seem obvious, yet a number of editors seem to regard it as infra dig and routinely change it to *in which,* even in such sentences as the following:

In buildings where the elevator shaft is centrally located....

It's paradoxical that editors who daily wrestle sesquipedalian terms to the mat can be daunted by four words that most first-graders can cope with. Maybe it's because we are quick to look up complex terms, but we assume we know all there is to know about the short ones.

The result is that many of us continue to edit uneasily around the scary spots, offering up superstitious proscriptions like hush money when asked why. Perhaps we all should reach for the latest edition of a style guide or dictionary before we sharpen our blue pencils. And check more than one if we don't like the answer we get! Usage may well have changed since last we looked. And what if we never check? Now, *that's* scary.

—*Lee Mickle*

prone/prostrate/supine

Although *prone* and *prostrate* both mean "lying face-down," they are often used more generally as synonyms for "lying flat," regardless of position. This usage is acceptable except where precision is at stake: More carefully, a *prone* figure is one that is resting against a supportive surface, whereas a *prostrate* posture implies submission, defeat, or physical collapse. "Blondie sighed as she eyed Dagwood's prone figure on the sofa and Daisy on the floor, prostrate with wistfulness."

Supine is the opposite of both words and always means "lying down on one's back, faceup." A *supine* position could connote inertness or depression. "Silent and *supine,* she spent the long winter nights tracking the cracks in the ceiling over her bed."

By the way, many people mistakenly refer to the male prostate gland as the "prostrate" gland, presumably because *prostrate* is the more common word. (Careful writers don't take such errors lying down.)

Promotional Writing That People Will Believe

The secret is to build in the benefit

It's easy to understand why advertising has earned itself a pretty bad reputation. More than anything else, advertising is known for its "hype," which the *American Heritage Dictionary* (third edition) defines as

1. Something deliberately misleading; deception. 2. Exaggerated or extravagant claims made especially in advertising or promotional material.

The key words here are *deception, exaggerated, extravagant*—what most of us think of when we think of advertising.

"Guaranteed to grow hair on a billiard ball!"

"Lose 70 pounds in one week or your money back!"

"Four out of five doctors recommend...."

The reason we think of those things is pretty obvious: The goal of advertising is to compel people to act, to make them do something. But the fact is, advertising won't ever make anyone do something they don't want to do. You can lead a horse to water, as the saying goes, but not even a frontier stump-winding snake oil salesman could have convinced gullible settlers to buy and drink bottles of magic elixir unless they felt they had something that needed fixing.

Straining at credulity

Advertising has no credibility because everyone who reads carefully knows that ads are manipulative, that the "truth" is slanted, that the whole perspective is shaded in favor of the product. "Nine of out ten doctors who recommend aspirin recommend ours." What the copywriters leave out is that the same doctors cite other brand names in the same recommendation. "More hospitals use our brand of ibuprofen than any other analgesic." Yes, and they use it because they get it at a deep, deep discount. Our jaundiced eye can fill in these blanks.

Still, some advertising works. (If it didn't, corporations wouldn't spend as much as $1.5 million for 30 seconds of commercial time during the Super Bowl broadcast.) Print advertising works when it speaks to a consumer's genuine need. Good copywriting communicates so forcefully, so passionately that it compels readers to act on real needs or desires—even if unaware of them before reading the ad.

The differentiator makes an ad believable

In copywriting school, they taught us how to write an ad that works. They told us that an ad without a differentiator is not an ad at all. They also taught us that an ad must have a couple of benefits to support the differentiator and a feature to prove every benefit. What they didn't teach us was that hype no longer works. If you want to write an ad that people will believe, tell the truth. Here's how.

A *differentiator* is the one characteristic that makes a product unique. The hype problem occurs when the differentiator isn't real. What differentiates a Ford from a Chevrolet? Just the spelling. But copywriters, questing after that special something, talk about the heartbeat of America (if America has a heartbeat, one hopes it's more in tune with the Constitution than with a Chevrolet) and quality as job number one (as if none of the subsequent assembly steps on the Ford line involved quality).

How do copywriters convince readers that the differentiator is indeed something about which they care? That's the role of the *benefit*. The simplest definition of a benefit is the attribute that answers the customer's need. In other words, a benefit is something that the customer derives from the product or service. The benefit of aspirin is, obviously, relief from pain.

Copywriters get into trouble by citing benefits that aren't real or can't be proved. Is it true, for example, that on the Miracle Diet Plan you can lose 70 pounds in one week? Only in conjunction with major surgery.

The feature as the attraction

For a benefit to be believable, it must be supported by a *feature*—a demonstrable element of a product or service. Unlike the ephemeral benefit, a feature is something that actually exists within the product. One way some copywriters remember the difference is to label benefits as subjective and features as objective: We can disagree on whether something is a benefit, but features are facts and therefore indisputable. An analgesic's feature is its pain-relieving medicine. Attributes prove the products can deliver what they say they can.

The benefits in an ad are the implied promises that a product will solve the reader's needs. When an ad leaves out the features that can be shown to be true, it offers only so many empty promises. In other words, hype. And finally, an ad without benefits to support the differentiator sounds exaggerated, extravagant, deceitful.

The key, then, is this: Find out what people want or need, then let them know you have it.

—*Craig Tyler*

Shifts in Construction

Careless shifts in tense, voice, mood, person, or number can distort meaning and confuse readers. In the following sentences, identify the shifts—sometimes called *mixed constructions*—and improve the sentences by making inconsistent elements parallel, supplying missing elements, or correcting pronoun-antecedent ambiguity. In some cases, it's better to rewrite the sentence.

1. If there are no signs of breathing or if no signs of a pulse are evident, take the first step in artificial respiration by placing one hand under the victim's neck and then you should put your other hand on the forehead of the victim so the forehead can be tilted back.

2. When a victim loses consciousness often scares a rescue worker.

3. Immediately after he accidentally cut his arm, his shirt was soaked with blood. His friend places a clean cloth directly over the wound and presses firmly.

4. If a person is suffering from food poisoning, you may feel the symptoms within a few minutes.

5. If a food poisoning victim has severe symptoms, they should notify a doctor.

6. In the morning, the first-aid students learned about remedies for frostbite; in the afternoon, the Heimlich maneuver was demonstrated.

7. The tourniquet was a temporary first-aid attempt but which was necessary.

8. The instructor explained that treating a burn with ice or cold water is preferable to when you adhere to the old wives' tale of using butter or oil.

9. Anyone can learn CPR if you try.

10. The Coast Guard instructor told us not to transport a drowning victim to shore first but that we should begin CPR while the victim is in a boat or floating in the water.

ANSWERS

There are several acceptable edits for these sentences. I've offered a few.

1. The compound dependent clauses lack parallel structure; the independent clauses shift from the imperative to the indicative mood.

> If there are no signs of breathing or there is no pulse, you should take the first step in artificial respiration: Place one hand under the victim's neck and then put the other hand....

> OR

> If no pulse or signs of breathing are evident, take the first step in artificial respiration by placing one hand under the victim's neck and then putting the other hand....

2. An adverb clause is trying to serve as the subject of the sentence.

> When a victim loses consciousness, a rescue worker often becomes scared.

> OR

> A victim's loss of consciousness often scares a rescue worker.

3. The tenses shift needlessly from the first to the second sentence. The action is all sequential, and the same tense should be used throughout.

> Immediately after he accidentally cut his arm, his shirt was soaked with blood. His friend placed a clean cloth directly over the wound and pressed firmly.

> OR

> Immediately after he accidentally cuts his arm, his shirt is soaked with blood. His friend places a clean cloth directly over the wound and presses firmly.

4. The sentence shifts from the third person to the second. Use one or the other consistently in both the dependent and independent clauses or rewrite the sentence.

> If you are suffering from food poisoning, you may feel the symptoms within a few minutes.

> OR

> Persons who suffer from food poisoning may feel the symptoms within a few minutes.

5. The sentence shifts in number from singular in the dependent clause to plural in the independent clause.

> If a food poisoning victim has severe symptoms, he or she should notify a doctor.

> OR

> A food poisoning victim who has severe symptoms should notify a doctor.

6. The sentence shifts awkwardly from active to passive voice.

> In the morning, the first-aid students learned about remedies for frostbite; in the afternoon, they saw a demonstration of the Heimlich maneuver.

7. The sentence shifts from a noun to an adjective clause.

> The tourniquet was a temporary but necessary first-aid attempt.

> OR

> The tourniquet was a temporary first-aid attempt, but one that was necessary.

8. The subject of the first dependent clause is a gerund and the subject of the second dependent clause shifts to *you*.

> The instructor explained that treating a burn with ice or cold water is preferable to adhering to the old wives' tale of using butter or oil.

9. The sentence shifts from third person to second.

> Anyone can learn CPR if he or she tries.

> OR

> You can learn CPR if you try.

10. The sentence shifts from a noun infinitive phrase to a noun clause. Use either phrases or clauses.

> The Coast Guard instructor told us not to transport a drowning victim to shore first but to begin CPR while the victim is in a boat or floating in the water.
>
> —*Ellie Abrams*

Humor Your Readers: The Uses of Wit

The funnybone's connected to the backbone of a message

Well-minted humor is a writer's hard currency: It will buy reader interest even when an article's content is debased coinage. People will pay money, stand in line, stay up too late, or learn how to program a VCR for something that makes them laugh. The wise writer will take advantage of the law of supply and demand. Don't think you have to be an Oscar Wilde to imbue your copy with wit or a Robin Williams to add a dash of amusement to an earnest article. Even if you are no wittier than most, you can often *quote* from someone with a gift for turning a quip.

Nor does humor require cracking jokes. In fact, in most writing, jokes and funny anecdotes are to be avoided; humor is a treacherous business. If you place a big bet on an obvious attempt at a knee-slapper or zinger, blow it and you've lost credibility. Subtle humor is better, because if it works, your winnings are just as large, and if it doesn't, it may pass unnoticed or at least look more like a tiny misfire than a sophomoric dud.

A 'stitch' in time helps readers unwind

Samuel Johnson said that "a good pun may be admitted among the smaller excellencies of lively conversation." The sort of humor I'm recommending is more likely to produce a smile or a chuckle than a belly laugh. Such humor entails viewing an idea or a subject in an uncommon light, from an odd angle, or by way of a slightly off-the-wall metaphor. Consider the following examples.

Illustrate serious points in a nondidactic way. No matter how weighty your subject, unless it's a funeral oration or a declaration of war, you can express an occasional thought amusingly while maintaining the appropriate tone overall.

Suppose you are assigned to do a piece on interest rates. (If you are a financial writer, you will probably write many.) Your article will no doubt mention the Federal Reserve Board, an august body whose job at times is to hold interest rates down to stimulate the economy, while at others it is to keep interest rates up to discourage inflation. You could write this:

> Leading economists expect 1994 to present low inflationary pressures, consequently encouraging Federal Reserve policies driven by prudent restraint.

Yawn. Or you could make the same point the way the writers of a *Business Week* piece did. They quoted economist Edward E. Yardeni:

> The Fed should just take 1994 off and call in for messages.

Vary the routine. For the sake of completeness, sometimes you must include information that is obvious or an idea that is commonplace. Humor allows you to follow the prescribed drill but in a lively, nonclichéd way.

Have you read a story about a company that still does things the old-fashioned way, clinging to long-standing traditions of craftsmanship in the face of automated corner-cutting? Of course you have. In fact, you have probably read this kind of "made-in-the-Black-Forest-by-elves" screed many times, and on the whole, you would prefer not to read it again.

Here's how *New York* magazine writer Bernice Kanner used humor to combat *déjà lu.* Her feature story on Brooks Brothers, the 175-year-old gentlemen's clothier specializing in the Old-Guard Establishment look, was headlined "Seams Like Old Times," and the piece was accompanied by a photo captioned "Sleeves of New York."

When it came to describing the buttons on Brooks Brothers shirts—can you *imagine* how boring this might have been?—Kanner delivered the information with a light touch:

> Though the retailer had used the same button supplier for a decade, a sudden rash of complaints prompted it to change vendors—and institute a new test. "We press buttons dry-cleaner style, 40 or 50 times," says [a marketing vice-president]. "Few break, but just in case you meet a sumo wrestler, we attach an extra button on the shirttail."
>
> ...One New Yorker reported that his shirts withstood the "bungee iron drop" at the neighborhood laundry, "where they have perfected the art of button-crushing." A rueful correspondent penned a requiem for a button, bemoaning the expiration of one on a favorite shirt that "had served with high distinction under the stresses of war, sport, bad laundry machines and a tough economy." Brooks sent the man a new shirt and a sympathy letter pointing out that the replacement had buttons that had been "briefed on the hazards of modern cleaning technology, catsup and inclement weather."

Take the sting out of criticism. From time to time, you will have to write something uncomplimentary about a person or company. Even if you feel the criticism is deserved, you may prefer to say it in a way that minimizes embarrassment or (if you happen to be influential) adverse economic effects. Humor can be the answer.

Steve Deyo, in *ComputerUser* magazine, recently wrote a critique of the biblical software on the market (that's right—programs that allow you to access and search the scriptures, for spiritual or scholarly purposes). Rating such programs as QuickVerse, Verse Search, and Bible Master, the author found them all useful but had some reservations about PC Study Bible, mainly because of his allergy to the DOS platform. Making deft allusion to the trend in software as well as the fate of sinners, Deyo wrote:

In a world that's going to Windows in a handbasket, it's awfully hard to get excited about monospaced fonts and DOS cursors.

Deyo sounds like something of a DOS curser himself, but he expresses his aversion wryly:

> However, for PC users who are abstaining from Windows, for whom DOS is a kind of purgatory (by preference or by limited purchasing power), PC Study Bible offers a lot of power....

Minimize verbiage. When your language must go on a diet because of space limitations, humor can present a case in fewer words than a formal argument. Sometimes a telling point is made by carrying a premise to its absurd conclusion.

For years, there has been a fierce debate among audiophiles (people who are serious about high-quality sound reproduction) over the value of interconnects. These are very fancy and very expensive (sometimes over $100 a foot) cables that send an audio signal from one piece of equipment to another. One school of thought says that interconnects make the sound clearer and purer, while the other team maintains that a wire is a wire. A correspondent to an audio magazine wrote:

> I am waiting for the golden-eared interconnect worshippers to tell me that I should use only electricity imported from Washington state, generated by water power, rather than unclean coal-generated electricity from here in Ohio.

Nobody likes a bully

Humor can backfire. When it does, it's usually because the joke is made at the expense of a vulnerable target or is tainted with vindictiveness or moral superiority. Check yourself on these points.

Relevance. Always ask yourself: Does this witticism advance the purpose of my writing, or is it a diversion I can't afford? When you interrupt the momentum of a piece, even for an amusing interlude, you and your readers must both work to get rolling again. Remember that the humor must be relevant not just to the *subject* you are writing about, but to the *purpose* of your writing.

For instance, Amtrak is currently running a billboard campaign promoting its Metroliner service between Washington, DC, and New York City. One of the boards proclaims that the train is

THE POIFECT WAY TO GET TO MIDTOWN NEW YAWK.

New Yorkers may not think this mimicking of their accent is funny, but for the sake of discussion, we'll call it amusing. But does the humor give you a reason to take Amtrak instead of flying or driving? No.

Taste. There are few taboo subjects anymore, but vulgarity is still bad form. Off-color humor rarely serves a useful purpose and is out of place in most publications. It is also tasteless to apply humor to situations involving real suffering or misfortune (by "real" I mean more than a wound to someone's ego). A good illustration is contained in *The Word: An Associated Press Guide to Good News Writing*, by Rene J. Cappon. Cappon quotes a human-interest story that begins this way:

> So you think you've got problems? Wait till you hear the story of Chuh-Chuh the shih-tzu from Howard Beach.

Having primed you to laugh and encouraged you to identify with the dog, the story then punches you out:

> The dog's owners filed for $5.1 million in damages...claiming they had suffered distress and psychological pain, while the dog suffered prolonged pain following castration by a veterinarian. Chuh-Chuh died in August, nine days after the operation. The veterinarian said the owners' attorney...had a bark that is worse than his bite.

The animal's suffering and the owners' grief turn this flippancy sour.

Offensiveness. Is humor acceptable if someone finds it, or may find it, offensive? Yes. You risk getting kneecapped by the Political Correctness Mafia, but as far as I'm concerned you are within your rights to use humor for advancing an argument or expressing an idea. Motive for using humor is the key. If your main purpose *is* to offend someone, you cross a line that should not be crossed.

Snide or condescending humor is almost always a mistake. A good example of high-horse humor is this excerpt from an editorial that leveled several hundred holier-than-thou words at a jargon-ridden Bell Atlantic brochure. The writer ended this way:

> For one thing, the writer has gone acronym berserk....Sorry, Mr. Ding-a-Ling. We just can't follow your trail....Thankfully [sic], Bell Atlantic promises "design and consultation assistance."...It's so comforting to be taken care of. Truly, Bell Atlantic is the mother of them all.

Even in a column labeled "Sound-off," there is no place for mean-spiritedness. The assumption is that readers will enjoy or identify with sarcasm directed against the corporation everyone loves to hate. But from the headline ("Many thanks for solving the problem you created") to the final smarmy "mother" reference, 'tain't funny, McGee. You want to leave readers laughing, not wincing.

—Rick Darby

49

Writing Short without Cutting Essentials

What you leave in matters as much as what you leave out

T rimming your own writing to meet a word requirement is no easier than trimming your own hair—it's hard to maintain an objective angle. You write and revise, write and revise, but can you tell when your prose begins to resemble a bad haircut?

Clarity and accuracy are just as important as brevity. Before cutting your own copy, safeguard the essential parts of your message by asking yourself the following questions:

- **Is your prose style appropriate to the content?** Short, punchy sentences and paragraphs don't suit all types of material. If you're narrating a tragic event or dissecting a complex issue, you'll need to lay your thoughts out more slowly. The rhythms of your prose affect your message, so listen to them.

- **Are you giving a step-by-step guide to a process?** If you're writing a software manual or a cookbook, you'll need to retain all the details of a sequence of commands or functions. Shortcuts that collapse steps may skip past installing the software or adding the eggs.

- **Are you making an argument?** Don't neglect the examples that support each of your points. Without them, your ideas will seem like mere opinions. A statement that a particular company excelled in 1995 requires an account of what the company's goals were and how they were achieved.

- **How much context will most readers require?** Consider how much they're likely to know about the issue you're addressing. If you're writing an appeal for donations for a relatively unfamiliar cause, your readers will need the fullest history of the topic that space allows. Similarly, a journalist writing on a current event in a country rarely covered in the news needs more space to sketch the background for the story.

- **How technical is the material?** Again, assess your audience's familiarity with your topic. If you're writing a chemistry article for a journal read exclusively by chemists, the terms being used will require little explanation. Science writers who publish in general interest publications, however, must not only explain the newest cure or discovery but also discuss it in terms that let the audience understand its significance.

- **How important are quotations from sources?** While you *can* briefly paraphrase what your sources say, it's not always the smart thing to do. Direct testimony carries a force that indirect reference lacks. If quotations have been chosen carefully for effect, they're worth the space they take.

There are, however, places that are almost always safe bets for trimming and reshaping. As William Strunk and E.B. White said, "Vigorous writing is concise." Here are some places to look at twice when you've been prolix:

- **Cut empty expressions.** "The rising interest rate had the effect of excluding many potential home buyers from the market" could be edited to "The rising interest rate excluded many potential home buyers from the market" or even better, "...kept many potential home buyers out of the market." Although people tend to default to wordiness in speaking, clunky phrases should be cut from writing. In his book *On Writing Well*, William Zinsser advises writers to "strip every sentence to its cleanest components."

- **Cut nonessential adverbs and adjectives.** Watch out for surplus indefinite qualifiers like *very, really, extremely, rather, some, somewhat, sometimes, partial, often, frequent, seldom, most,* and *many.* "Much research suggests that many people may find that the costs of psychotherapy are somewhat prohibitive but can sometimes be offset by partial insurance reimbursement" is a less than useful statement. Clarify or delete imprecise qualifiers whenever possible. (Sometimes an estimate has to be worded loosely, however.)

- **Cut down on jargon.** Even language specific to technical types of writing can often be rewritten more simply. Just because readers are *capable* of reading highly technical language doesn't mean they want to encounter it in, say, a newsletter or a summary report. A little of the likes of *repurposing* goes a long way.

As Alexander Pope wrote, "Simplicity is the mean between ostentation and rusticity." Writing short means writing simply—without oversimplification.

—*Elisabeth Dahl*

On Kindly Teachers and the Generic *He*

The right word in the right place doesn't get there by accident

Whenever I read something by Garrison Keillor or Anne Fadiman, I find myself wishing I'd said that first. This month, two examples stand out.

Pathetic protozoa?

When Keillor mercilessly lampooned entries to a poetry contest he judged (*Atlantic Monthly*, February 1996), he probably wasn't surprised that a spokeswoman for the contest's sponsor, the St. Paul AAUW, protested in print (Letters, ibid., May 1996). She claimed to have expected more sympathy because Keillor "seemed to understand how much it meant to those inspired, pathetic protozoa who submitted their absurd elegies to their dead cats, their odes to Vietnam buddies 'blown away yesterday,' their lyrics on wedding receptions, their memories of Duluth, and assorted other laughable 'painful truths.'"

To which Keillor, in his response, had the courage to denounce "kindly teachers" like his critic, who "encourage bad writing." Attacking his critic for referring to the amateurs as "pathetic protozoa," Keillor said he viewed them as "ambitious, intelligent persons who deserve better teaching. Writing requires discipline, and it can be taught, but you don't find it in turgid poems about Bad Daddies and The Struggle to Be Me and all the other flat, morbid, narcissistic writing that is encouraged by bad teaching...."

Her, too

Meanwhile, Anne Fadiman may have made the most persuasive argument yet for abandoning the idea that "or her" is understood in constructions such as "to each his own." In an essay titled "His, Her, His'er" (*Civilization*, May/June 1996), she recounts her difficulties in accepting "his or her," "their," or any mutations ("his'er"), as well as the awkwardness of casting every sentence in the plural.

She also reports her ambivalence about the value of the United Church of Christ's new "inclusive" hymnal, in which, for example, "Dear Lord and Father of Mankind" has been replaced by "Dear God, Embracing Humankind." She endorses the aim while deploring the means, saying "I'm not sure I want to be embraced by a God with such a tin ear." (Others might be even less charitable, especially with respect to the hymnal's complete rewrite of the beautiful poetry of "America the Beautiful" as a paean to hemispheric solidarity: "How beautiful, two continents, and islands in the sea...Americas! Americas!....")

Anyway, to investigate just how "understood" the female was in the generic "he," Fadiman decided to ask her father, writer-editor Clifton Fadiman, what was in his mind when he wrote these sentences long ago: "The best essays [do not] develop original themes. They develop original men, their composers."

"Be honest," she said on the phone, and he replied:

> I was thinking about males. I viewed the world of literature—indeed, the entire world of artistic creation—as a world of males, and so did most writers. Any writer of 50 years ago who denies that is lying. Any male writer, I mean.

Anne Fadiman concludes:

> I believe that although my father and E.B. White [whom she described as her "beloved role model" and who also wrote in masculine terms: "the essayist/he"] were not misogynists, they didn't really *see* women, and their language reflected and reinforced that blind spot....

> What I am saying here is very simple: Changing our language to make men and women equal has a cost. That doesn't mean it shouldn't be done. High prices are attached to many things that are on the whole worth doing....

'The right man in the right place'

Anne Fadiman says that women's "invisibility" was first brought home to her 15 years ago when a 1946 book of which her mother, Annalee Jacoby, was coauthor, *Thunder Out of China*, was reissued in paperback. In the foreword, Harrison Salisbury mentioned the other author, Theodore H. White, 19 times and Jacoby, once. His first sentence, in fact, was "There is, in the end, no substitute for the right man in the right place at the right moment."

When Fadiman called this imbalance to Salisbury's attention, he responded, "I am entirely guilty.... It is just one of those totally dumb things which I do sometimes." [Ed. note: I find this an adorable but unacceptable, as well as ungrammatical, apology.]

Appalled as I am at the prospect of abandoning "God shed his grace on thee, / and crown thy good with brotherhood / from sea to shining sea" for "God grant that we may be / a hemisphere where people here / all live in harmony," I think Anne Fadiman makes a lot of sense.

—*Priscilla S. Taylor*

Honoring Diversity in Business Writing

Writers must weigh their words for accuracy and inclusiveness

"**W**ords are what hold society together," said Stuart Chase, an American economist and author. Unfortunately, the words chosen by many speakers and writers often push people apart. Words make a difference; writers and editors who use them well have an enormous influence on reader attitudes.

The U.S. workforce includes men and women of all races and ethnic backgrounds, religions, ages, physical and mental characteristics, and sexual orientations. Employees should be defined by the skills they bring to the workplace, not by physical or cultural characteristics that are irrelevant to their jobs.

Traditionalists argue that we shouldn't alter the language "just to appease a few extremists." They're right; we shouldn't. But the number of "nontraditional" workers (that is, not white males) in the labor force is more than "a few." In fact, it's more than half, according to the Hudson Institute's *Workforce 2000.*

Customers are diverse as well. It's plain bad business to use sales letters, training manuals, press releases, and presentations that are likely to alienate potential clients. Most of us prefer to do business with companies that show us some respect, and inadvertently referring to a woman as "Sir" or "Mr." in correspondence is careless.

Of course, changing "the handicapped" to "people with disabilities" in your employee handbook will not transform people's attitudes. But over time, such language can contribute to an atmosphere in which employees' abilities are seen as more *important.* Besides, the real reason for using bias-free words has more to do with clearness and accuracy. Many exclusive terms (*workman, manpower*) are misleading, confusing, or incorrect.

Communication involves more than the writer's intent. If readers have to pause to determine the intent, the writer has introduced unnecessary ambiguity. Why not use one of the clearer options that are available? Some of the most useful and appropriate words are the simplest and most objective ones. For example, your company's "Manpower Study" might easily be retitled "Staffing Study."

Many commonly used terms carry negative connotations, even when the writer's or speaker's intended meaning is innocuous. The editorial style guide to *The Economist,* noted for its flouting of political correctness, advises writers that "the *hearing-impaired* are simply *deaf.* It is no disrespect to the *disabled* sometimes to describe them as *crippled*." That recommendation is an anomaly to the most of the publishing world. General business communications will do well to avoid referring to people as secondary to their physical condition.

Job descriptions bring up another compelling reason to avoid gender-biased language: Exclusive language can leave a company vulnerable to Equal Employment Opportunity lawsuits. Any systemic bias—against

The number of 'nontraditional' workers is more than a few. It's more than half

gender, age, race, physical condition, or the like—infused throughout your organization could open the door to "environmental" harassment and discrimination lawsuits. If your company has job titles that specify sex (such as foreman, chairman, or salesman), change them to encompass all potentially qualified applicants—even if the current job holders are men. Studies show that when masculine terms are used for supposedly gender-free concepts, both women and men are likely to read "men only" (as reported in *The Nonsexist Word Finder*, by Rosalie Maggio, Oryx Press). The solution is often as simple as using *courier* instead of *deliveryman* or *press worker* instead of *pressman*.

In general, people should not be made uncomfortable by what they are called—but those terms must be accurate and clear. If you find yourself reaching for a muddy or ludicrous euphemism (*sewing personnel, seamster*) to avoid a possibly offensive word (*seamstress*), remember that there is *always* a way to say what's meant (*garment maker*) in a clear *and* sensitive way.

—*Catherine Petrini*

The Grooves of Academe

The habit of writing long is honestly come by and hard to shake

The vast majority of scholarly authors have two pet locutions, which the vast majority of copyeditors smite hip, thigh, and blue pencil at every opportunity. Perhaps the highly educated among us, having been properly trained to eschew four-letter words, assume that *most* and *than* are a bit risqué. That might explain why copyeditors can stay employed changing sentences like this one

> The vast majority (73%) of respondents agreed that teenagers are more likely to drive recklessly compared to adults.

to read

> Most respondents (73%) agreed that teenagers are more likely to drive recklessly than adults.

It's curiously rare, too, to encounter *majority* by itself, even when the accompanying percentage shows it to be no more than substantial or even modest. Academic writers seem to feel that a majority that isn't vast is no majority at all. Could they be unconsciously swayed by political reporting?

A more subtle point of usage deals with *compared to*. It's generally accepted that when comparing similar subjects, the preposition of choice is *with* rather than *to*. This leaves *compared to* with comparatively little to do except lounge back and act poetic:

> Shall I compare thee to a summer's day? Relative to a summer's day, thou art more lovely and more temperate.

Alert readers will notice that the preceding is a paraphrase. *Relative to* is the kissing cousin of *compared to;* both look down their noses at poor but honest *than*.

It should come as no surprise that academic authors tend to err on the polysyllabic side. From high school or even earlier, students are conditioned to believe that in writing, more is better; that if a two-page paper is worth a B+, two and a half pages will earn an A. (For an entertaining view of a teacher who grades her students' notebooks by thickness, read Daniel Pinkwater's *The Snarkout Boys and the Avocado of Death*, which is at least as funny as its title.) Small wonder that "writing long" comes naturally by the time authors reach the postgraduate level.

Fortunately for you, however, I'm a graduate-school dropout.

—Lee Mickle

The Struggle for Gender-Free Language: Is It Over Yet?

No, and don't hold your breath

A ll current style manuals address in one form or another the need for bias-free, inclusive language. Most writers and editors deal with this issue regularly—we've installed mental alarm systems that go off when we sense bias or something that can be construed as bias.

Does gender-free writing still present problems? After all these years of practice at being evenhanded, consider several litmus tests.

The all-purpose *he* we love to hate

Perhaps the first and best evidence of how popularized the issue of fairness has become is the case of what's called the "generic *he*." At this point, it probably should be replaced for more than issues of social justice: The "universal" masculine pronoun is likely to stop most readers because they see it so seldom. No matter the writer's intention, the risk is that *he* won't be considered inclusive and will annoy readers.

Editors are all too aware that write-around-the-problem strategies present problems of their own, not the least of which is sounding forced. Recasting a sentence into the plural or using second person instead of third works well as long as the revision fits in with the surrounding text. But if the discussion has been in the third person all along, changing persons simply calls attention to the problem without solving it. And while it's true that the passive has a place in our language, it pains us as editors to hobble an active verb, no matter how just the cause.

Other fixes for replacing the generic *he*, such as *he or she*, too often lead to imprecision and wordiness. And although it's not difficult to find sources that favor using *their* despite the disagreement in number (after all, writers as different as Jane Austen and Ernest Hemingway used it this way), this usage is still far more acceptable in spoken than in written language.

One term for all and all terms inclusive

The second, closely related challenge in gender-free writing has been to substitute inclusive terms for gender-specific ones. The move to many of these words has been painless. *Police officer, firefighter, flight attendant, sales clerk, mail carrier, anchor* or *newscaster, weather forecaster*, and the like all have gained general acceptance. No meaning is lost, and there's nothing particularly awkward or silly about any of these terms.

But not all gender-free language rolls off the keyboard quite so easily. In a survey with no scientific pretenses, I asked some of my editing colleagues to review a list of problematic words and their suggested alternatives from Rosalie Maggio's classic, *The Nonsexist Word Finder*. Here are their reactions to three words people are likely to come across in formal writing:

- **chair.** Most of those polled had no problem with this term, but some preferred committee *head* or *chairperson*. Chair obviously doesn't work as part of a formal title, and the Associated Press style guide, among others, recommends *chairman* and *chairwoman* for that usage. None of these alternatives was particularly helpful to the *Editorial Eye* subscriber

Not all gender-free language rolls off the keyboard easily

we heard from who was the only woman in a group of fellow (oops!) corporate vice presidents who were all *chairmen* of various committees. She believed that all the committee heads should be called the same thing: Calling her something different singled her out as a woman, but she didn't want to be called a *chairman*, which she found sexist. Her male colleagues refused to budge. They wanted to be called *chairmen* and resisted terms like *chair* or *chairperson*, which they found too impersonal. ("We *are* men," they told her. "Call yourself a *chair* if it bothers you.") Evidently, nothing's as simple as it seems.

- **layman.** As far as most respondents were concerned, this can easily be *layperson*, while a *congressman* can be called a *representative* or a *member of Congress*. No one wanted to replace *ombudsman* (the Swedish use is inclusive because "man" means "one") with *ombud* or *ombuds*, but this word suffers from the same drawback as other "man" words. The alternatives sound odd and a bit awkward—*service member* for *serviceman* and *jury supervisor* for *foreman*—but so does "Jane Smith is the foreman."

- **forefather.** Although *ancestor* and *forebear* were generally seen as acceptable substitutes for *forefather*, several people pointed out that the alternatives don't have exactly the same meaning. We are the direct descendants of our ancestors, but our forefathers include a broader group of those that preceded us. Nevertheless, these two substitutes are likely to find more favor than *forefather* and *foremother*, which Maggio says are acceptable if used gender-fairly. My colleagues agreed that, used gender-fairly or not, *foremother* is not a particularly euphonious or graceful way to solve the problem.

Reinventing the flat tire?

And in a third category are alternative words Maggio proposes that may not be obvious candidates for change because they seem to work.

Mastermind seemed just fine to everyone surveyed. Despite the "master," it did not strike anyone as being a biased term, and the alternatives— *genius* or *plotter* for the noun and *oversee*, *guide*, or *originate* for the verb— didn't have the same connotation; likewise for *craftsmanship*, *gamesmanship*, *straw man*, and *straight man*.

It's clear that despite good intentions and conscientious efforts, it's not over yet. Some current alternatives feel like sand on the tongue, while others slip into the language. As time goes by, constructions we resist now may grow on us. It's probably safe to say that our children will wonder what all the fuss was about, but in the meantime, writers and editors must work toward making certain that gender-free language doesn't become substance-free.

While extremists may have been instrumental in starting the movement toward gender-free usage, they won't be the ones who finish it. As *Webster's Dictionary of English Usage* quotes from Ebbitt and Ebbitt, "the hard choices in word selection with respect to sexism have to be made by middle-of-the-roaders; the partisans—the militant feminists and the entrenched elderly males—have already made up their minds and are seldom in doubt."

I, for one, am still wrestling with "Dear Sir or Madam."

—*Jane Rea*

The Craft of Editing

Why Edit?

Because it matters

Where do I start? Perhaps with narrow escapes...like the editor who correctly changed "lowering" (the drinking age) to "raising" it in a document meant for national distribution, or the editor who noticed that the signature line for a letter signed by James Madison should not have read 1924. Or, more to the point, perhaps with horror stories...like the editor who did not notice that John Adams was referred to as the third president of the United States in a letter signed by Prince Charles and Princess Diana. This letter appeared a few years ago in the *Washington Post* in conjunction with the Treasure Houses of Britain exhibit, and the press had a field day.

In each case, someone merely reading these documents for typos would not have caught the error—nor would the ubiquitous spell checker. Someone's brain had to be engaged; someone had to be reading with a critical eye; someone had to be processing the information. That someone is often an editor.

Who or what is an editor? Ideally, someone with an eye for detail who checks spelling, grammar, consistency, and conformity to style. On a deeper level, someone who clarifies the author's meaning but leaves the author's voice intact; someone who acts as the reader's advocate and points out where ideas are muddled, logic is flawed, or the argument bogs down in unnecessary detail or endless repetition. Every piece of writing can benefit from an edit.

For many writers, an editor is simply the enemy who takes a piece of perfectly adequate writing and mucks it up. Undoubtedly, some writers have been victims of the meat-ax school of editing: There are as many bad editors out there as there are bad writers, and it takes only a few bad experiences to sour writers on editing and editors forever. But the fact of the matter is that writers tend to be concerned with content and editors with its expression; writers focus primarily on meaning and editors on form. Together they can produce a document that says what it means to say clearly to its intended audience. Often a writer is so close to the subject matter that he or she thinks a sentence or phrase will be crystal clear when in fact it will not. Readers depend totally on the written word; no body language or inflection guides them as in conversation.

Why edit? Because the little things you think that no one will notice or care about can come back to haunt you. Because an editor just might save you from looking foolish in print.

—Mary Stoughton

Not by Intuition Alone:
Taking Stock of Editing Habits

Let's resolve to be clear about why we're doing what we do

I t's surprising how many editors rely on their intuition and how few seem aware of their editing techniques. The habit of editing by hunch is common to new editors as well as to those who have been editing for years and now work almost automatically. But editing is like performing: Doing it well requires both art and craft, innate skill and training.

I was reminded of this connection recently when I attended a performance of Jim Cartwright's play, *The Rise and Fall of Little Voice*. The main character is a young woman who sings brilliantly and ingenuously, with no sense of her own artistry. Another character asks her, "How do you do it? You wouldn't know, would you? The true performer never does." Natural talent obviously comes into play. But with editing, as with singing, intuition alone is not enough to sustain a career unless every assignment calls for the same approach.

Because most editing jobs require making reasonable (and defensible) judgment calls, I encourage the students in the workshops I teach to take editing out of the realm of pure intuition. I urge them to look for general principles and specific rules by asking them such questions as "How did you know it needed fixing?" and "What made you choose this solution instead of that one?" The education of an intuitive editor—and of a veteran editor—can be undertaken on two levels: by using consistent work habits and by resisting the occupational hazards of introversion and stagnation.

How can editors develop organized habits?

Make multiple passes. One of the most reliable techniques is to make multiple passes through a manuscript. Susan Colwell, associate technical editor for *Byte* magazine, says, "I used to try to do everything at once, but I've realized that I do better by focusing on certain things individually." Colwell now uses her first pass to correct style problems and her second to address the content; other editors attend first to substance, later to style. Many make a separate, quick pass to review head levels, check figure titles and sources, or examine the format of lists.

The point is not that "Thou shalt only edit thus"; as long as your technique works well, it's legitimate, but be aware of what it is. You can always deviate from your standard if the document warrants it—for instance, when editing a short brochure—but only if you have a conscious standard to begin with can you avoid getting sidetracked in large, complex, or dense editing jobs.

Use flags for different types of problems. It's also helpful to develop a system to make the most of the manual or electronic tools that can help organize a job. Many editors use self-stick notes to flag the problems in a document; later they find themselves pawing through pages bristling with yellow in the vain hope of finding a certain query. Why not invest in a rainbow of colors? Use one for queries, another for statements to be checked, a third for format inconsistencies to be resolved later, and so on, and you can then focus on particular problems systematically.

Electronic markers—"hidden comments" or notes and queries entered directly in the text—should also be used consistently. Mark them with a unique combination of characters, such as **??** or **xxx**, so that you can search for them easily.

Use a style sheet. Maintaining a record of editorial decisions—a style sheet—is one of the best ways to deliver editorial consistency. But have you examined your criteria? Some editors record virtually every decision they make; others enter only issues that are not specifically treated in their main style guide. In any case, start the style sheet during the early stages of editing, scan it before your final read of the document, update it, and file it for future reference.

Again, there are many reasonable approaches. The exact format of the style sheet matters less than using it each time as a matter of objective quality control. Readers notice inconsistency.

Use an editorial checklist. Perhaps the best tool is a comprehensive checklist. The kind of publications you edit will determine the items on the list, and not all items will be checked for each job. For a book you might include reminders to complete the permission forms, check pagination for the table of contents and the index, and cross-check the acknowledgments against the bibliography. A checklist for a brochure might include a reminder to verify the address and to cross-check the order form with product prices in captions. There are two basic kinds of checklists:

- One checklist can be used at the start of a job to define the appropriate level of edit for a specific manuscript or client. An editor may be directed to impose a certain format on bulleted lists but to refrain from changing first person to third. This approach starts a job off on the right track and avoids wasted effort.

- A second checklist, used for quality control, can save editors from their worst nightmares. This out-the-door checklist is the last chance to correct the things that can sabotage a completed manuscript: copy repeated or left out, incorrect color specs, transposed placement of photos and captions, and the like. Even if you consider yourself a careful worker, never assume that you will always remember to check for everything. We all need memory aids.

How can editors keep learning—about everything?

Remember that no editor is an island. Especially if you're an introverted sort (true for many of us in this field), bringing the "people" part of the publishing equation into the open can be a big help in managing the editorial process successfully. And we can learn from our mistakes.

Consider, for example, the project that Carmen Drebing, of Sandia National Laboratories, says "almost crashed before I could get a good grasp on what was happening." Drebing, responsible for editing and coordinating a major report, realized with dismay that she and the lead writer simply weren't on the same wavelength. "I wasn't getting the detail I needed, and the writer kept thinking that I should know where to put the various elements." All ended well, but only "after we each became aware that the other person wasn't wrong, just different." Adds Drebing ruefully, "The traumatic experiences are the ones you learn from."

The more insular your work environment is, the more important are outside sources of knowledge and stimulation. I'm always surprised that editors don't make more time for general reading—science fiction, cookbooks, history, political essays—for pleasure. Outside reading can provide perspective while adding to your knowledge.

Professional reading should be regular fare. Some editors set aside time to actually read reference books, beyond just looking things up to document specific decisions. Reviewing a section of a particular usage manual each Friday afternoon almost surely will help an editor spot a useful rule or explanation that escaped earlier notice.

Get back to, and away from, the basics. Regardless of the subject matter, a class can provide the benefit of cross-pollination that comes from exchanging viewpoints with like-minded colleagues. The best editor is often a generalist. So why not stretch your muscles? An advanced grammar class will arm you with technical explanations you had forgotten and enable you to make decisions more expeditiously. A writing class will renew your appreciation for the writer's task and help you develop judgment about style and organization. A computer or design course will open your eyes to a world of form beyond page margins—and open eyes are the editor's best habit.

—Diane Ullius

English as She Is Spoke

Transcriptions are an unusual editorial challenge

I recently had the interesting experience of editing the transcript of a three-day conference on a moderately technical topic. One of the things that made it interesting was that my assignment was to copyedit the transcript; my client assured me that a substantive editor had already reviewed it. Nonetheless, my eye fell on the following phrases:

Without further adieux, let me proceed.

The question is whether the existing networks will be vulcanized.

I'll give you a quick antidote to illustrate my point.

It's a phrase that is deigning some currency.

This shows what the medium locals are thinking.

(The last one stumped me for a few minutes; after a careful examination of the context, I figured out that *medium locals* were *media moguls*.)

Aside from the fact that one editor had managed to miss these errors, it was interesting to note that they appeared in what was, in fact, a remarkably clean, well-produced transcript. Imagine, then, what pitfalls lie in weight (get it?) when a transcript is produced under less-than-ideal conditions.

For less-than-ideal conditions, of course, we need look no further than the federal government, which customarily chooses transcription services primarily on the basis of price. A member of my family deals with transcripts of hearings on medical conditions. The deck is definitely stacked against the transcriber; the subject matter is quite technical, and neither the transcriber nor the speaker is likely to be familiar with the terminology. Those conditions lead to such valiant attempts as

Arthur's optotree (*arthrotomy*)

Chain smokers restoration (*Cheyne-Stokes respiration*)

Charcoal Mary's tote syndrome (*Charcot-Marie-Tooth syndrome*)

The Pasture (*Pasteur*) Clinic

Sick-as-hell anemia (*sickle cell anemia*)

My favorite malapropism, however, comes from a paper—ostensibly not a transcript at all—written by a Ph.D. I choose to assume that it was transcribed by a fairly competent word processing operator. The spell-checking program had obviously been run, but the program saw no reason to flag a reference to *inappropriate sexual morays* (*kinky, promiscuous, and casual*). After reading that, my advice is, Don't go near the water!

—*Lee Mickle*

Keeping Things Consistent When You're the 'Guest' Editor

The biggest favor you may do is watching out for blindspots

Consistency is the cornerstone of intelligent editing. In these days of leaner staffs and smaller budgets, however, many organizations don't employ full-time editors and depend on contract or freelance editors to make sure their publications are written in a consistent—and thus coherent—manner.

Take, for example, the case of a large telecommunications company that bought out a smaller competitor's hot new software product, which was intended to work with an existing office phone system through an interface designed by the telecommunications company. The immediate need was for documentation and online help to facilitate the user's interaction with the software.

What's so unusual about enforcing consistency? Because this company no longer had an editor on staff, two freelance technical editors (I was one) were hired to work with a team of writers assembled from several areas in the company. We kept coming across major inconsistencies in the information that would be supplied to users.

Although dealing with inconsistency is nothing new, particularly on a large project, we were surprised at how enterprising we had to be to resolve the writing problems we found.

Because of recent companywide cutbacks, the telecommunications writers and project leaders were working on more than one project at a time—starting new projects before finishing others. As "guest" editors we had to honor our professional commitment to consistency and coherence while figuring out the rules—and the dialect—of the country in which we found ourselves.

Some of the most difficult of the problems we eventually identified and tackled were

- writers' random use across documents of different terms that mean the same thing;

- variations by one writer in describing the same set of recurring instructions;

- confusion over the proper terminology to be used for writing about different parts of the software and its interface; and

- different vocabulary used for different parts of the audience by seasoned writers and newer writers.

To our advantage, we were given responsibility for the overall quality of the content of this particular project. Here's how we approached these problems as they came up.

An outbreak of editorial consistency. We focused on striving for consistent use of new terms across documents and screens. Why did we consider this so important? Because consistent use of specialized terms signals careful thinking, and it reassures readers and allows them to do what they need to do without having to wonder, "Is my *station* the same thing as my *extension*?"

Pressed for time, swamped with research, and at the mercy of a graphics-intensive layout that made text editing slow and cumbersome, the writers tried to dismiss our vigilance over their erratic terminology as "an editorial disease." But our team outnumbered them: We brought their readers with us to the bargaining table.

We wrangled with writers every day over *facility* versus *trunk* and *trunk* versus *line*. As we nailed down what was going to be called what, other aspects of the instructions tended to become clearer, too. Hearing the explanations for choosing one term over another gave us a crash course in the product and some insight into how the writers had approached their sections.

Variation: It ain't necessarily elegant. Inconsistent terminology, however, was not the only discrepancy we faced. Descriptive paragraphs kept surfacing in different sections with slightly different wording. Readers, not knowing whether it was new information or not, would become frustrated.

Elegant variation, the practice of changing the wording for descriptions of the same thing for the sake of variety, can be desirable in fiction writing, but it obscures information in business and technical writing. Processing similar but not equivalent vocabulary hinders both quick understanding and cumulative learning: People look for differences, not connections, when the wording changes. When we pointed this problem out to the writer, he said that he liked to use variety to keep the reader interested. "Please," we said. "Save it for your novel." Sheepishly, he agreed. (There was a novel!)

Many writers, a plural point of view. A problem inherent in any cooperative writing project is that factions may, with all good intentions, take a point of view based on reasonable but faulty assumptions. For this project, the terms used in the online help screens were not the same as those used for equivalent subjects and items in the documentation. It's easy to see how this happened: The writers responsible for writing the newly designed help screens used the terminology of the developers with whom they had been working closely, whereas the document writers used terms that mainstream readers were likely to be familiar with.

A staff editor accustomed to reconciling multiple vocabularies could have headed off the extensive reworking that was necessary once we began comparing notes with the two groups of writers. Unfortunately, that didn't happen until well into the project, but we were then able to resolve discrepancies that would have reduced some users to growls of frustration. A guest editor can't take such near-misses to heart—scoring late in the game still counts.

A confederacy of voices. The audience for our documentation was a mixture of field technicians from the telecommunications company and system administrators at the customer site, that is, people who ranged from trained technicians to those whose background was largely clerical. As editors, we took our lead from the seasoned writers in the group. If they said the term to use was *facility* instead of *trunk*, we agreed. But then we discovered that while the seasoned writers were using language appropriate for trained technicians, some of the newer writers were using a less technical vocabulary geared to system administrators.

We did a thorough search of dictionaries and we paid a visit to the human factors group—specialists on the user interface who helped us choose some key terms appropriate for both audiences. Armed with our research, we instituted our own weekly meetings (or haggling sessions, depending on your perspective) with the writers. They all voiced their opinions, and then we editors presented our research. Finally, we voted on preferred terms. The democratic process worked for these technical writers, typically rugged individualists that they were. To back up our decisions, we created a database of terms and definitions that all the writers could use.

One writing style for all and all for the audience. Writers may have a hard time recognizing inconsistencies in their work, regardless of the content, especially if they're part of a team or working on different parts of a large project. The indispensable role of editors is to guard against both elegant nonsense and clumsiness, in the form of puzzling and erratic writing that will disturb readers. Maybe someday all technical publications departments will have staff editors, but in the meantime, many publications will continue to benefit from the efforts of "outside" editors with a regard for consistency and coherence.

—Judith Goode

How to Edit Long Documents Online

The pros and cons of editing complex material electronically

Problem: I supervise a publications department for the Army Corps of Engineers. We publish approximately 400 highly technical (and extremely lengthy—generally 200 to 300 pages) documents a year. They are filled with complex mathematical formulas, tables, and color and black and white graphics. My boss has tasked me with implementing online editing and review/approval of our documents. As a former editor, I am resisting this "task." I find it difficult to edit 200 pages of technical material for content and grammar online and prefer the tried-and-true red pencil and hard copy method. I do use the spell check and search features available online. I need advice on editing lengthy material online.

Solution: Software packages such as Red Pencil allow you to insert electronic editing marks and provide an electronic trail. You don't say in your note that you are using one of these packages, so I'm assuming that you are simply editing on screen instead of on paper. As a working editor, I know how difficult it is to edit long, technical documents online. That said, let me note that, whether we like it or not (much less whether we learn to love it), online editing is the way of the future.

Let me summarize the pros and cons. First, online editing has real advantages:

- It streamlines the process; the same person can decide on the changes, key them, and proofread them if necessary.
- It allows several people to work on the same document at the same time.
- It minimizes the need for hard copy.
- It creates a file that can be sent electronically for typesetting or approval.
- It provides helpful editorial features such as search and replace, spell check, and word counts.
- It lets editors move large blocks of copy instantly.
- It facilitates global changes necessary to accommodate style decisions made late in the process.
- It lets editors embed queries in the text (either visibly or using the hidden text option) or print them separately.
- It lets authors review clean copy without the distraction of editing marks and spares them the pain of seeing their writing chopped up and dissected.

Online editing is extremely useful for stylistic edits and for substantive edits or rewrites. You can move, copy, and delete with amazing rapidity, but problems do remain. Some of the pros have a flip side that can turn them into cons, and you need to be aware of them:

- Online editing streamlines the process, but that may mean that no one checks behind the editor.

- Several people can be working on the same document, but they can be working at cross-purposes. Having several people working on a document also means that the chance of their using the wrong version or creating multiple versions increases greatly. Most of us are reluctant to destroy earlier versions—especially for documents that have to pass committee scrutiny—but tracking versions can become a nightmare. (As programs like the Quark Publishing System become more common, this problem will become less serious.)

- Many editors find it difficult and tiring to do everything on screen. Having a full-page monitor helps, but checking complex format, equations, or head levels still presents problems, eyestrain among them.

- It can be difficult for authors to track extensive editing changes.

Editing electronic files is the norm for many journals; it works best if the editor can simply present the author with clean copy. Trying to preserve an electronic trail, given the current state of the art, is often counterproductive. Existing software packages work well for stylistic or simple edits; they are less helpful for complex edits where a line may have many changes. Programs like CompareRite work for short, relatively simple documents, but no one will have the fortitude to plow through its "markup" of 200 pages of extensive changes. If editors have to move into the 21st century, so do authors. For them, electronic editing means that they will have to take the time to review the editor's work carefully to make sure that the meaning has not been changed.

Finally, we hope your boss remembers that online editing is only as good as the person doing the work, no matter how computer literate he or she may be. A bad editor is a bad editor, whether that person works on screen or on paper. Good luck to you.

—*Mary Stoughton*

Some Ways to Make Online Editing Less Wearing

Take advantage of shortcuts

- Editing on screen doesn't altogether eliminate the need for hard copy; you will want to print pages to check format or head levels or to correct equations.

- If you are trying to learn the software by the seat of your pants, you may need to ask your supervisor for formal training. Most of us use only a fraction of the features our word processing programs have. You will be a lot less frustrated if you have a grasp of more sophisticated features like creating macros, coding equations, using table mode, and so on. If you are a rotten typist, swallow your pride and take a basic course in keyboarding, or buy a software package that teaches typing.

- If several people are working on a document at the same time, use the date/time feature to put a header or footer on each page to be sure that everyone is using the correct version.

- Take the time to read the document through before you start, even if it's long. Take notes and get a feel for the author's style and for the main arguments or findings. You will make fewer mistakes that have to be undone later.

- Develop habits that take advantage of the shortcuts and avoid the drawbacks of working online. Try to work on long documents in sections, and take a break every hour. Get up and walk around. Print pages once in a while, especially where you've made extensive changes, as a stimulus and a checking step. Embed notes to yourself in the text (preface them with your initials or else use QQQ as we do at EEI) and switch back and forth between screens to keep your style sheet and acronym list current as you work.

- Display the document double spaced and change the font if necessary so that you can see the whole line at once. Most word processing programs can change the display without changing the underlying font.

- Allow time for review by another editor or else be sure you print and read the document yourself when you're through. This is time well spent.

—*Mary Stoughton*

The Considerate Editor:
The Art of Criticizing Colleagues

The peers you edit today may be editing you tomorrow

Professional writers and editors try to grow thick skins that will blunt the sting of criticism when it eventually comes, as it must. But the truth is, it's always painful to be edited by peers with whom one must maintain a working relationship—especially that particular peer whose edits make you want to stuff a dictionary down her throat. Could *your* editing of *her* work be what makes her so nasty? People on small staffs such as my own often edit each other, and it can get ugly.

You may be on the other side of the red pen someday soon, and what's good for you—tact, respect, support—is good for the people you edit. Whether you work online or mark hard copy for the writer to revise, consider practicing the small niceties listed below.

- Don't be pedantic, no matter what your mood. Being "objective" is not the same as being rigid—equating the two is a bad professional sign. Experience and education should make an editor flexible. (I can recall one editor who carefully typed long passages from the *Chicago Manual of Style* and then taped them to my manuscripts. I don't miss him.)

- Craft your criticisms so they are positive and constructive. A successful editor is one whose suggestions are given close consideration and implemented; negative comments are likely to be resisted. Put yourself in the writer's place. Would you prefer to hear "Long direct quote is good, but interrupts the flow—let's trim," or "Delete! Confusing!"

- Provide positive feedback as well as identify problems. Almost every piece of writing has *something* good about it. A "Nice!" or "Interesting" (if you mean it) can go a long way toward getting a better reaction to your corrective edits.

- Don't mix messages. People are not fooled by such manipulative statements as "This is a good analogy, but it's probably not necessary." If it's so good, why is the editor suggesting cutting the analogy out? Be straightforward.

- Don't be patronizing. A good writer or editor will be as offended by a gratuitous compliment as a callous edit. Using a note or query to flash one's training makes it hard for a writer to be grateful for the attempt at improvement. Anybody would balk at absorbing a comment like "Nice try, but I'm wondering whether you're familiar with the rhetorical flaw of tautology?"

- Pick your battles, especially when someone's trying to engage you in Style Wars. You can build a fortress around your desk with reference books to defend your work, but daily full-scale battle is tiresome. Save your energy for the big things. This advice is predicated on a reasonable definition of what the big things *are*. Has meaning been compromised? Then fight for a rewrite.

- Address the big issues in person, not on paper. Written criticism can sound harsher than you intend it to, but respectful, concerned inflection can soften the exchange. Friendly laughter and self-deprecating humor on the part of the editor are also legitimate ways to make straight shooting less painful. (Watch out for writers who have no sense of humor about being edited.)

- Examine your own editing style. If you are unnecessarily critical, you may be inspiring tit-for-tat editing of your work. The result is a stressful competition to find fault—and that ante only goes up.

- Phrase edits in the form of questions rather than imperatives when you can. But avoid cryptic wording. Try, for instance, "Sentences seem to be backward—can you rework?" instead of "Rework" or "Logic?" Nobody likes being on the receiving end of commands, and it's frustrating to be left wondering what a one-word comment means. Better yet, wherever possible rework the passage yourself.

- Resist the temptation to use underlines, exclamation points, un-smiley faces, and anything else that may rub salt in the wound. These little graphic inflections don't make editing seem more human: They make criticism seem more personal.

- Be tidy. Edits are hard enough to swallow as it is. Spare the recipient time spent deciphering what, after all, is an error message.

- Consider the cumulative effect on a writer of several tiers of editing comments. In my office, we use different colors so we can identify comments from different editors. Fortunately or unfortunately, I wield the wicked red pencil, so I try to keep my marks small and restrained. Although writing small doesn't necessarily indicate tact, it's symbolically a smaller mote in the eye.

- When edits are many and serious, jot a quick note at the top of the manuscript enumerating its better points. It costs nothing to be nice, and the return in goodwill is worth the effort many times over. One of these days when you're on the receiving end of a stem-to-stern, you'll be glad to see a few kind words prefacing your own bout with humility.
  —*Catharine Fishel*

Do unto Authors...

Editors who want respect from writers will return it

As editors, we tend to feel that we have a lock on the communications process, but there is some evidence to the contrary. Editors may need to be reminded that communicating with readers is half their task; the other half is communicating with authors.

Are there rules for communication between editors and authors? There is at least one, and it is golden: Treat authors as you would like to be treated. I hear complaints from some of my colleagues that authors don't respect them as professionals. Without question, there are curmudgeons out there who simply don't deserve the privilege of having their work reviewed by a professional—but surely they aren't the majority. An editor who finds most authors hostile needs to seek the source of the problem closer to home.

The editor-author relationship can be played out in several scenarios:

- Both work for the same organization.
- The author is under contract to the organization that employs the editor.
- The author is submitting a manuscript for publication by the editor's employer.
- The publisher has hired an outside editor to review the author's work.

But whether the author is down the hall or across the country from the editor, the golden rule of communication remains unchanged.

Say 'how do you do' and shake hands

In the first scenario, authors may already know the in-house editorial staff, but in a large organization that may not be true. Even in a small organization, it's not a bad idea to say something along the lines of "Sarah, I'm going to be looking at your section of the proposal tomorrow." In less intimate circumstances, a phone call or a note serves the purpose. Because ours is a consulting firm, our editors are usually in the last scenario. Some of our clients perform the introduction for us, through a letter or phone call to explain to the authors that an editor from our firm will be reviewing their work. If not, on first contacting an author, we explain who we are. Otherwise, authors would be justifiably bewildered to find their work in the hands of someone other than the publisher. And bewilderment is hardly the best start for a cordial working relationship.

What's your query, dearie?

Most editor-author communications concern queries. Here again, there are several variants—from something as informal as dropping into a colleague's office, page in hand, and requesting clarification, to sending a typewritten list of queries to an author in another state. In any case, tact is crucial. Precious few authors construe editing as anything other than a form of criticism, and people who claim to welcome criticism are lying.

One simple way to make queries tactful is to ban the word *you*. However well meant, it has an accusing tone. Compare the following:

> On page 40, you say that 37 thousand housing units need to be built; on page 85, you say that 38 thousand units are needed. Which is correct?

> Page 40 says that 37 thousand housing units need to be built; page 85 says that 38 thousand units are needed. Which is correct?

This guideline applies to oral as well as written communication. Even though both you and the author know perfectly well that a manuscript doesn't write itself, it's more tactful to point out the manuscript's inconsistencies than the author's.

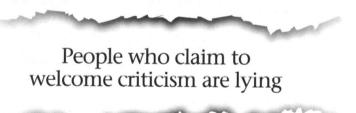

People who claim to welcome criticism are lying

A pet peeve of mine is editors who simply write "awkward" or "unclear" in the margin of a manuscript and expect the author to respond. If a section is awkwardly written, it's part of the editor's mandate to rewrite it so that it is graceful. (As a co-worker of mine puts it, that's why we make the big bucks.) If a section is unclear, an editor should take his or her best shot at rewriting it, coming as close as possible to what the editor believes is the intended meaning.

If the editor's guess is on target, the author is saved some work. If the editor has failed to grasp the author's intent, the rewrite serves as a graphic demonstration of how the text could mislead a reasonably intelligent reader. Few authors are eager to concede that they've been unclear, but by shifting the focus to a failure of the editor's interpretation, you have tactfully made the problem obvious.

If you are completely at a loss as to the meaning and feel unable to attempt a rewrite, say so in the margin and ask the author to rephrase the passage. The question "Will the readers understand?" can be useful, but there's a danger that the author may simply reply, "Yes." For this reason, it's better not to phrase complex queries as yes-or-no questions.

When communicating with authors, show that you respect their schedules. If you're calling or seeing an author in person, make an informal appointment—if only by asking, "Is now a good time for you? It will take about half an hour to go over this material." If you're sending written queries, call first. Not all authors, many of whom travel, have office staff to contact them or forward packages.

When sending a manuscript for an author's review, include a cover letter defining your expectations—"We need to have your responses by May 12. You may fax them, send them, or call me." If at all possible, you should build some leeway into your due dates so that when May 12 arrives and the responses do not, you can give the author a friendly reminder without having to quell the edge of panic in your voice.

Please and thank you

Those "do-bee" words have been drummed into our heads since we first learned to talk—but do you remember to use them in your professional communications? Any request, from "define the acronym ABCXYZ" to "review the enclosed chapter," should start with the magic P-word. And every communication, written or oral, should end with "thank you very much." It works!

—Lee Mickle

How to Query Authors Effectively

Writers will wrap up the loose ends—if you don't fray their nerves

How can you tell when an editor's query is effective? When the author provides an answer that ultimately benefits the reader. The basic characteristics of an effective author query are legibility, tact, clarity, and concision.

For the purpose of this article, I'm defining a *query* as a written question or comment to an author whom the editor does not know. The definition in *Merriam-Webster's Collegiate Dictionary*, tenth edition, serves us well: "a question in the mind." When a question about the content of a manuscript occurs to an editor, and when the answer isn't to be found in a general reference book or elsewhere in the manuscript, a query is appropriate. Comments or questions concern any loose ends (material that seems confusing, contradictory, or incorrect) and may be framed formally or somewhat more personally ("I'm puzzled, maybe it's just me—will the reader understand?").

Legibility

Editing on paper usually means writing queries in a small space, either in the margin or on a query slip. Despite this disadvantage, the author must be able to read every word of your query. Illegible queries pose two threats: (1) The helpful author who wants to answer the query may misread it and therefore answer incorrectly, and (2) the overly sensitive author, put off by the sight of a hastily scrawled note, may not answer at all.

Use printing or script, whichever will be most legible. Always repress the desire to scrawl in frustration; your attitude may come across and your query may go unanswered. Many editors also type up a page-by-page query cover sheet that explains the marginal notes more fully. That way, the editor can go into as much detail as necessary—and everybody can read a word-processed cover sheet.

Tact

No author enjoys having mistakes pointed out, but authors enjoy having their mistakes find their way into print even less. If your queries are tactful and courteous, the author is more likely to be cooperative (and sometimes even grateful that you caught the problem). The following strategies may help you frame your queries.

- Address the query to "Author." This shows respect for the author's role and also avoids the possible confusion of such headings as "AU" or "QA," which the beginning or hurried author may not recognize.

79

- When you're asking an author to go back to the source and check a quotation or a detail on a reference citation, use "Please" to show that you know you're asking for extra work and appreciate the effort involved. Don't overuse it, though, or you may appear obsequious.

In querying, you seesaw between sets of priorities

- If you provide information that proves the author wrong about something, put the information in parentheses. For example, for the sentence *Elvis Presley gave his last concert in 1985*, a tactful query might read as follows:

  Author: Are both the date and the name correct? (Elvis Presley died in 1977.)

  Putting the correct information in parentheses makes the point, but softens the blow of having one's attention called to an embarrassing mistake.

- Avoid emphatic markers such as the use of all capital letters and exclamation points. These markers can make a simple query look like a challenge—the emotional equivalent of "AUTHOR: THIS CAN'T POSSIBLY BE CORRECT!!!" Your redlining software program may dictate the appearance of queries (e.g., they may appear boldfaced and all caps and be surrounded by brackets, with question marks on both sides of the query). The purpose of the formatting is to make sure that the author sees the query and responds. However, the editor must be aware that the more obvious the query is, the more the author may object to it. If the style at your office is boldfaced, all-capital, in-text queries, the content becomes even more important. An unassuming query is a good query.

- Be sure to word your query so you get the answer you're looking for. For example, a query such as *"Author:* Can you clarify this statement?" has two possible answers, and one is "No." That won't help you or the reader. Instead, use wording like this:

  Author: Do you mean that the institution is too old-fashioned or that the students are too radical? If neither, what is your exact meaning?

- Don't make changes when you can't be sure about the change without the author's input. Suppose you find a glaring arithmetic error such as this: *in 10 (24%) of the 100 patients*. Don't simply slash through the

24%, write 10%, and then write "Author: 100 X 24% does NOT equal 10!!!" You can't know for sure which of the numbers (*10, 24, or 100*) is incorrect. Instead, call the author's attention to the problem in a polite query:

> *Author:* The arithmetic does not seem to be correct (24% of 100 = 24, not 10). Which number needs to be changed?

Clarity and concision

Queries, by nature, should be brief. You must phrase them in the fewest possible words that express your concern clearly. But brevity isn't quite all there is to being clear. Even short queries can be dangerous if they are hastily written. Such queries are often too messy to read and too vague to be answered. For example, the common query "Author: Please clarify!" tells the author nothing about the nature of the problem. Therefore, authors sometimes answer this two-word request with a three-word statement: "Leave as is!" This exchange of exclamation points helps no one.

And quips have no place in author queries. Not only are flippancy and sarcasm impolite and insulting, but they are always vulnerable to misinterpretation. Of course, funny comments occur to all of us when we find an unwitting juxtaposition, but we should never write them down for the author to see.

I learned this the hard way, when a Post-it note to another editor was inadvertently left on a manuscript. The note concerned a photo of a patient's legs, with a legend saying "55-year-old woman with rheumatoid arthritis." My ill-advised "joke" note read something like "Evidently this author sees women only as legs." When the author saw that wisecrack, he became angry and rejected all my suggested editorial changes. Needless to say, I no longer put my one-liners on notes.

In her article, "Rules for Substantive Editing" (see page 115), Mia Cunningham lists three guidelines, paraphrased here, that will help make the content of author queries both clearer and more concise:

- Be businesslike (cutting down on chattiness cuts down the length of the query).

- Suggest solutions (proposing alternative wording gives the author a quick way out or illustrates the problem with the present wording).

- Avoid confrontation (insults are unprofessional and counterproductive).

Querying is a balancing act

You must always anticipate the author's reaction as he or she reads the query: The response you're working toward is "Oh, that does need work.

I should find a better way to explain that." And the query must be clear, without insulting the author's intelligence, and short, without sacrificing the clarity of your question.

In querying, you seesaw between sets of priorities. You're trying to avoid alienating the author with unintelligible questions and avoid leaving readers with unresolved discrepancies.

Because you're the reader's advocate, you want to write queries that net reasonable answers from the author. So after you've finished editing a manuscript, go through it just to read the queries you've written. Do they meet the balancing test? Are they clear enough that they can be answered and tactful enough that they will be?

After 17 years as a professional editor, I recently learned something about my own queries. Looking over old manuscripts, I found that I had underlined words for emphasis in my queries when I felt the author's mistake was particularly egregious or a sentence was maddeningly unclear. I came to the conclusion that the use of underlining made some of the queries seem somewhat snippy rather than helpful. I'll avoid that mistake in the future.

When you query effectively, you're relaying the friendly questions of a careful reader. Most times you'll get the answers you need. But be prepared: The author may reply, "Elvis lives! He just doesn't play Vegas anymore!" Sometimes all we can do is take a deep breath and stet the original sentence. Even then, as some famous editor should have said, "It's better to have queried well and lost than never to have queried at all."

—*Elizabeth Whalen*

Editing a Moving Target

Time won't stand still, so figure out a way to streamline your efforts

Does this scenario sound familiar? It's 3:00 p.m. and a proposal due at close of business the next day finally arrives for editing.... Or how about this one? It's 9:00 a.m. and the CEO asks for copies of your annual report to take to the board meeting that night. Now you have eight hours to finish what you expected to have three days to do.

I'd like to assume that most of us find ourselves having to edit a moving target only occasionally, but from the horror stories I've been hearing, it seems that more and more people are being expected to edit well in a ridiculously short time.

What matters most when the deadline's too soon?

There's no simple answer to this question. To illustrate why, take a look at the following list of basic editorial flaws. In theory, everything matters, but different people would prioritize these things differently. Try numbering them on the basis of their importance to you.

- **Content**

   A wrong total in a table of numbers

   An illogical conclusion

   Redundancy

- **Typos**

   An error in the spelling of your company president's name

   A word that's spelled correctly but is the wrong word

- **Grammatical problems**

   Subject-verb disagreements

   Misplaced modifiers

   Unnecessary passive voice

- **Format**

   Too much white space

   Paragraphs that seem endless

- **Stylistic errors**

   Inconsistent number style or capitalization

   Abbreviations defined more than once in a chapter or section, or not defined at all

What's involved in editing a moving target?

We're going to look at things from two points of view: that of the editor and that of the project manager who are deciding what to fix and what to leave alone.

These two people usually come at the problem a little differently although their interests naturally converge. To some managers, editing looks expendable until the company's major stockholder opens the report to page 29 and finds that the net profit line is missing a zero. To some editors, a document isn't presentable until every flaw, however minor, has been eliminated.

In the best of all possible worlds, every document gets the attention it needs, but in reality what gets fixed depends on the priorities mentioned earlier, as well as on the answers to the following questions.

If you're the project manager...

Here are the questions you need to ask:

How large is this document? Even if it's small, you may still have a problem: You may have only half an hour to check a brochure full of addresses and prices. But you can usually fix a small piece even if you're already in final pages. It's just going to cost you. If it's large, however, how much of a problem you have depends on the answers to the questions that follow.

How visible is it? Is it just an internal report or is it going to the media and members of Congress? Obviously, there's a lot in between. An internal report should be fixed as much as possible in the time you have because, after all, it reflects on you and your organization. But if there are errors in it, only your company will know. If the report is going to be seen by others, the question is, Which others?

Who is the audience? Are your readers researchers, policymakers, stockholders, clients, people in the publications field, or the public in general?

For researchers and other technical specialists, you can assume that they're more interested in the content than in the style or format, so you really need two edits—a content review and a style edit. If you were planning to skip the review by a subject-matter expert, think again. The two edits can and should proceed simultaneously, but in this case the style edit is much less important than the content review.

If this document is meant to convince policymakers, persuade your clients, or inform your stockholders, you pull in every available resource on the premise that everything is important. And if by any chance there are publications specialists in your audience, they'll find every extra space and misplaced comma.

So you may have no choice: You have to do a full edit because the document is highly visible or because the audience demands it. But another factor has a bearing here: the production cycle.

Where are you in the production cycle? Are you working with draft copy, or are you already into formatted pages? If the document went directly into final format, then the first thing you need to do is accept the fact that the production cycle imposes certain time constraints. The second thing you need to do is vow that this will never, ever happen again: Editing early in the cycle saves a lot of grief later on.

Now take a realistic look at what's there in terms of the complexity of the text; the number of pages; the number of tables, figures, or references; and the absolute drop-dead deadline. Remember too that you have to allow time to incorporate the corrections and proofread them. To determine just how much time you need to get the document into final form, the rule of thumb is to allot half of the total time for editing and half for correcting and proofreading.

Next, see whether there are any shortcuts you can use to streamline production and buy some time: Can you get a few extra days added to your other deadlines and set those projects aside temporarily? Can you authorize overtime? Can you set up an assembly line (that is, divide the work into batches and have several people editing, making corrections, and proofreading at the same time)?

Once you've tentatively decided on the level of edit and determined how much time you have, you need to find an editor who can do the work. Also, you need to find someone who can take that person's calls and pick up the other work that will languish in the meantime. This brings us to the last question.

Is there someone who can drop everything and work on this job exclusively? You need to find the right person for the job. It may be that you have only one in-house editor and no money to hire a temp or freelancer, and so you have no choice. Let's assume, however, that you do have a choice. How do you decide which of the available editors to choose?

Some people have only one speed; doing something "quick and dirty" goes against their nature. Perhaps they're perfectionists, or perhaps they can't compromise or make quick decisions. Save these people for the day-to-day work that still needs to be done while your chosen editor focuses on the moving target.

Sit down with this lucky editor and decide on some ground rules. Discuss the level of edit you've tentatively decided on and make sure that the editor thinks it's appropriate for the document in terms of what it is, where it is in the production cycle, and how much time you have left.

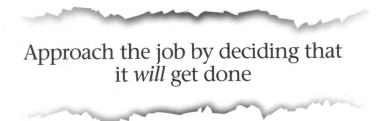

Approach the job by deciding that it *will* get done

Once you've done everything you can to make the production end of things go smoothly, step back and give your editor some room to work, but make sure you're available to answer questions.

If you're the editor...

Somehow you have to pull this off:

Psych yourself up. The first thing to do is realize that this project will consume you for the next few hours or days. If you have personal plans, cancel them. If you're going to be working through the night, try to go home and change into comfortable clothes and grab a few hours of sleep before you start. Lay in a supply of coffee and sandwiches to keep you going.

Determine the level of edit. Now you need to look at the document realistically and decide what you can do in the time you have. It may be that you physically can't do what the project manager wants, in which case negotiations are in order. Don't jump to conclusions, though. Remember that tasks often look insurmountable until you get started.

Approach the job by deciding that it *will* get done but that it's up to you to figure out how. To determine the level of edit you can do in the time you have, edit the first few pages at your best speed (as fast as you can do them accurately). Then take into account that you need to make more than one pass and that you'll have to go more slowly as you get tired so you don't make mistakes. If this exercise tells you that you can't edit in depth, scale back.

In any case, go over the first part of the document—the abstract, the executive summary, the introduction—and the conclusion meticulously on the premise that people tend to read the beginning and the end of a document. Also pay close attention to the rest of the front matter. No one will thank you if you find a minute error on page 20 and leave a typo on the cover.

Pace yourself. As you work, try to set a rhythm; don't get bogged down. If something is badly worded and the fix doesn't come to you right away, mark the passage and come back to it. Try to work as long as you can at a stretch, but remind yourself to get up once in a while. Look away from the copy or the screen so that your eyes don't give out before you're done.

If you've decided to edit online, remember that the speed of an online edit depends on your keyboarding skills and those of the person who created the electronic file. For example, if hard spaces were used for indents and formatting, a handsome document will rewrap in strange ways when you start making changes. Then you'll have to add reformatting to the list of tasks you are already hard-pressed to finish.

Can you get help? Can any revisions be made automatically? If you are editing on paper, don't waste your time marking things that can be fixed globally, like spacing or capitalization or particular terms that need to be changed. Can someone else check the format while you fix the words? Can other editors help with sections? (You would have to review their work and make sure everything is consistent.)

Whatever you do, keep moving—and above all, keep thinking. Work with one eye on the clock and the other on the copy. Ask another editor or the project manager to take a quick look at what you've done before you turn it in for corrections.

A postmortem now can save you out-of-body experiences later

When the dust has settled, hold a postmortem so that everyone on the project team can learn from this experience. If you're the project manager, write things up while they're still fresh in your mind, and try to see patterns. If editing is always an afterthought, you have serious problems with your production cycle.

Whether you're the project manager or the editor, don't berate yourself for missing things that you ordinarily would have caught. After all, editing, like politics, is the art of the possible. If you follow these guidelines, you'll be doing the best you can in the time you've got.

—*Mary Stoughton*

Communicating Story Ideas to Writers

If you can't explain what you have in mind,
nobody can write it for you—or whistle it, either

Editors who rely heavily on freelance writers to generate the content of their publications sometimes become frustrated with submissions that don't meet their needs. This situation often arises when an editor must deal with freelancers who are subject matter experts instead of trained writers. Every editor has experienced at least once the frustration of working with a writer on a story only to have the manuscript be a disappointment that requires extensive revisions or is unsalvageable. What can we editors do to ensure that we get appropriate, publishable material from our freelancers?

The screening phase

If you often receive material you aren't happy with, perhaps you need to review the ways you screen potential writers. Read other publications in your field looking for good authors whose talents you can also use. Seek out as authors well-respected and well-spoken authorities in your field and speakers at your industry's conferences. Send writers' guidelines and sample copies of your publication to prospective writers to help them grasp your editorial style. In return, ask for writing samples before you give an assignment to a new writer. Finally, review your pay rates to make sure they are competitive; remember the adage, "You get what you pay for."

Communicating your vision

When assigning an article, you, like most editors, probably envision the story clearly, but you may have trouble communicating the idea to the writer. The ways you discuss a story will differ depending on the type of writer you use. Editors with limited budgets can't always afford experienced professionals whose skills—and fees—are greater than those of less experienced freelancers or subject matter experts. Those editors will need to give their "writers" more direction.

Discuss assignments face-to-face, when possible, or over the telephone if the freelancer isn't local. If you propose an idea to a subject expert rather than a professional writer, ask whether this aspect of the subject is one the person feels comfortable with, is interested in, and feels experienced enough to write about. You have an advantage if you work with professional writers; they have developed the ability to research and write on almost any topic. Subject experts may be more hesitant. If you sense reluctance, determine its source by asking questions: "Do you have time to write an in-depth article? Are you concerned about the long-distance charges for this telephone survey? Have you written in this style before?" Such questions should draw out the writer's concerns about the assignment.

In addition to providing writers' guidelines, include sample copies of your publication (specifically, issues dealing with a similar subject), background material on the topic, and samples of outside articles treating the topic or written in the style you wish to follow for this assignment. Explain what you like about the samples so that the writer will know how to shape the article. This discussion should be specific; if you use a formula for writing certain types of articles (book reviews for example), diagram the various parts of the review for the writer. You may want to send this material after your initial conversation, give the writer a day or two to review it, and then call to discuss any questions.

To create a workable manuscript, the editor and the writer must share common assumptions about the focus of the piece. As you communicate your vision of the article to the writer, discuss the story's overall purpose, specific goals, audience, tone, and style. Why is the topic important? What needs to be said? What do you hope readers will learn? Should the style be reportorial or human interest? Serious or casual? Will the article

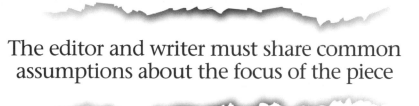

The editor and writer must share common assumptions about the focus of the piece

take the form of an interview, profile, survey, or analysis? Will the topic require extensive research or interviews? How long should the piece be? As you discuss these questions, the story will take shape in the writer's mind.

Sometimes untrained writers are reluctant to ask questions or to admit that they don't follow your train of thought. Encouraging them to recap their impressions of what you want will tell you whether you have clearly communicated your needs. You may even want to have a colleague listen in on your end of an assignment discussion and suggest ways to improve your techniques.

If the topic and the writer aren't a good match, don't force the issue even if this person is your last resort. Writers produce their best work when they are interested in the assignment. Instead, offer a different story or assure the writer that future assignments will be forthcoming.

The nurturing phase

No matter how experienced, many writers will require some initial guidance to ensure that the manuscripts you receive do indeed address your publication's needs.

Help the writer list and prioritize questions and issues you would like to see answered and discussed. Summarize these questions and issues in a follow-up letter. If you are working with an untrained writer, consider providing a rough outline of the article. It will help ensure that the first submitted draft is what you expected and requires little editing or rewriting. We've found that no matter how experienced, freelancers usually appreciate an outline with pertinent questions and issues laid out.

Following up

Call periodically during the assignment to see how the writer is doing and to answer any questions. Stories can take a different turn once the writer delves into the topic, and your guidance will be appreciated. To ensure that you have communicated your needs, ask to see a revised outline before the writing begins. You may also ask for a rough preliminary draft to make sure the writer is on track. These measures can help both of you avoid frustration later.

The editing phase

When the manuscript arrives, let the writer know you have received it, even if you aren't yet prepared to discuss it. Review the article promptly, and call the author immediately. This discussion should occur while the article is still fresh in the writer's mind. Go over the article's positive points first. Then discuss areas that need to be strengthened. If your editorial suggestions are detailed, follow your conversation with a marked manuscript or a memo. When a manuscript requires substantive reorganization, some editors number the manuscript's paragraphs to make their suggestions easier to follow: "Move para. 3 to p. 4, and insert new material after para. 12." Some editors prefer to note all questions and comments on a separate sheet; others insert comments manually on a printout or insert their comments online in text. Still other editors and writers prefer to work through an edit on the phone while both have the document on their computer screens. Use the techniques that work best for you both, but be sure to put your comments and suggestions in writing.

The revision phase

If the revised draft fails to meet your expectations, and you know the author has your suggestions in writing, you should ask why they weren't acted on. The reasons may be legitimate: Perhaps a suggested transition didn't work as smoothly as the one the writer supplied. Or the addition you suggested after paragraph 12 worked better after paragraph 17. Or the emphasis you wanted in a certain section didn't jell with the writer's research. If the manuscript was heavily edited, perhaps the writer missed a few of your comments or simply disagreed with you. (If so, the writer should discuss the point with you rather than ignore your suggestion.) Finally, and unfortunately, a few less experienced writers either don't want to take the time to do a revised draft or don't think their work requires one. These are the freelancers whose work you end up rejecting or rewriting (and whom you use only once).

Despite occasional disappointments, most freelancers aim to please, because they take pride in their work and their livelihood depends on doing so. These strategies will help you develop a more reliable roster of writers whose manuscripts will require fine-tuning instead of overhauling.

—*Ann R. Molpus*

gibe/jibe

To gibe means "to taunt or jeer at." The word also has a noun form. *To jibe* with something is "to match or correspond with it." Because these words are pronounced identically (with a long *i*), and because some dictionaries allow the use of *jibe* as a synonym for *gibe*, writers and speakers should make sure the context gives clear clues as to the intended meaning. *Jibe* is also a sailing term meaning "to move a fore-and-aft sail from one side of a boat to the other." "The old sailors mercilessly *gibed* the new crew member who was knocked off the boat by the boom when the captain *jibed* and came about."

Do Scholars Need Editing?

Yes, indubitably—arguably more than some

In his book, *Wonderful Life: The Burgess Shale and the Nature of History* (W.W. Norton, 1989), Stephen Jay Gould has this to say about his approach to science writing:

> I have fiercely maintained one personal rule in all my so-called "popular" writing.... I believe...that we can still have a genre of scientific books suitable for and accessible alike to professionals and interested laypeople. The concepts of science, in all their richness and ambiguity, can be presented without any compromise, without any simplification counting as distortion, in language accessible to all intelligent people. Words, of course, must be varied, if only to eliminate a jargon and phraseology that would mystify anyone outside the priesthood, but conceptual depth should not vary at all between professional publication and general exposition. I hope that this book can be read with profit both in seminars for graduate students and— if the movie stinks and you forgot your sleeping pills—on the businessman's special to Tokyo.

Would that other scholarly writers held to the same philosophy and were as successful at implementing it as Gould. Scholarly publications—books, research reports, conference volumes—abound. Do they need editing? Yes. Are nonspecialist editors competent to edit scholars' writing? Yes, assuming they keep alert, work with care, and use appropriate reference resources.

Why scholars need editing

Scholarly writers have most of the same problems that other writers have, plus a few others:

Poor word choice. Many scholars are oblivious to Fowler's five commandments to "prefer the familiar word to the far-fetched, prefer the concrete to the abstract, prefer the single word to the circumlocution, prefer the short word to the long, and prefer the Saxon word to the Romance." In fact, if a scholar had had a go at Churchill's defiant, Saxon-loaded challenge to the Nazis, "...we shall fight on the beaches, we shall fight on the landing grounds, we shall fight in the fields and in the streets, we shall fight in the hills...," the end product might well have been something like, "In terms of defense, we shall endeavor to focus our attention on repulsing the opponent...."

Similarly, scholars tend to prefer the original foreign word to the anglicized (*Zeitgeist* to "zeitgeist") and italicized Latin phrases to English translations (*ceretis paribus* to "all else remaining the same").

Misspellings. Scholars may misspell fewer words than other writers do, but the words involved are more esoteric (*paleaeoanthropology* instead of *paleoanthropology*). I've also noticed a particular tendency toward confusion among double consonants: *dessicated* for *desiccated* (as misspelled in the May 1991 issue of *The Atlantic*), *mocassins* for *moccasins*, and *grafitti* for *graffiti*. And many scholars lean toward British spellings: *defence, spectre, speciality, politicise.*

Overkill. Scholars tend to write long and repetitiously, perhaps because they fear that the reader will not get the point if they do not labor it or because they are used to classroom teaching. This characteristic not only works against readability but also may have disastrous results. In *The Path Between the Seas*, a history of the Panama Canal, author David McCullough comments on a two-year delay in the publication of Dr. Henry Rose Carter's report on how yellow fever was spread: "Publication of Carter's vitally important observations had been delayed because the editor of a medical journal returned his paper saying it was too long."

Verbal tics. Some scholars pepper their work with throwaway phrases like "It is, I think, fair to say..."; "I submit..."; and "I might add that...." Some favor legalisms like "can and should," "does and ought to," "some though not all," and "if and only if." Others go in for indirect language like "hardly uncontroversial" and "not infrequently."

Some scholars demonstrate a tendency toward excessively cautious language that ends up being simply redundant or wrong. They use vague nouns like *matters* and verbs like *involves* and *affects* (how?); introduce every list with *includes* although the list is complete; and may begin a parenthetical note with *e.g.* and end it with *etc.*, as if to be sure to cover all bases. Many overuse or misuse phrases such as *on the other hand* (when they simply mean *in contrast to* or *however*).

Jargon. Unlike Stephen Jay Gould, many scholars fear that any simplification of their writing will destroy its integrity or impair their reputation with peers, but such writing is hardly intelligible to nonspecialists: "There are of course multitudinous modalities in institutions and policies that might be employed, if appropriate perspectives could be created in the peoples of the world, to improve the global constitutive process of authoritative decision toward a more secure, free, and abundant world public order." (There are many paths to peace?)

A desire to obfuscate, for any number of reasons, including a desire to hedge their bets about research conclusions or policy recommendations. In her entertaining account of *What I Saw at the Revolution*, President Reagan's speechwriter Peggy Noonan describes Bud McFarlane's obfuscatory way with words and says she first suspected that his aim was to silence questioners with incomprehensibility. "They cannot challenge him because they cannot understand him. They fall back on form and nod sagely: Ah, yes, I take your point." Subsequently, Noonan says, she changed her mind, concluding that

> McFarlane decided long ago, as young people sometimes do, that intelligent people speak in an incomprehensible manner. He adopted the style. In time, he was no more capable of a simple public utterance than of a private one, [so] that when dining with his wife, he would not say "Pass the butter," but "The stationary oleaginous object which is now not within my grasp or the grasp of others within this administration would be desirable, though not necessary, within my sphere and on my muffin...."

Other common problems. Scholars tend to have the same writing problems that other writers have with elusive pronoun references, nonparallel constructions, organizational lapses, and noun strings. Many scholars are

Scholarly writers have the same problems that other writers have, plus a few others

careless about making sure that in-text references match the reference list, and that in-text descriptions of tables match the information on the tables. Scholars have as much trouble as other writers making the appropriate distinctions between *forgo* (do without) and *forego* (go before), not to mention *since* and *because* and *loath* and *loathe*. And an article in a recent *American Scholar* has this double negative: "cannot help but."

Do scholars welcome editing?

It depends. Jacques Barzun, who is on record as believing that editors should be restricted to "the correction of typos, the striking out of hyphens at the ends of lines, the indication of em-dashes, together with the assigning of point size to heads and subheads" (*The Editorial Eye*, November 1985), represents one formidable extreme. Scholars in general invest more ego in their writing than other writers, and to meet with their approval the editing must represent an obvious improvement over the original. When it does, and when the editor saves the scholar from the embarrassment of having an error appear in print, the scholar may be quite grateful.

Obviously, the same point can apply to all writers, scholarly or otherwise. Peggy Noonan illustrates a writer's need for a good editor "to catch your dumb mistakes" with this story: She describes the infighting among the State Department, the National Security Council, and herself in the White House over imagery in a speech that President Reagan was to deliver in China. They went back and forth about whether "history is a river" and "the tide is high" represented Communist propaganda or poetry. Only after the presidential party had reached China did somebody finally note a factual mistake—oceans, not rivers, have tides. At the last minute, the text was changed to "the current is swift." Noonan comments:

> What I learned was that I would have to watch out at the White House, as I did at CBS, for the kind of editors who want to sit around and give you their opinions on things instead of concentrating on the text and catching your factual mistakes. Catching mistakes is hard; you have to know things like facts and numbers and names; you have to be awake. Anybody can have an opinion....

In summary, everyone—scholars included—can benefit from the watchful eye of a skilled editor, and that editor should not be intimidated by an author's degrees or reputation. After all, scholars perhaps more than other people want their writing to be perfect, and the editor who catches their mixed metaphor or nonparallel construction or just plain dumb mistake may even earn a nod in the acknowledgments.

—Priscilla S. Taylor

How to Edit Instructions

If a recipe makes short work of creating a new dish,
thank an editor

Imagine the mother of a three-month-old baby puzzling over this instruction: *You may feed your baby as much as half a baby food jar of two different things at each meal.*

Actually, I don't have to imagine this mother because, many years ago, I was this mother, and I spent the better part of an afternoon asking myself, "Half a jar made up of two different quarters or one jar made up of two different halves?" As a mother, I outgrew my dependence on precision feeding instructions, but as an editor I've never outgrown my impatience with ambiguous and inaccurate instructions.

When I teach courses on editing, I devote about one-third of the sessions to editing instructions. Why? True, there's always a demand for someone who can edit technical manuals or cookbooks, but my real reason is that working on instructions gets you into editorial shape. It hones your ability to keep readers and their needs always in mind, to weigh each word for accuracy, and to be sure that every sentence means what the writer intends.

If ambiguous and inaccurate instructions were an issue only for jargon-jammed pamphlets on operating VCRs or assembling appliances from countries where English isn't the first language, we editors could excuse ourselves and go back to business as usual. But many writers and editors of basic instructional material seem to depend too much on the common sense and goodwill of their readers rather than the clarity of the writing. With instructions, readers are at the mercy of the writer; the reason they're reading in the first place is that they *don't* know what they're doing.

Several practices are useful when editing instructions. Most important, the editor should constantly picture the readers trying to follow directions and should ask at every step, "Will this work for them?" Here are some methods to make sure the answer is yes.

Separate the components

Although other kinds of text and the editing of it usually proceed from line to line, instructions often do not. They are made up of pieces that aren't necessarily read in sequence—an equipment list, a photo or diagram of the finished project, headnotes,* the actual how-to (the step-by-

---

*A headnote is a comment or note of explanation that precedes the instructions.

step part of the instructions), tips, and information on timing. The editor has to juggle all these pieces. The easiest way to keep them all in the air is to separate them (which may mean making copies of some pages) and array them so that you can see and edit all the pieces at once in a circle. As you look from one component to another, you'll see what I mean by "editing in a circle." Here are some examples.

- Side by side, compare the equipment list with the how-to instructions to be sure that every item in the list is used and every item used in the how-to is listed. I use a double-check system. As I edit the list, I find each item in the how-to and put a check mark at the left of it; when I edit the how-to, I put a check mark at the right of the item, noting any item not found in the list. It's a kindergarten procedure, but this observation in a cookbook review by Florence Fabricant (*New York Times*, April 12, 1995) shows the necessity for it: "A wonderful-sounding plum cake called for a quarter-pound of melted butter that was never incorporated into the recipe."

- If there is a picture or diagram of the completed project, check carefully to make sure that everything described in the how-to shows up in the picture—and nothing more. And is everything in the picture covered in the equipment list? No one wants to run out for one more item.

- Keep referring to the headnotes. Is the project that's billed as "easy" really simple for everyone? When I put this query to the author of an exercise book, she responded, "For me, yes. You must be out of shape." No matter how out of shape I was, if this book was billed as being for beginners, I should have been able to do the exercises. Does the headnote match the how-to? For example, if the headnote for a recipe says chopped nuts are optional, does the how-to reiterate that we may leave them out?

- If instructions indicate the total time required for a project, make sure it's accurate. In a book of carpentry projects for parents and children, the authors didn't include the drying time for the varnish. Picture the parent—or, worse, the ten-year-old—who reads

  Time required: three hours

  only to find out later that the beautiful picture frame can't be used for eight hours more while the varnish dries. Drying time varies from one finish to another, so I edited it this way:

  Time required: three hours, not including drying time for paint or varnish

  Again, check to see that varnish is listed with the equipment and that the finished project in the picture has a nice gloss.

Editors are guinea pigs

Instructions are written to be followed. With your readers in mind, always try to follow them, physically if necessary (thus my exercise question). To show you what I mean, here's another comment from Fabricant's *Times* review: "If the very first and most basic recipe in the book...is baked in the regular nine-inch layer-cake pan as specified, there will be cake batter all over the oven."

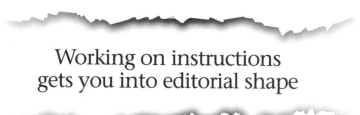

Working on instructions gets you into editorial shape

But do editors have to personally test every instruction? Must they have a working knowledge of the subjects they're editing? The answer to both questions is no. Authors have the ultimate responsibility for what they write, and editors, or book editors at least, rely on the author's knowledge. However, editors who work for periodicals, especially newsletters, often find themselves rewriting; they do need a working knowledge of the subject. Some editors have built-in help to confirm results. Specialized magazines and publishers often have test kitchens or hire outside specialists such as knitters, carpenters, and computer whizzes. But for most editors a healthy skepticism will suffice:

- Cultivate a questioning frame of mind: Try to picture whether the batter will fit into the pan. If you sense a possible problem, query the author. It's also helpful to consult other books in the field to familiarize yourself with the terminology.

- Is the information in the right sequence? In one gardening manual, this note came at the end of all the planting instructions: "Take great care in handling the fertilizer and always wear gloves. The fertilizer is highly toxic." As the editor of the book observed, the careless gardener could be poisoned by the time she had finished planting.

- Remember that people don't usually read instructions from start to finish; they may read only what they need to know for the part of the project at hand. Make sure they have all the information for every part *when* they need it—not sooner or later.

Edit the artwork, too

Editors are great at editing words, but they often lose their instincts when they look at pictures, maps, or diagrams. The illustrative material in instructions is as important as the text and must be edited with the same care and skepticism that you apply to the text. A book on fly tying that I edited had a picture of a fly in progress in someone's hands. Contort my hands as I might, I could not get them into the position shown in the illustration. Finally I gave up and queried the author. "Well," he said sheepishly, "we were trying to cut down the number of illustrations, so I combined two. But I forgot that both pictures showed the right hand."

Artwork is one of the components you separated when you started editing, and you should regularly consult it as you work on the text. First establish whether the artwork supplements the text or illustrates it.

- If the art supplements the text, be sure that it doesn't run ahead of or behind the written instructions. If the readers have been told to take off their shoes before doing their stretch and tone exercises, the exercises shouldn't be illustrated with a picture of someone sporting new Reeboks. If the map accompanying a bike tour tells the readers to follow the road for two miles and then take a right, check the mileage scale and that right turn.

- If the art illustrates the text, photos or drawings of parts should closely resemble the physical model the reader will be looking at. Nothing is more infuriating to someone who's bought a new lawnmower than being confronted with a set of assembly instructions for another model. If you're asking the reader to adapt instructions from a prototype, specify when and how the steps differ.

Check for consistency

People often do more than one project suggested in a book or an article, especially if the first attempt is successful. It's important that instructions for similar procedures be phrased consistently; in fact, if certain steps—for example, folding in egg whites or attaching wires—are repeated exactly from instruction to instruction or step to step, it's a good idea to develop standard phrasing for the procedure. Otherwise, readers will wonder why the same procedure is described another way in a second project.

The best insurance for consistency is to edit each new instruction against the previous one to see that similar steps are discussed in similar language. This method also spotlights previous steps that need rewording if better language or an improved approach comes up later in the manuscript. Editing the new against the old also works for tables, charts, and lists.

Keep tabs on what your reader is doing

My favorite example of forgetting the reader involves the directions for an original worship service. Working in a burst of pure inspiration, without checking against a formal service, the writers asked the worshipers to rise—and then left them standing for the rest of the service.

Remember, if you drill a hole, you put a screw or dowel into it; if you buy bobbins for a sweater, you wind yarn onto them; if you have wires in the equipment box, you attach them to something. If you've ever ended the day with designer mushrooms that didn't get sprinkled on the pizza, brass studs that somehow were never used to decorate a reupholstered chair, or a male plug with, alas, no female socket, you know how frustrating flawed instructions can be. Only a good editor stands between the reader and that frustration.

—*Maron L. Waxman*

as bad as...or worse than

The *as bad as...or worse than* comparison is more often than not honored in the breach. The misusage that omits the second *as* from this phrase—as in *as bad...or worse than*—is an example of what Bernstein calls "incomplete alternative comparison" and is rampant especially among media reporters. Correct usage of this comparison separates the careful writer or speaker from the careless one.

Perhaps the *as bad...or worse than* comparison seems complete because the *worse than* phrase is immediately followed by the object that completes the thought. For example, in the sentence, "This earthquake was as bad or worse than the last one," the second part of the comparison, "worse than the last one," makes sense, but the first part of the comparison, "as bad...the last one," does not.

One way to avoid this problem is to say, "This earthquake is as bad as the last one—or worse." Another is to rewrite: "This earthquake was at least as bad as the last one."

Getting Ducks in a Row: The Rules for Displayed Lists

Make information easy for readers to absorb

When is a list not a list? When it's not recognized as such by the reader. A good displayed list is the mental equivalent of a line of cheerful ducklings behind their sensible mom on their way to an invigorating dip. A short series of items can often be run smoothly into text, but lists longer than eight lines or so tend to stray in the reader's mind from the preceding thoughts. A run-in list that becomes estranged from its lead-in context is worthless.

When does a reader dread seeing a run-in list? When it's so dense it seems like being back in junior high, memorizing the causes of World War I.

Displayed (also called vertical) list format makes the information more approachable and has been shown to help readers absorb—and retain—three or more relatively complex items more easily. This article contains variations on list style; we've assembled the basic rules from some of our favorite sources.

Displayed lists aren't foolproof

Vertical listing isn't a magical format, however; in fact, considerable care in writing and editing is necessary to make any list meaningful to readers. Lists establish either sequential or coordinate relationships among ideas or facts. The two most common flaws in writing lists are (1) camouflaging coordinate information with inconsistent writing or punctuation and (2) formatting sequential items erratically so that readers are distracted or miscued. (The preceding sentence is a run-in list that would look long in a columned layout, a consideration when choosing list style.)

Three conventions affect the usefulness of displayed lists:

- List style: dingbats and indention
- Parallel construction: form and grammar
- Consistent formatting: capitalization and punctuation

Choose the right list style for visual order

Use numbers and letters for list items only when sequence or hierarchy matters; numbers imply priority. If "the following four steps must be followed" to open the emergency exit when the plane crashes, please use numbers. But if there's no reason to emphasize the number of items or their order, and if you won't be referring to the items by number later in the text, use bullets instead. Whether using numbers or bullets, remember this advice:

> In lists numerals with periods are preferable to numerals with parentheses.
> —*Words Into Type*

> In lists with 10 or more numbers, the periods should be aligned.

> Bulleted items look best when set with hanging indention, which may appear [as an indented block]...or with further indention of runover lines.

> Hanging indention is preferred for numbered list items, but paragraph style is acceptable when (1) every item or almost every item is about one-third of a manuscript page long or longer or (2) the page is to be typeset in two or more columns.
> —*New York Public Library Writer's Guide to Style and Usage*

What kinds of bullets are best? Round, square, diamond, or any other shape that your software can produce—just go easy on the somewhat clichéd icons like checkmarks and pointing fingers, and avoid the asterisks reminiscent of typewriter mock-dingbats. A formatting point:

> Bullets should be checked for positioning—the same amount of space should be used before each bullet and after each bullet throughout the text. They should also be checked for consistency—the same types of bullets should be used for the same levels of text throughout the document. For example, a square bullet could be used for the main elements in the list and a star-shaped bullet could be used for the subsections. Care should be taken not to use too many types of bullets within a single document.
> —*Error-Free Writing: A Lifetime Guide to Flawless Business Writing*

Make items parallel in form and grammar

Making elements in a list parallel when they're not can be annoying, but it's worth the trouble. Parallelism is the principle that says the parts of a sentence or a list that are parallel in meaning should be parallel in form. Why? To emphasize coordinate relationships. Here's the rule for structural parallelism:

> Items in a list should ordinarily be parallel in construction—that is, all phrases or all sentences—but if one item in the list is a complete sentence and therefore requires a period, then each item in the list, including phrases, should end with a period. Otherwise no periods are necessary on lists of phrases.
>
> —*Words Into Type*

Here's an example of grammatical parallelism doing its work well; parallel terms are italic:

> To achieve its mission, the National Breast Cancer Coalition focuses on three goals:

- *research—increasing appropriations* for high quality, peer reviewed research and *working within the scientific community* to focus research on prevention and cure;

- *access—increasing access* for all women to high quality treatment and care and to breast cancer clinical trials; and

- *influence—increasing the influence of women* living with breast cancer and other breast cancer activists in the decision making that impacts all issues surrounding breast cancer.
  —from a National Breast Cancer Coalition flyer

Although grammatically parallel, these bulleted items could be improved. The first word in each item should be capitalized, the unit modifiers (high-quality, peer-reviewed) need hyphens, and the end punctuation for each phrase is unnecessary. Some people would object to the use of *impact* as verb. But writers and editors will decide differently about such things. See the rules for punctuation and capitalization below.

Punctuate and capitalize lists consistently

Phrase- and sentence-style lists can be mixed in a document, but it is always the choice of lead-in sentence or phrase that determines the punctuation that precedes the list and the options for punctuation and capitalization within the list. The one rule without an exception is that a sentence fragment introducing a list should not be followed by a colon. Here are the basic guidelines.

For lead-ins—

A colon is used after an introductory statement that contains the words as *follows* or *the following*; either a colon or a period may be used after other statements introducing lists.

When the introduction is not a complete sentence and one or more of the items on the list are needed to complete it, no colon or dash should be used.... An exception...is that a colon may be used to replace a comma when the statement preceding a displayed list ends with such words as *for example* or *that is*.

In lists, between a word and its definition a comma, a colon, or a dash may be used: a comma when the definition is a simple appositive, a colon for a more involved construction. A dash is often used in a glossary.
—*Words Into Type*

Within lists—

When the list items that follow a complete introductory sentence are not complete sentences, the items may begin with either uppercase or lowercase letters and end with either periods or no punctuation. Whatever style is chosen, it should be followed throughout the publication for the same type of list.

When the list items that follow a complete introductory sentence are complete sentences, each item should begin with an uppercase letter and end with a period.

If none of the items in the list has an internal comma, each item ends with a comma instead of a semicolon.... [A]nother widely accepted approach...[is the]...type of list in which the first word of each item is capped and end punctuation is dropped entirely.

—*New York Public Library Writer's Guide to Style and Usage*

Use different types of lists for different content

And lists and *or* lists need to be handled differently. They need a different lead-in and clear internal reminders of the nature of the list. That's because list content can be one of three types:

- *Exclusive.* A, B, and C are a comprehensive list, a closed unit. Items are equally weighted and function as coordinates or as a sequence or chronology. Example: a list of the airplane emergency exit instructions.

- *Representative.* A, B, and C are a list of samples in the same category or a list of equal factors only one of which is key at a given point. Items show a range or pattern. Example: this list of the three types of list content.

- *Inclusive.* A, B, and C are independent variables that cross categories but are equally key. Putting them in a list together implies an interrelationship. Example: the causes of World War I.

Notice that the previous list is introduced by a complete sentence that clues the reader to the type of content: "...content can be one of three types." The mixed pattern of phrases and sentences, including examples, in the bulleted items would be difficult to follow without parallel syntax, capitalization, and punctuation.

Don't introduce an exclusive list with phrasing like "The four reasons include..." if what follows are all four reasons. Saying a list includes several items implies that others have been left out.

Like too much of anything good, displayed lists can become monotonous, and writers who use them as a shortcut to telegraph difficult material or mask inadequate research give lists a bad name. But well-constructed displays earn their keep in copy with several valuable services:

- They help readers understand and remember multiple items, factors, and ideas.

- They break up copy visually so that even complex information seems approachable.

- They clarify the relationship among list items and the nature of the content.

Displayed lists prevent ringers

Structural and grammatical parallelism are just two aspects of clarifying relationships among list items. Common sense is important when ordering items, no matter how duck-like they look on screen or on the page.

For example, we found a run-in list that, by virtue of the final element in the series, seems to make light of homelessness. If this had been a vertical listing, the apparent attempt at humor would have shown up for what it is, a mistake: *sales of ice cream cones* rings wrong.

> The record-breaking cold came hard on the heels of a week of driving rains, stinging ice and yet more snow. And as people around the region hunkered down and tried to keep warm, slippery patches of ice blanketed sidewalks and roads; homeless men and women sought shelter; brittle icicle-laden trees snapped and fell; and sales of ice cream cones dropped precipitously.
> —*New York Times*

Carefully edited bulleted lists will keep you from linking incongruous items, because the ringer has no place to hide.

—*Linda B. Jorgensen*

Singin' the Blues

Don't set yourself up for abduction by aliens

T he first time I got a real taste of the blueline* blues was more than 10 years ago. The wounds have healed, but the scars.... I was a naive young project manager dealing with a naive young client (a dangerous combination—never put a green rider on a green horse). The client wanted to publish a packet of information materials for association members. At our first meeting, I described the steps the packet would go through—writing, editing, production, proofreading, and printing. I explained that the client could review the draft at each step up to and including page proofs. Then someone piped up, "I've heard of something called bluelines—we can make changes there, too, can't we?"

As I said, I was naive. Instead of answering, "I'm afraid you were misinformed. It's physically impossible to make changes on bluelines. In fact, the last person who tried it was abducted by aliens," I attempted to explain that while it was *possible*, it was a terrible idea from a financial and scheduling point of view. Needless to say, the bluelines went back to the printer three times, and the client was angry at me because the job came in late and over budget.

To understand what you should and should not do with a set of bluelines, it might help to think about whose work you're reviewing at each stage of editing and production. When you edit a draft manuscript, you're reviewing the author's work. When you proofread a set of galleys or pages, you're verifying that the keyboard operator has followed the copy and the layout artist formatted it correctly. When you check bluelines, you're reviewing the printer's work, which consists of reproducing whatever you have provided.

Editors can leave participles dangling, but printers don't. Typesetters can make typos, but printers don't. Project managers can forget to verify that the table of contents matches the revised text, but printers don't. If you find those mistakes in the bluelines, it's because you failed to catch them earlier. You can correct them, but you'll pay a stiff price to do so.

---

blueline proofs—one-color proofs made on photosensitive paper exposed to final film. These are generated for one- or two-color projects (the second color usually appears as a lighter image) and in addition to color proofs to show format. A blueline proof is a chance to check the registration of all the images and placement of stripped-in elements and shows how pages will fold and bind.

—adapted from *Electronic Design and Publishing Business Practices* by Liane Sebastian (Allworth Press, 1992)

Recently I participated in a panel discussion on the subject of newsletters. The members of the audience belonged to nonprofit associations, and they were doing good works with tight budgets. Nonetheless, some of them, like my lamented client, were under the misapprehension that proofreading or editing could wait till the blueline stage. They "just didn't have time" to do those tasks any earlier. This kind of thinking is exemplified in the saying, "There's never time to do it right, but there's always time to do it over."

If you don't have time to edit or proofread your piece carefully before it goes to press, why bother to do it afterward? Those tasks take just as long at the blueline stage; the only difference is that the later you do them, the more they cost.

Even if time and money were unlimited, there's another reason that making changes at the blueline stage is inadvisable. Printers schedule their print jobs carefully so their presses don't stand idle. When you make changes, your job has to be rescheduled, and the printer may end up having to rush it through so other deadlines don't slip. As a result, you may end up with less-than-perfect print quality.

Granted, to err is human, and anyone can find himself or herself making text changes in bluelines—once. If it happens to you more than once, though, you need to take a hard look at your production process. Are you spending too little time at the editing or proofreading stages, with the idea lurking in the back of your mind that you can make those last few corrections on the bluelines? If so, you're just setting yourself up to be abducted by aliens.

—*Lee Mickle*

Pin Down Vague Terms of Measurement

When my second child was born, the pediatrician suggested that I nurse the baby for a long time because of allergies in the family. When we returned for my son's two-month checkup, the doctor asked how the nursing was coming along. I said, "Oh, I'm finished; he's weaned." The doctor looked at me in sheer amazement and objected, "But I said to nurse him for a long time!" I replied quite honestly, "I did." To me, two months was an enormous amount of time. Clearly, the doctor's concept of a long time and my concept of a long time were two different things. Had the doctor given me an exact figure, perhaps eight months or so, I would have said either "Okay" or "You must be crazy!" But at least we would have been communicating within the same realm.

Each of the statements below contains a subjective measurement or proportion open to misinterpretation. Isolate the ambiguity and identify the missing information needed to make the point clearer. In some cases, the measurement may not need to be more specific because a great deal of detail isn't essential to the meaning of the sentence.

1. Virtually all the women at the seminar chose to attend the Macintosh design workshop rather than the IBM spreadsheet workshop.

2. Please have your manager answer this letter as soon as possible.

3. If you buy photocopier paper in bulk, we can offer you a substantial discount.

4. I've only asked you to work late a time or two lately.

5. High winds caused terrible destruction in the small community.

6. The guest of honor was visibly upset because his children arrived at the awards banquet late.

7. The candidate won by a slight majority.

8. For someone who's been at the newspaper for only a short while, you've made more than a few good contacts.

9. They drove at breakneck speed to the beach.

10. This project should require a minimal amount of effort from the editor.

ANSWERS

1. *virtually all*. What percentage of the women present went to the Mac workshop? It's hard to guess where the emphasis belongs: on the preference of women as opposed to that of men for the design seminar or on the preference of women for design as opposed to spreadsheet training. If men were present, what percentage of all participants went to the Mac seminar?

2. *as soon as possible*. When should the letter be answered? By the close of business or by the end of the week?

3. *in bulk/discount*. What cutoff point defines a bulk purchase? What is the retail price and how much will it be discounted? What is the savings over retail?

4. *a time or two/lately*. How many times has it actually been in the past week? In the past six months? How many other people are regularly asked to stay late? (Also note that *only* is misplaced.)

5. *high winds/terrible destruction/ small community*. What was the force of the wind in miles per hour? What was the estimated property damage? What is the population and the size of the area affected? If millions of dollars in repairs are needed for a few square miles, the magnitude of the damage is clear.

6. *arrived late*. It doesn't really matter how late the children were. Being only a few minutes late could still embarrass their father.

7. *slight majority*. What was the margin? What percentage of the eligible voters did the majority vote represent? This victory could still have been significant if the narrow margin represented a large popular vote.

8. *a short while/more than a few*. How many years have you worked for the paper? Does that include the time you were a gofer or just since you've been a reporter? How long does it usually take to develop contacts? How many of them do you have? Three? Twelve? The way this sentence is worded, it's a slightly invidious compliment.

9. *breakneck speed*. How fast were they driving? What was the speed limit? Are they teenagers who go 70 miles per hour without realizing it or retirees pulling a trailer who feel reckless at 55 miles per hour?

10. *minimal effort*. How many hours will the editor have to work? How many pages will he or she have to read? Is the effort minimal because it's a big but easy job or because the editing is a small part of it?

—*Ellie Abrams*

Where Do Errors Lurk?

Check all pagination. If the front matter is paginated with roman numerals, are they in the proper sequence? If the document will be printed double-sided, will all odd-numbered pages fall on the right and all even-numbered pages fall on the left? Do all new chapters or sections begin on a right-hand page? Have blank pages been inserted in the proper places, and have they been accounted for in the pagination?

Check the table of contents against the text. Are all the head levels listed? Is the wording exactly the same as it is in the text? Are the page numbers correct?

Read all running heads and running footers. Do the running heads reflect the correct chapter title, and is the wording exactly the same as it is on the first page of the chapter or suitably abbreviated? Also, don't read only the first one and assume that all the rest were generated automatically and must therefore be correct.

Read all heads. Chances are that they've only been skimmed by everyone along the way and may still contain errors.

Read the first few lines after each head. Errors are overlooked here.

Read page transitions. Look carefully for dropped or duplicated text.

Check anything in alphabetical order. An index, a list of references, acknowledgments with a list of names—these are the places where alphabetization errors lurk.

Check the order of numerical listings. If the text says that there are five steps to assembling the product, make sure that five steps are actually given and that they are numbered consecutively. Likewise, if the head levels are numbered, make sure that the numbering tracks throughout the document.

Check all endnotes and footnotes. Are they mentioned in the text? Are they numbered consecutively?

Look for pairs. Parentheses, brackets, and double and single quotation marks must come in pairs. Read all equations, even if you don't understand them, and look for pairs.

Look for "placeholders"—symbols or letters used to hold the place for information that will be filled in later. For example, XXX might be used in cross-references ("see page XXX for a more detailed description of this item") until the pagination is final. These placeholders are often forgotten and make their way into print.

—*Robin A. Cormier*

Substantive Editing:
The Words-Upward Approach

Copyeditors may be doing more of this work than they realize

What's your image of a "substantive" editor? Someone who lunches with authors? Or someone who assesses the overall content and length of manuscripts, moves chapters around or deletes them, and makes recommendations about tone and content?

The latter image is partly right. For doing such work at the manuscript level, an editor is armed with a broad brush. Indeed, some manuscripts may require no more than rearranging a few paragraphs to make the whole thing fall into place and read more smoothly. But editing substantively calls for a magnifying glass too; that skill is the focus of this article. Most editors do substantive editing at some point: All editors work toward helping a manuscript say what it means and mean what it says.

What is substantive editing?

I define substantive editing as the *editing of meaning*. Consequently, substantive editing has to happen not only at the manuscript level but also at the word, sentence, and paragraph levels: After the broad brush comes the magnifying glass.

At any level, substantive editing is based primarily on *analysis*. Analyzing means "separating or distinguishing the component parts of something...so as to discover its true nature or inner relationships." Whether I'm using my broad brush or my magnifying glass, I have to analyze the manuscript—examine its components and understand its inner relationships.

The specific tasks that are part of each step are not mutually exclusive; for the purpose of this discussion, I treat them as more neatly compartmentalized than they may be for a particular manuscript. Details that must be analyzed with both broad brush and magnifying glass, though with necessarily different emphasis, include examining the topics of chapters, moving large sections or chapters, deleting irrelevant and redundant material, recommending a change in a term throughout a manuscript, supplying missing words, replacing incorrect or unsuitable words, reorganizing sentences within or between paragraphs, and moving sentences and paragraphs. An editor who is knowledgeable about the subject matter may also have to do some rewriting.

In summary, the substantive functions of editors are as follows: analyzing, filling gaps in thought, reducing, reorganizing, rewording, and rewriting.

The words-upward approach

When the broad brush has been brandished (in a pass through the whole manuscript), I pick up my magnifying glass and start literally at the word level and begin working upward. That is, to understand the meaning being conveyed by the manuscript, I must first understand what the words mean and how they are related in each sentence. Then I can understand how the sentences in each paragraph are related and how the paragraphs are related.

This words-upward method comes naturally to inductive thinkers, people who learn and understand by getting a grip on the specifics first and working their way up to the big picture. Of course, deductive thinkers (the folks who work from the big picture down to the details) can also make fine substantive editors. But the words-upward method, which is what I use and teach, works so well that even deductive thinkers should try it.

Substantive word flaws

Editors are familiar with word flaws at the copyediting level; many of these same flaws, and others, become substantive when the editor has to make decisions about their *meaning*—that is, when the meaning of a word or term is so unclear that the editor must try to figure out the author's intended meaning. This is not to say that substantive editing is always hard or that it's necessarily harder to do well than copyediting—which in some ways is more of a challenge precisely because the editor can't go as far. What, then, is the special challenge of substantive editing? Let's look at some examples.

Clarifying pronoun antecedents is a good example of a word-level copyediting task that becomes substantive when a meaning decision is involved. The pronoun *this* is a good example. The guideline I use for clarifying *this* antecedents is that every *this* needs a noun to modify. When supplying that noun is easy, I'm copyediting; when supplying it is hard, I'm editing substantively. (There's the possibility that I will be wrong no matter how careful I am being. That's one of the calculated risks of substantive editing; when I'm afraid to take it, I'm better off querying the author.)

Here's an example of a *this* that needs substantive editing:

The lymphocytes are mixed with myeloma cells in the presence of polyethylene glycol. This fuses the cellular membranes of the two cell types.

This *what* fuses the membranes? Neither the context nor my own knowledge provided the answer, but I could see at least two choices, and I had to query the author: Either the act of mixing fuses the membranes—

This *mixing* fuses the cellular membranes of the two cell types.

or the polyethylene glycol does it—

> The lymphocytes are mixed with myeloma cells in the presence of polyethylene glycol, *which* fuses the cellular membranes of the two cell types.

That was a simple example. To come up with precisely the noun that will clarify a truly obscure antecedent requires some expert knowledge on the editor's part—unless, of course, the issue can be sidestepped by supplying a generic noun or by rewording. This example stumped me:

> Virtually everyone responsible for the missile program assumed that the next step in the missile's growth would be the designing of a semiactive homing version of the missile, both to give the missile greater range and to allow it to intercept aircraft approaching at low altitudes, where shipboard radar often failed to distinguish between an aircraft and its reflections from the water. *This* presented a problem in the design of the missile radome....

This *what* presented a problem? I couldn't find an appropriate noun in the long sentence preceding *This*. My technical knowledge of the subject is nil, so I wasn't able to supply my own noun by synthesizing the preceding sentence. Further, none of the generic nouns I keep up my sleeve for this purpose seemed to work—*this condition, procedure, point, finding, situation,* and so on. By default, I reworded:

> Consequently, there was a problem in the design of the missile radome...

Faulty logic is another word-level substantive flaw. Here is an example:

> Iraq's invasion of Kuwait so plainly violated the United Nations charter and directly challenged the major powers as to be unique in important aspects. Not only was the boldness of the aggression exceptional, but few other aggressors are likely to miss as many opportunities to sow confusion in the Security Council.

Logic tells me the intended meaning is that few other aggressors are likely to *find*, not *miss*, as many opportunities to sow confusion as Iraq found. Faulty logic is easily overlooked when it occurs in a sentence that is otherwise correct. Hence the need for the magnifying glass.

Vagueness is a substantive word flaw of epidemic proportions. The vague words in the following example constitute a mix of copyediting and substantive editing problems:

> Project staff are charged with operationalizing viable health education programs using interpersonal, community, and mass media channels.

I think *interpersonal* is clear enough, and it's defined in *Webster's*, so I stopped attacking it years ago; perhaps I've lived too long in Washington, DC, vagueness capital of the nation. *Operationalizing* and *viable* are worth some effort, however. The vague *operationalizing* could be replaced with the more precise *carrying out*, a copyediting fix, if the context contained no indications of any other meaning.

The decision about *viable*, however, is not so easy. One of the meanings of *viable* would be particularly appropriate here: "capable of existence and development as an independent unit." But I would have to analyze the context; if the author mentions that programs must be capable of existing on their own after the project is over, then *viable* was used properly; otherwise, it is probably just a buzzword and I would delete or replace it.

The word *using* is also somewhat vague in this example, but the vagueness has to do with the word's role in the sentence, not with its meaning. Changing *using* to *by using* or *through* would clarify that the staff is doing the using, not the programs.

The following example of word vagueness is all substantive for me:

> Reading is a processing skill of *symbolic reasoning* sustained by the *interfacilitation* of an intricate hierarchy of *substrata factors* that have been mobilized as a *psychological working system* and pressed into service in accordance with the purpose of the reader.

I had no text to help me with this one, because it was a lone sentence pulled from a collection of bad writing samples. My own knowledge doesn't help me, either. Faced with a sentence this mysterious in a real editing job, I would take a whack at rewriting it—just plain guessing, if necessary—and query the author, as I do here:

> Reading is a processing skill that involves interpreting signs and is reinforced by several other intricately related factors that people subconsciously press into service when they read.

> (Author query: Editing okay? Is this the meaning? If not, please clarify the meaning of the terms *symbolic reasoning, interfacilitation, substrata factors,* and *psychological working system.*)

The topic of vagueness alone could fill many pages, and wrong meaning, wrong connotation, and jargon are other word-level flaws that also require substantive editing. The words-upward approach may help editors doing substantive editing to work more systematically. I expect that some editors will discover they've been doing more substantive editing than they realized—or have been credited with.

—*Mia Cunningham*

Rules for Substantive Editing

The good news and the bad news: Few hard-and-fast rules apply

The good news about substantive editing (the editing of meaning or content) is that it has few concrete rules of its own—good news, because someone who has command of copyediting and writing skills probably already knows most of the rules for editing substantively.

Of course, the *bad* news is that it has few concrete rules of its own—bad news, because the criteria for substantively editing a manuscript are almost entirely subjective. Consequently, substantive editing is hard to teach; students want to learn the "right way" to do things, and rarely is there one and only one right way to fix a substantive editing problem.

Substantive editing, like writing, is a highly creative process that leaves much room for interpretation and judgment. But here are four basic rules:

1. Always call a thing by the same name. For this discussion, a couple of terms need defining. The two basic types of writing are *creative writing* (e.g., novels, short stories, poems, essays), the purpose of which is to transmit experience, and *expository writing* (e.g., nonfiction, reports, manuals, regulations), the purpose of which is to transmit knowledge.

Variety of expression is used intentionally in creative writing to stir the imagination and arouse in the readers the same feelings that inspired the writer. But in expository writing, intentional use of variety is risky. Used where it should not be, variety of word choice is a major confounder of clarity.

Intentional but inappropriate use of variety is called *elegant variation.* Here's an example:

> Assignments of spaces to carpools shall be based solely on the number of regular **passengers** in a carpool. Carpools with the highest number of regular **occupants** shall receive priority; for example, if there are a limited number of spaces available for assignment to carpools, a carpool with six **employees** shall receive a parking space before a carpool with five **members**. In determining the number of regular **participants** in a carpool, an **individual** who travels less than on a daily basis or who travels only one way shall be counted on a pro rata basis.

The people who ride in carpools are intentionally called by six different names for the sake of variety, and nothing but confusion is gained. The confusion that results from *unintentional variety*—that is, from thoughtlessly calling a thing by different names—seems to grow in proportion to the number of words in the term and the number of pages between mentions. For example, let's say you find the term *Surface Missile System Project* on page 5 and the term *surface missile systems program* on page 15. It may

115

be impossible for anyone but the author to know whether the use of different names is an unintentional inconsistency or the intentional use of two similar but different terms.

2. Do what is necessary to "tell the story" clearly. Even the driest expository writing has a story to tell. Like a story, an expository manuscript has a beginning, a middle, and an end. In the middle, the facts are laid out in one or more kinds of order by means of induction, deduction, or comparison and contrast.

To help the author tell the story, the substantive editor first has to analyze the manuscript in terms of the principles of good writing—unity, coherence, and emphasis—and then apply the substantive editing functions: reducing, reorganizing, rewording, and rewriting. These principles are developed very clearly and with good examples (though from creative, not expository, writing) by Theodore A. Rees Cheney in *Getting the Words Right: How to Rewrite, Edit & Revise* (Writer's Digest Books).

3. Assume every new manuscript is a first draft. Until editing reveals otherwise, it's a good idea to assume every new manuscript received for editing is a first draft. The personal computer has made it possible to turn out half-baked first drafts faster than ever before. It's too bad for us substantive editors, because the process of rewriting is actually the process of rethinking, and when that process is skipped, the chances of a first-draft manuscript containing a complete "story" are poor.

Treating the manuscript as a first draft gives the substantive editor an entirely different slant on the job. Manuscripts are somewhat like jigsaw puzzles: A carefully written draft can be expected to contain all the necessary pieces of the story, which simply have to be arranged in the proper order. But first drafts may contain duplicate and irrelevant pieces that have to be eliminated, and new pieces may have to be created to replace unsuitable ones. Pieces may even be missing or obscure, and then the only recourse is to query the author.

4. Develop a strategy for querying authors. Since authors must be queried about missing and obscure pieces of the story, editors need a strategy for querying. The following are the three most important elements of my own strategy.

- **First, be businesslike.** It's important to show authors that you have the querying process, like the entire editing process, under control. You can do so by making appointments for in-person and telephone conferences and suggesting a time limit, even if the author is in the adjoining office. Have all your questions ready in advance.

- **Second, suggest solutions.** Don't just dump editing problems in the author's lap by writing or saying, "This is unclear." Remember, *it's clear to the author.* Make your best effort at editing and query, "Is the editing okay? Is this the meaning?" If you can see another possible meaning, add "...or does it mean such and such?" Authors are reassured by an editor's ability to see alternative meanings.
- **Third and most important, avoid confrontation.** You and the author are actually on the same side—the reader's side—so there is no reason to be combative. When I was new at editing, I took personal ownership of every manuscript I edited, and of course every author conference became a confrontation. In fact, the strongest emotion editors need to show is regret—regret that the readers may not understand the meaning that the author has tried to convey.

Here's one simple but amazingly effective way of avoiding confrontation. When writing memos or asking questions, avoid using the second person; that is, don't say "What do you mean by...?" or "On page 6 you say A, but on page 7 you say B; which is correct?" Instead, use the third person: "The text on page 2 says A, but page 4 says B; which is correct?" Or even better, align yourself with the author by using the first person plural: "How can *we* say the same thing in fewer words?"

Unlike copyediting, which is guided by the concrete rules of grammar, punctuation, spelling, and style, substantive editing is about meaning. It's abstract, its rules are abstract, and it therefore requires full, unremitting engagement of the brain.

A wonderfully perspicacious client once told me that he did not necessarily want me to work 40 hours a week on his manuscript. He would be satisfied with only 20 hours, he said, provided that all 20 were the "freshest" (he meant brain-engaged) I could possibly give. That client understood the abstractness of substantive editing and the puzzle-solving quality about it that make it so intensely frustrating and rewarding at the same time.

Concrete rules are much easier to teach and learn, but there are few concrete rules in substantive editing, which is second only to writing in creativity. The rules for substantive editing, such as they are, only point the way for editors to use their own skills and experience.

—*Mia Cunningham*

How Careful Should Editors Be?

Pretty careful. But perfection's not possible

Three recent incidents prompt me to ask, How careful do editors have to be in checking facts? Is it possible for publications people to be too careful?

A misspelled famous name. I noticed that *Wallace Warfield Simpson* was used in the text and in the index (at least he was consistent) of Anthony Cave Brown's mammoth book *Treason in the Blood* about Kim Philby and his father St. John Philby. (Published by Houghton Mifflin in 1994, it's a terrific read.) There's one reference to Wallis's husband as *Edward VII* instead of *VIII* in the text as well.

The names of well-known persons are easy enough to check in almost any good dictionary, and this misspelling of one of the best-known personages of the 20th century really is surprising, especially since the author is of the generation that lived through the abdication crisis. And it should be easy enough to avoid confusing Edward VII with Edward VIII in the same book—an eye for consistency alone should be enough to call that VII into question.

The lengths to which editors should go to check the spelling of unknown persons' names is what's negotiable here. I generally settle for querying the spelling of any name I can't find in a common reference, especially if the spelling is unusual (e.g., *Conoly*).

Place names are another problem (*Veracruz* or *Vera Cruz?*) and should routinely be checked, particularly in historical works. Remember that the spelling of names may change over time.

A wandering *the*. Several sharp-eyed readers of the newsletter I edit alerted me to the fact that the title of Darwin's pathbreaking work is *The Origin of Species* (not *Origin of the Species*, as it had appeared in the newsletter), and that misplacing *the* in this instance is meaningful and has deeply disturbing implications. (The fine points of the meaning were generally not elaborated upon, though one correspondent did ask if the error meant that "we" were Creationists.)

Obviously, the Darwin title would have been easy enough to check. It just looked "okay" as it was given to me and I didn't check it. Biologists know better. A lot of what we editors catch or don't catch relates to how specialized our knowledge is; when we're outside our field of expertise, we need to check things more carefully.

Trademark symbols. I've worked on reports for government agencies in which the word processors had been carefully instructed to add ® or ™ to every product name, mostly drugs, used in the text. They were going nuts trying to make sure that every proper name (e.g., Anacin) had the appropriate symbol (® being reserved for trademarks registered with the U.S. Patent and Trademark Office and ™ for trademarks that are not registered).

In this instance there was great rejoicing when they learned that although companies try to plaster symbols on their products' names wherever they can, that does not mean the rest of us have to use the symbols in ordinary text.

As the *Chicago Manual of Style*, 14th edition, puts it:

> Dictionaries indicate registered trademark names. A reasonable effort should be made to capitalize such names:.... The symbols ® and ™, which often accompany registered trademark names on product packaging and in advertisements, need not be used in running text.

I would add that the "reasonable effort" should extend to punctuation as well (*Coca-Cola, Jell-O*).

Incidentally, a check of two dictionaries on trademarked product names turned up some anomalies. For example, *Merriam-Webster's Collegiate*, tenth edition (1993), lists *Levi's, Ping-Pong, Vaseline*, and *Xerox* with the designation *trademark*, whereas the *Oxford Encyclopedic English Dictionary*, second edition (1995), omits *Levi's*, lists *ping-pong* only with the definition "table tennis," lists *Vaseline* as a proper noun and *vaseline* as a transitive verb, and lists *Xerox* as a proper noun and *xerox* as a transitive verb. It's that lowercased use of names as "transitive verbs" that causes companies to plaster their symbols everywhere.

None of us can promise perfection (except, perhaps, in a second edition)

Moreover, whereas the *Washington Post Deskbook on Style* lists *ChapStick* and *Saran wrap*, these names are spelled *Chap Stick* and *Saran Wrap* in both *Words Into Type* and the U.S. Government Printing Office's *Style Manual*. The *Post*'s guide also says that "in any trade or brand name, only the first letter is capitalized"—ambiguous advice at best, considering its own listings of *Alka-Seltzer, Band-Aid, Day-Glo, Kitty Litter, Ping-Pong, Q-Tip*, and *Seeing Eye dog*.

At the same time, the *Post*'s guide offers some sensible advice on avoiding the use of a trade name for a generic product unless you're sure the product bears that name and there's some reason to mention the brand. (Not all facial tissues are *Kleenex*, not all scouring pads are *Brillo*, and not all jeans are *Levi's*.) It also points out that some trade names—including *Frisbee*, *Gatorade*, *Kool-Aid*, *Laundromat*, and *Velcro*—have no simple generic synonyms.

It may be worth mentioning here that company names (the *Xerox Corporation*), as opposed to product names (*Xerox copier*), should never bear the trademark symbol.

A modest proposal for grace errors. All editors strive for perfection. However, as I wrote to Thomas Campbell, an editor in Washington, DC (who gently called to our attention the inadvertent substitution of the word *subjective* for *subjunctive* in a previous *Editorial Eye* blurb), none of us can promise perfection (except, perhaps, in a second edition).

Consider this proposal: Given the conflicting signage and the extraordinarily diligent parking enforcement in the District of Columbia, I admit to perpetual anxiety about the possibility of getting a parking ticket when I routinely park my car near my office. My husband has tried to assuage this fixation by suggesting that he has budgeted for X number of parking tickets a year, and since I've not had one in 10 years, I should strive to relax.

May I suggest that we editors consider that we have a budget of errors for the year, a modest balance to draw against in time of factual inaccuracy? Chances are, most of us will end the year way under budget.

—*Priscilla S. Taylor*

Are Editors on Their Way Out?

No, but they may never be paid what they're worth

A reader recently sent up a flare for help. "This is a request for a reality check," he wrote. "My question is simple: Are editors an endangered species?

"Based on the trend where we work (a large engineering corporation), based on what we read and hear generally, and based on the quality of what we see more and more in print, my co-editors and I are feeling akin to the little Dutch boy, with our fingers in the dike trying to hold back the floods of... what, we are not sure: ignorance, indifference, the bottom line? It is as if the whole world is rapidly coming to the conclusion that there is no value added by the services of a good editor.

"So, not only are we apprehensive that our department's days are numbered, but we are also starting to wonder if our very profession's days are as well. Anything you might be able to say to dispel at least the latter concern would be most welcome. Sans that, we are open to suggestions regarding suitable life jackets for when the dike bursts."

The Editorial Eye replies: If it's any comfort, people have been predicting the end of editing and editors for as long as I can remember, certainly since the dawn of the computer age. How could any mere mortal compete with the mechanized wonder of spell check, electronic thesauruses, and, later, grammar programs?

Well, as we all know, it's not that simple. Although nobody doubts that ignorance is increasing, it can be argued that this situation will dictate more emphasis on careful editing rather than less. Of course, the extent of reader indifference may be the key to the future of editors, but I can't help feeling that although nobody wants to pay editors a living wage, everybody wants the published product to be perfect. Some publishers care enough to pay for near-perfection (as we all know, perfection comes only with the second edition).

We hear a lot about how editing and editors are vanishing: Fewer editors do actual correction of manuscripts—more simply oversee the production process; many editors in government offices and elsewhere are not replaced when they retire; and more offices are expecting everyone who writes a document to edit it as well. And we all see shoddy products from publishing houses we used to respect.

At the same time, to take only one person's experience, my husband has been surprised, and pleased, to have his work edited more carefully by the publishing houses with which he has dealt as the years progress (and, he thinks, as he has improved as a writer!). Charles E. Tuttle, in 1961, and W.W. Norton, in 1970, published his first two biographies without changing a word. In contrast, Doubleday, in 1989, had his biography of a general edited by a military specialist, and both HarperCollins, in 1991, and Brassey's, in 1994, had two other biographies edited by freelancers.

The main problem is that more publishers are looking for the cheapest editor they can find, and this means freelance rather than on-staff. As long as there are good freelancers available—who are paid by the job or the hour and work at home, perhaps sporadically or temporarily in an office, on varied projects and for varied employers—staff editing jobs may indeed be unable to compete when an employer's paramount concern is economy. At the same time, on-staff editors acquire expertise that may be difficult to duplicate outside the office, especially in a technical field such as yours.

In sum, I think the extent to which editors are an endangered species depends—on the priorities of the employer, the health of the company's finances, and the skills and adaptability of the editors. As long as people desire not to look ridiculous in print, there will be a need for editors, but whether editors will be able to feed their families on what they get for saving others from embarrassment is another question.

—*Priscilla S. Taylor*

One Last Look:
The Final Quality Control Review

This is your best chance to catch maddening errors under your nose

Virtually everyone in the publications field has a story to tell about "the one that slipped through"—a horrible, glaring, embarrassing error that went undetected and made it into print. My personal worst was the time the company I was working for sent a proposal to the Joint Chiefs of Staff at the Pentagon, and our proposal cover said "Joint *Chefs*...." There's always plenty of blame to go around when these errors occur, but the problem is usually a faulty error-prevention system.

QC review, editing, proofreading: What's the difference?

An examination of the editorial processes of many organizations will reveal that an important step is missing: the final quality control (QC) review. Proofreading has traditionally been the last step in the publications process, but there's lots of evidence to indicate that even several rounds of thorough proofreading aren't enough. We at EEI believe that a final look by a "fresh pair of eyes" is critical. The concept is simple: *When you think everything is perfect, add one more review.*

The final quality control review is entirely different from editing and proofreading. Instead of looking at the meaning of the words—as an editor does—or looking at each character of the text—as a proofreader does—the QC reviewer looks at the document as a whole—as the reader will. The editor doesn't always see the document in finished form, and the proofreader frequently doesn't have the entire document at once, so errors can still slip through.

What kinds of errors can a QC review unearth? Both large and small:

- an introduction that mentions a glossary that doesn't appear in the document
- a subtitle on the title page that no longer reflects the content
- a figure without a caption
- a running head that doesn't match its chapter title
- an empty box that was supposed to contain a photo
- a format inconsistency between the preface and the rest of the document

These errors, and many more, can occur when a document is being prepared on a tight schedule, when changes are being made at the last minute, or when the text is divided among several proofreaders and no one person sees the entire document at once.

Who should perform the QC review?

Ideally, it should be performed by someone with strong editorial skills, a sharp eye for detail, and familiarity with document production methods and conventions. Under less-than-ideal circumstances, when such a wizard is not available, the review can be performed by any detail-oriented co-worker who has not seen the document before.

How do you QC a document?

For an effective quality control review, two requirements must be met:

1. The document must be complete. The cover and title page must be included, all graphics must be in place, the index must be complete, and every last error that has been marked by the proofreaders must be corrected and checked. The review will not accomplish its intended goal if the document is given to the reviewer in pieces.

2. The review must be performed by someone who has never seen the document before. A fresh pair of eyes is essential. The QC reviewer should never be the person who has shepherded the document through all the steps in the process and is intimately familiar with it. The bigger the error, the less likely this person is to detect it at this stage of production.

What do you look for when you are performing the QC review? The answer depends on the time available and the level of quality desired. As a general rule, check the most basic elements first; then move on to the details as time allows. You will not receive congratulations for finding an extra space between two words on page 322 if there's a typo on the cover. Here are some additional pointers:

- Ask the person responsible for the document to point out any special areas of concern. For example, if the proofreader found a lot of errors in the graphics, they should get a close look. If time is short, ask for a definition of the priorities. ("We know the sizing of the figures isn't consistent; don't worry about that. Just be sure they're numbered consecutively—we had to add a few at the last minute.")
- Look at the document as the reader would. Start at the beginning, and glance at each page to become familiar with the document before you take a closer look.

- Look at the overall visual effect of the pages before reading the words.
- Mark everything you find—except the most egregious errors—on Post-its that can be removed easily if it turns out that the page is acceptable as is. There may not be time to fix everything, and some decisions may have to be made about what can be fixed and what can't.
- Flag anything that looks odd or seems confusing to you. Do not get too bogged down trying to figure out what was intended. If something is not obvious to you, it is likely that the readers of the document will react the same way.
- Speak up the minute you find a major problem. For example, if the first thing you notice is that the running head that appears on every page contains a typographical error, let someone know immediately. If time is critical, corrections can begin while you continue your review.
- Use a checklist, particularly if you don't perform QC reviews regularly. Customize the checklist to reflect the priorities established for the document at hand.

What comes after QC?

The most important part of planning the review step is allowing enough time to fix any errors that are found. This point may seem obvious, but there's a tendency to schedule the QC review for the day the document is scheduled to go out the door. The assumption, of course, is that everything will be perfect—or that corrections will be so minor that they will take only a short time to make.

But if a last-minute QC review turns up something major, you won't have time to fix it. As a rule of thumb, allow one-fourth of the total time it took to lay out or format the document for making final changes. For example, if the layout step took four days, schedule the QC review for two days before the final deadline to allow one day for final corrections.

There's no magic involved—just good planning

There's nothing magical about the QC review—it just requires a little extra planning. Obviously, the more experienced the reviewer, the better the review will be. Some organizations designate one person as QC reviewer for all products; others have the editors serve as reviewers for one another. And of course, not all types of publications warrant the same level of scrutiny. But for documents that must be perfect, the final quality control review can mean the difference between success and embarrassment.

—*Robin A. Cormier*

Usage and Grammar

Changing American English in Times of Change

For better and worse, language mirrors who we are

"Language changes every 18 or 20 miles," says a Hindi proverb. The English language—particularly American English—admits change more rapidly and in greater quantity than perhaps any other language.

The language was forged by three invasions and a cultural revolution in Britain, transplanted to the brave new world of the colonies, and transformed over time by the multicultural strands constituting the people of the United States of America. In the 1990s, *change* is more than ever the word that represents the condition of American English.

For better or worse, linguistic change is a mirror: It reflects the import, scope, and sequence of societal change. Language *is* people, and popular attitudes, beliefs, behavior, and deeds have strong, immediate, and often lasting influence on the words that gain sustained currency from generation to generation.

It is a great editorial challenge to chronicle this rumbustious language of ours, formed as it has been over the centuries by a diverse multitude of individualistic, often quarrelsome folk. At the same time, dictionary editors must record the language with precision, concision, grace, and accuracy. It's somehow fitting that electronic database tools, which have increased the communications channels through which change races, also make analyzing the changes possible.

Dictionary editors as chroniclers of change

Editors of dictionaries are the scribes of linguistic and social history. We observe, collect, analyze, chronicle, and from time to time comment critically on examples of changes.

To do all this we rely on citational evidence: printed and oral examples of words as they are actually used by educated speakers and writers. We seek relatively long-term evidence of usage—usually five to seven years' worth—by a diverse group of speakers and writers in a broad array of sources—general and technical, fiction and nonfiction.

In the past, editors relied solely on accumulations of manually marked, manually alphabetized, and manually filed citation slips. Such collections give us only a worm's-eye view of the linguistic landscape. In a world where events can alter the names and boundaries of nation-states overnight and new words can enter the parlance just as fast (*AIDS* being

129

the prime example in our time), editors must rely on computerized databases to obtain the essential global view. Only with these data can we assess the potential longevity of new words, analyze new meanings of existing words, verify variant spellings and stylings, and track shifts in usage.

Weighing the evidence for variants

A few examples make the point. When we were compiling the third edition of the *American Heritage Dictionary (AHD)*, we were aware of the variant spelling *ambience* as opposed to *ambiance*. We needed to determine whether to make the two words equal ("**or**") variants or unequal ("**also**") variants*; a frequency analysis (to determine the relative predominance of occurrence) was in order. Our examination of 6,000 electronically generated citations for both variants yielded 4,000 instances of the *-ance* spelling and 2,000 for *-ence*. On the basis of this 2-to-1 ratio, the editors chose to enter the *-ence* variant as an unequal—or less frequently occurring—variant of the main entry word *ambiance*.

Validating editorial decisions

In matters of usage, electronic citations are similarly invaluable in validating or canceling editorial decisions. Once the editors have identified an issue, instances of it can be pulled up and studied. Such was the case with the noun *bias*. We needed to find out whether *bias* is being widely used to denote not only "a preference or an inclination, especially one that inhibits impartial judgment," but also "an unfair act or policy stemming from prejudice." Analysis of the citations enabled us to report in the Usage Note at *bias* that this second usage has become increasingly acceptable—a judgment that would have been shakily grounded otherwise. Here is a representative citation backing our view:

> The report also notes "remarkably consistent" *biases* in administration R&D budget requests. *These* included emphasis on military R&D and...basic research.
>
> —*Christian Science Monitor*

Still another example of the utility of electronic citations as the formative basis for usage judgments is *sneaked* vs. *snuck*. Analysis revealed that of 10,000 instances of both forms in print, *sneaked* was still preferred, by a ratio of 7 to 2, over the 19th-century American dialect form *snuck*. This was true despite such examples as these:

---

* For your dictionary's labeling and usage policies, be sure to check the fine print in the front of the book. This is where you'll see evidence of prescriptive or descriptive intentions. The number and kinds of labels (e.g., *Informal, Nonstandard, Usage Problem*) and the types of usage notes are the true indicators of how the entries are intended to be used.

A man armed with dynamite who held six small girls and their teacher hostage was killed this morning by police who *snuck* into the classroom as he dozed.

—Associated Press

Raisa Gorbachev *snuck* away yesterday afternoon for a 65-minute helter-skelter tour of San Francisco.

—*San Francisco Chronicle*

This trove of evidence was critical in composing the Usage Note at *sneak*: the existence of the 7-to-2 ratio in favor of the standard form despite recent increasing use of *snuck* clearly backs up the 65 percent disapproval verdict against *snuck* handed down by the 173 members of the *AHD* Usage Panel.

Adding new words

Space is a major constraint in entering new words into a dictionary, so *AHD* editors relied heavily on electronic citations when deciding which ones to include. One word that did not pass muster was *womyn*. The evidence showed that it is used chiefly in the literature of women's issues, and that when it does occur in general sources, more often than not it is enclosed in "shudder quotes" or briefly glossed, often in a jocular manner.

Existing words have taken on new meanings

The use of such quotation marks and glosses is a standard warning to editors that the word in question has not yet gained widespread currency. *Waitron*, on the other hand, is and has been widely used in running texts and want ads; on the basis of that kind of evidence, it gained entry to the third edition of *AHD*.

New senses of existing words can also be discerned through study of electronic citations. Having identified possible new senses, editors can then search for and analyze new usages in their contexts to determine whether they warrant inclusion in the dictionary.

The criteria used for new additions are quantity, longevity, and breadth of sourcing. If a new sense, or a new word, for that matter, occurs for only a year or so in one or two sources, chances are that it will not make the cut. Citations are extremely helpful not only in writing definitions but also in choosing restrictive subject or usage labels such as *Sports* or *Slang*.

Finally, citations can be a rich source of quoted illustrations that force meaning, attest to the existence of the word or sense in question, or show the word in action in a well-written sentence. Examples of existing words that have taken on new meanings are *virus, catastrophic, family,* and *slam-dunk.*

No more blind spots

Never will a problem like James Murray's difficulty over *appendicitis* recur: Though the word was current in 1885, the year in which the section of the *Oxford English Dictionary* that ought to have contained the word was published, Murray excluded it on the advice of the Regius Professor of Medicine at Oxford. *Appendicitis,* dubbed a "crack-jaw medical and surgical word," was omitted for the sake of time, money, and space in a period when there was strong pressure to include a host of newly emerging scientific words. This misjudgment became apparent in 1902 when Edward VII underwent an emergency appendectomy, an event that caused postponement of his coronation. *Appendicitis* became a household word as a result of print media coverage. Today a database search would preclude such flawed decision-making.

And so, in an era fraught with changes that often overtake definitions, the lexicographer's methods of staying au courant have changed. Through constant reading and listening, dictionary editors identify shifts in usage and the emergence of new words and new meanings of existing words; computers then attest to the frequency of occurrence and longevity of changing lexical items. In essence, the new methods are a marriage of the human brain and the computer.

—*Anne H. Soukhanov*

Passing Whose Test of Time?

To some of us, new usages will never sound right

Decisions about whether something has passed the test of time are not always immediate and universal. To some editors, *prioritize* will never sound right, echoing to them as it does verbs like *backwardize* and *permanentize*—mentioned by Theodore Bernstein as examples of "expendable novelties" that never caught on. Bernstein says, however, "The suffix '-ize' is one of the devices that have helped the English language grow."

The Usage Note at *-ize* in the *American Heritage Dictionary* (1995) differentiates between the acceptability of words like *Americanize, nationalize,* and *jeopardize,* which are fine, and *accessorize, incentivize,* and in particular *privatize,* about which it says, "Coinages of this sort should be used with caution until they have passed the tests of manifest utility and acceptance by reputable writers."

Success with Words (*Readers Digest,* 1983) has a rather temperate discussion that puts the matter in perspective:

> Many of these coinages in *-ize* may...seem, to some people, unnecessary, irresponsible, or nasty. But our language is extremely democratic. No matter who first invents or promotes a word, it takes its chance on its merits and is judged by the community at large.... When winterize was first used by the housing industry, it was denounced by purists, but it has since become a well-established and unmistakably useful word.

Just be aware that some people may disdain your choice of an *-ize* form in anything other than casual writing. (I confess to viewing *prioritize* with particular caution. One of the academics to whom I once sent a form letter requesting a ranking of preferences on some subject sent it back with a note: "Thank you for not saying *prioritize!*")

—*Priscilla S. Taylor*

The Right WORD

abbreviation/acronym/initialism

Abbreviation is the general term for a shortened form of a name or word, such as *FL* or *Fla.* for *Florida*. Standard written English uses only the most customary abbreviations—that is, for words that are rarely seen spelled out: *Mr., Mrs., Dr., Ph.D., a.m., p.m., RSVP,* and the like. Abbreviations were devised by scribes and early typesetters to save time and space. Most abbreviations should be defined at first use.

An *acronym* is composed of the opening letters of a group of words; the letters can be pronounced as a word. Over time, an acronym may completely supplant the original words, as in the case of *radar* (*ra*dio *d*etecting *a*nd *r*anging) and *modem* (*mo*dulator *dem*odulator). The wish for a snappy acronym has led some groups to devise one first and then make the spelled-out version fit the letters: *MADD* (Mothers Against Drunk Driving) is a good example.

Some use the term *initialism* to mean an abbreviation that is composed of the initial letters (or syllables) of the words in a name or term, but that is pronounced letter by letter (YMCA is an example). This term is not yet commonplace, though *Merriam-Webster's Collegiate Dictionary*, tenth edition, includes it.

The wide range of initialisms and acronyms represents

- organizations (CARE, UNICEF, NATO, UL-approved),
- medical and scientific terms (mph, MMPI, AIDS),
- computer systems and processes (DOS, WYSIWYG, ASCII), and
- conversational shorthand (gone AWOL, a COB deadline, do it ASAP).

As for punctuation of new abbreviations, the style trend is toward fewer periods and decreased capitalization. The most comprehensive reference work for what abbreviations mean, with 480,000 definitions, is the *Acronyms, Initialisms, and Abbreviations Dictionary* published by Gale Research.

Skirting the Generic *He*

Why invite trouble when recasting is almost always easy—
and sometimes clearer?

The trouble with using *he* as a generic to mean both *he* and *she* is clear: Not everyone perceives *he* as being inclusive of both men and women. In *The Nonsexist Word Finder* (Oryx Press), Rosalie Maggio explains further why generic *he* usage is problematic:

> Defenders of the convention most often claim that it is a point of grammar and certainly not intended to offend anyone. That it does in reality offend large numbers of people does not appear to sway some grammarians, nor does the fact that their recourse to the laws of language is on shaky ground. While *he* involves a disagreement in gender, singular *they* involves a disagreement in number [as in "to each his own" and "to each their own"]. Eighteenth-century (male) grammarians decided that number was more important than gender, although the singular *they* had been in favor until that time.

Contemporary grammarians generally agree that the need for a gender-neutral pronoun reference supersedes the convenience of convention. But that mandate is more easily endorsed than enforced—the English language does not offer all-purpose third-person pronoun forms and sometimes resists simple recasting.

The familiar use of passive constructions to avoid the generic *he* can lead to dull writing; *he and she* or *his and hers*, or *he* and *she* alternated in the same document can boggle readers and ultimately lose them. The singular *they* has had strong supporters for almost two centuries, and Maggio says that "In less formal language, its acceptance rate is fairly high." But "there are so many other ways of replacing the 'generic' *he* that you should not have to rely on the singular *they* too often."

Politics aside, here are several ways writers and editors can avoid, replace, or defuse the potentially distracting use of *he* to refer to both genders. Why ask for trouble? As a bonus, the rewrites suggested below can sharpen your writing if you also pay attention to the context and common sense.

- Rewrite your sentence in the plural. This is often the easiest way. "A careful editor will couch his queries in neutral terms" suffers no loss from a rewrite to "Careful *editors* will couch *their* queries in neutral terms."

- Recast your sentence using *we/us/our*. "Each must do his best" can become "*We* must all do *our* best."

- Rewrite your sentence in the second person. "No man knows what he's got until it's gone" can become "*You* don't know what *you've* got until it's gone."

- Replace *he* with an article or with such words as *someone, anyone, one, the one, no one,* etc.; you can also omit the pronoun entirely, as the respective examples given show:

  > Clayton Rawson's "Can't a critic give his opinion of an omelette without being asked to lay an egg?" could be changed to "Can't a critic give *an* opinion...?"

  > "Everyone can laugh at a pratfall except he who has fallen" could be changed to "...except *the one* who has fallen."

  > "The average American travels in France with a few stilted phrases he has memorized from a guidebook" could be changed to "...phrases memorized from a guidebook."

- Replace the pronoun with a noun. "He who betrays a friend loses him" could be changed to "To betray a friend is to lose *a friend.*"

Obviously, although a statement like "To each his own" could be recast as "To all their own" or "To each his or her own" or "To each one's own," such straining for gender neutrality can do serious damage to euphony—a point that disgruntled commentators often make. Although many writers and editors feel pained at imposing such constructions on readers, it helps to think of this process as the growing kind of pain.

—Linda B. Jorgensen

Of Hyphenated Americans and Editorial Rigidity

Start with the small stuff and let go of some prejudices

When the *New Yorker*'s long-time editor, William Shawn, was eulogized by his colleagues after his death, two contributions caught my eye (in the Dec. 28/Jan. 4, 1993, issue).

In one, Philip Hamburger recounted a run-in with Shawn late at night over whether Evita Perón's hand was "stone cold" or "stone-cold." Shawn insisted on adding the hyphen. The impasse continued until 2:30 a.m., when Shawn capitulated, saying, "All right. No hyphen. But you are wrong."

In the other story, William Maxwell told how he "wore out one Artgum eraser after another" sparing fiction writers from Shawn's commas, semicolons, and dashes, for Shawn "believed that all prose should be punctuated for clarity and logic according to rules that are set forth in Fowler's 'Modern English Usage' and are as applicable to one piece of writing as to another."

Geniuses, of course, are always allowed their eccentricities, but the rest of us workaday editors can't get away with a rigid approach to our jobs. I thought of Shawn when I read an article about a black woman director who saw her film "as a chance to undo stereotypes about the inner city and African American teenage girls." Have you noticed how the hyphen has all but disappeared in all ethnic designations, adjective or noun? Most style books haven't caught up with the trend, but hyphenated Americans are becoming passé.

Among the sources I checked, **Afro-American** is the listing in both *Webster's New World Dictionary* and the *American Heritage Dictionary*, third edition. (The latter does direct users to the Usage Note at **black**, which then lists **African American: Afro-American.**) In contrast, **Asian American** appears in the *American Heritage Dictionary*, but it's **Asian-American** in the *Random House Unabridged*.

Standard style guides aren't much help on this subject. The *Chicago Manual of Style* only cautions users not to confuse **Latin American** ("always open") with "such forms as **Scotch-Irish, Austro-Hungarian**." The *Government Printing Office Style Manual* also cites **Latin American countries** but specifies hyphens in a **Mexican-American, Spanish-American pride**, and **Afro-American program.** *Words Into Type* is the only authority I found that specifically foreshadows the usage that is gaining acceptance, by differentiating between **Spanish American** ("an American of Spanish ancestry") and **Spanish-American** ("refers to the two countries").

Shawn, of course, had so many strengths as an editor that his idiosyncrasies became cherished anecdotes. Moreover, I happen to agree that a good editor's prejudices amount to time-saving mechanisms. I also share many of Shawn's prejudices, at least as detailed by another of the eulogists, Daniel Menaker:

> "We avoid," his Lilliputian hand noted in a galley's margin, with a spidery line leading to "smarts" or "urinal" in the text. We avoided, as I learned little by little, "photo," "intrigued" for "interested,"..."massive" as a description of anything but a physical object,..."home" for "house,"..."feisty," "workaholic," "prestigious,"..."quality" as an adjective, "tycoon," and "balding."

Not a bad list, but those of us editors who are not in Shawn's league—and who is?—might do well to consider William Bridgwater's contribution to that wonderful book *Editors on Editing* (Grove Press, 1993), which ends with the injunction that copyeditors must "be truly familiar, even intimate, with the English language and current English usage...[and] should know the old and outmoded usages as well as those that are current.... If the worst disease in copyediting is arrogance, the second worst is rigidity."

—*Priscilla S. Taylor*

compare with/compare to

Merriam-*Webster's Dictionary of Usage and Style* notes that *compare with* and *compare to*, particularly in the past tense, have become so interchangeable that the two no longer convey reliably distinctive meanings. The *Harper Dictionary of Contemporary Usage* recommends observing the distinction in formal speech and written communication, but observes that in informal speech the two prepositions have become interchangeable.

If the goal is to point out dissimilarities between persons, things, or objects, it is best to use *contrast with*: "The acid precision of Dorothy Parker's wit contrasts with Roseanne's antic comedy."

Maintaining Distinctions with a Difference

Do we really want to let sleeping dogs lay?

In his commentary titled "The Lay of the Language" for the *Atlantic Monthly* (May 1995), Cullen Murphy tackles the *lay/lie* confusion with erudition and resignation. His article, subtitled "The decline of a semantic distinction, and what it suggests about linguistic evolution," was stimulated at least in part by what he described as "irate letters from a number of readers" in response to the same magazine's publication of whisky ads recommending "a gift that's been laying around for 12 years."

Murphy describes the confusion between *lie* and *lay* as an old and understandable problem:

> Among other things, the verbs share a manifestation (*lay*). Moreover, when you *lay* something down, you cause it to *lie*. Also, there was once a reflexive pronominal use of *lay* (as in "Now I *lay* me down to sleep..."), which has undoubtedly sown confusion. And *lie* and *lay* as nouns, connoting a configuration of ground, can at times be used interchangeably ("the *lie* or *lay* of the land").

Still, he notes, the distinction between the two words was generally maintained over the past two centuries, until *lay* began to overtake *lie* not just in speech, but in formal writing in recent decades. In fact, Murphy attributes the growing acceptance of *lay* to the declining influence of the print media.

Does the apparent triumph of spoken over written English mean that we should give up on trying to maintain the distinctions between this and other confusables? Is the *lie/lay* distinction "fragile and impractical," as linguist Dwight Bolinger is said to argue? And if you give up on *lie/lay*, do you also throw in the towel on all the other confusables that your spell checker doesn't help you with?

Knowing the correct pronunciation can help writers avoid using *loathe* (hate) when they mean *loath* (reluctant), *loose* (not bound) when they mean *lose* (to experience loss), *suit* (apparel) when they mean *suite* (a grouping of furniture, rooms, or musical themes), and *prophecy* (noun) when they mean *prophesy* (verb). And using the preferred pronunciation for *route* (like *root*) can help differentiate this word (meaning a way for travel) from *rout* (an overwhelming defeat). But pronunciation doesn't help with *aid/aide, cite/site/sight, dual/duel, foreword/forward, forego/forgo, led/lead, principle/principal, pour/pore, palate/palette/pallet,* and similar land mines.

And how about those pesky apostrophes? According to Murphy, Richard Hogg, editor of the *Cambridge History of the English Language*, thinks that the apostrophe "may just decline of its own accord" and Hogg is on record as saying that he "would not go to the stake" to preserve the distinction between *its* and *it's*.

Well, we've all become accustomed to dropping the apostrophe in geographic names such as *Harpers Ferry* and *Hells Canyon*. (The editor of the *Government Printing Office Style Manual* once told me that only the citizens of *Martha's Vineyard* had prevailed against the U.S. government geographers in this regard—on a map, he explained, the apostrophe can be confused with a prime mark.) And we might almost be willing to accept *childrens* if it meant we'd no longer see *her's* and *their's*, not to mention *potato's* and *bean's*.

But to accept *lay* for *lie* would be admitting only the nose of the camel among confusables. The *Random House Dictionary of the English Language*, second edition, unabridged, lists 115 sets of "Words Commonly Confused."

To appreciate the scope of the problem more fully, consider the 84-page discussion of "Misused and Easily Confused Words" in *The New York Public Library Writer's Guide to Style and Usage*. And neither of those sources includes the commonly confused pair *degree/diploma*. (A high school graduate has earned a *diploma*.)

One solution is to develop a smarter mechanical spell/meaning/context checker; another is to learn about the distinctions that are the glory of a rich language.

—*Priscilla S. Taylor*

On Naming the Problem

Sometimes it's hard to put into words what the grammatical problem is

"**O**nce you can name the problem, you can find the solution," writes Robin Williams about graphic design in her nifty little *Non-Designer's Design Book* (Peachpit Press, 1994).

The same point applies to editing and writing; naming or at least recognizing the problem will help you find a solution. Here are some errors in written and spoken English collected from a variety of sources. Most of them fall into the "You know what I mean" category; naming the error can be more difficult than fixing it.

Error 1

"All noise is not bad."—attributed to the winner of an award for outstanding first-year teaching in a Maryland elementary school (*Washington Post*, Dec. 10, 1994)

All dictionaries are not alike. (from an ad for the *American Heritage Dictionary* in *Book World*, Dec. 4, 1994)

The modifier *not* is misplaced. The writers meant to say, "Not all noise is bad" and "Not all dictionaries are alike."

Error 2

Republicans plan drastically to revise the $30-billion crime bill so laboriously passed last summer.... (*Economist*, Nov. 19, 1994)

The writer is trying too hard not to split an infinitive and ends up implying that the planners are drastic, instead of simply saying "to drastically revise."

Error 3

"It's always a pleasure for Barbara and I to be here." (President Bush, at the National Defense University in Washington, D.C., in 1991)

"We love Dan and Marilyn Quayle and really wish they and their family only the very best," said Gary Koops, the Gramm campaign press secretary. (*Washington Post*, Jan. 12, 1995)

Why do politicians and their spokespersons tend to think that the nominative case sounds more grammatical than the objective? Bush means "It's a pleasure for *us*," hence "Barbara and *me*." And of course the press secretary should have sent his wishes to *them* not *they*.

Error 4

...Cisneros has produced a workable set of proposals that call for "dramatic restructuring" and saves money. (*Washington Post*, Dec. 9, 1994)

As competitive pressures increase, many doctors complain the fun and intellectual challenge is going out of their work. (*Wall Street Journal*, Jan. 6, 1995)

In the first sentence the pronoun *that* agrees with only one of the verbs. Solutions: "calls for...and saves money" or "call for...and save money," depending on whether *set* or *proposals* is the antecedent. (One can almost see the two authors arguing over whether their subject takes a singular or plural verb, and deciding to compromise on one of each.)

In the second sentence, the subject of the clause, "the fun and intellectual challenge," is plural and thus requires "are." (I'd add a *that* before the subordinate clause too: "many doctors complain *that* the fun....")

Error 5

This Christmas give a gift that won't be laying around for 12 years.... This Christmas give a gift that's been laying around for 12 years. (Two half-page ads for Glenlivet scotch, *Atlantic Monthly*, Dec. 1994)

The ad writer has confused two verbs: *to lie* and *to lay*. One *lays* something down, but it just *lies* there. *Lying* is the appropriate verb form for both sentences.

Error 6

The most distressing material in Mr. Bernstein's book involves primary and secondary education, where educators push the idea that America has no common culture nor anything redeeming to offer the world. (*Wall Street Journal*, Jan. 4, 1995)

Nor is misused here; the *no* carries over to the second part of the phrase, hence: "no common culture or anything redeeming...."

Error 7

Leaders throughout the world take [Jimmy Carter] seriously because he is of equal or higher status than they are. (Letter to the editor of the *Washington Post* from Dean G. Pruitt, Jan. 9, 1995)

The comparison is incomplete: "His status is equal to or higher than *theirs*," not *they are*.

Error 8

These streams of contradictory criticism share one thing in common: Both sides are frustrated because Clinton no longer looks like he's really going to change things. (*Washington Post*, May 25, 1993)

"Share in common" is redundant: They "have in common" or they "share," period. And of course that *like* should be *as if.*

Error 9

"I have seen dollars...but I have never held one in my hands," Lapshitz said as she prepared to leave the downstairs Soviet grocery clutching a few dessicated fish wrapped in an old newspaper. (*Washington Post*, Oct. 23, 1991)

Desiccated must be one of the most commonly misspelled words in English. Others in the same category are *graffiti* and *moccasins*. If you can't decide which consonant is properly doubled, resort to using a dictionary.

Error 10

Initially reluctant to sit in the *Masterpiece Theatre* chair, Cooke's daughter persuaded him to take the job 22 years ago. (*WETA Magazine*, Oct. 1993)

When phrases like this adjectival one (*initially reluctant*) begin a sentence, they must refer to the subject: "Initially reluctant to sit..., Cooke was persuaded by his daughter to take the job...."

—*Priscilla S. Taylor*

gamut/gantlet/gauntlet

Originally a musical term for a series of notes, *gamut* is now widely used to express the idea of an entire series, "a range that is run through," as here: "Steve Martin's face moved through a gamut of emotions when his daughter announced her engagement." A *gantlet* is "a course of abuse or a severe test that one must run through or endure." A *gantlet* is a traditional military punishment whereby the accused is forced to try to slip through two files of peers while they flail away at him. A *gauntlet* is "a glove, thrown down to signify a challenge." Some dictionaries give *gauntlet* as a synonym for *gantlet*, but the latter is more often found in journalistic writing. "Your readers may run you through a *gantlet* of disapproval if you throw down the editorial *gauntlet* of them for the generic third person singular pronoun."

Precision in the Choice of Words

Even the best editor can have a mental block about certain word choices such as *less/fewer* or *among/between*. The sentences below contain common errors in word choice. Find the errors and correct them, making sure you substitute the precise word.

1. Since Dale lives further from the convention center than I do, I will attend the conference.

2. After our company contracted with a new printer, our proofreader found less mistakes than usual.

3. Since I was anxious to buy a new car, I was thrilled with both my promotion and my raise.

4. The bonus money was divided evenly between the training, graphics, editing, and proofreading departments.

5. The client was disappointed with the printer because the newsletters were delivered late.

6. By next spring, everyone of the employees will be eligible to participate in the new training program.

7. To insure that our budget proposal is correct, our supervisor asked us to triple-check our figures.

8. Due to his poor health, Mr. Saltz decided to resign from his stressful job.

9. A large percent of registered voters went to the polls in inclement weather to support their candidates.

10. This manuscript has lain untouched on my desk for three days.

ANSWERS

1. Ideally, *since* should be reserved for use in the context of time: "since 1989." *Because* is the correct choice here. *Further* means "to a greater degree or extent." *Farther*, which is the precise word choice here, refers to actual distance. *Because Dale lives farther....*

2. *Less* refers to quantity or degree and is used with singular nouns. *Fewer*, the correct choice, refers to countable items and is used with plural nouns.... *the proofreader found fewer mistakes than usual.*

3. Note the explanation for *since/because* earlier. Both *anxious* and *eager* mean "desirous," but *anxious* implies fear or concern and is a negative term; *eager* is a positive term. *Because I was eager to buy a new car....*

4. Use *between* when referring to two persons or things and *among* when referring to more than two persons or things. *The bonus money was divided evenly among the training, graphics, editing....*

5. Use *disappointed in* when referring to a person, plan, hope, or result. Use *disappointed with* when referring to a thing. *The client was disappointed in the printer....*

6. When used as a singular compound pronoun, *everyone* is treated as one word. *Every one, any one,* or *some one* are two words when they are followed by an *of* phrase or when used to mean "one of a number of things." *Every one of the employees will be eligible....*

7. *Insure* means "to protect against loss." *Ensure* means "to make certain." *Assure* means "to give someone confidence." *To ensure that our budget proposal is correct....*

8. *Due to* introduces an adjective phrase and should modify nouns; it is normally used after some form of the verb *to be* (*is, are, was, were,* etc.): *The change in plans was due to the unexpected arrival of the president of the university.* The precise word choice here is *because of.* When used correctly, *because of* and *on account of* introduce adverbial phrases that modify verbs: *Mr. Saltz decided to resign from his stressful job because of his poor health.*

9. In everyday usage, the word *percent* should always be preceded by a number; for example, *30 percent, 0.2 percent, 120 percent.* Similarly, a column of figures in a table may be headed *Percent of Total, Percent of Return,* etc. (In American usage, *percent* is preferred to *per cent;* use of the percent sign should be avoided in formal text.) In all other situations, use the term *percentage. A large percentage of registered voters went to the polls....*

10. The verb *lay* means "to put or place." Its principal parts are *lay, laid, laid,* and *laying.* The principal parts of the verb *lie,* which means "to recline, rest, or stay" or "to take a position of rest," are *lie, lay, lain,* and *lying.* In the sentence, the manuscript has *stayed* on the desk for three days, so the verb *lain* is correct. *This manuscript has lain untouched....*

—*Ellie Abrams*

145

Cracking the Code: Making Verbs Agree with Collective Nouns

The wages of confusion is grammatical disagreement

I n 1961, when I arrived in New York, college bound, the main landmark of the upper West Side was a huge black sign with grimy white letters that covered the side of a tall building: THE WAGES OF SIN IS DEATH. The words, visible for blocks, made me uneasy as I walked with my fellow freshmen (this was in the days before "first-year student" became required tactful usage) down a seedy stretch of Broadway. I hadn't sampled much sin yet, but I *was* planning to be an English major. Why, I wondered aloud, did *wages* have a singular verb?

"Because it's the wages of sin," the lone sophomore among us replied. "In New York, sin is collective."

My friend, I now realize, had a better grasp of metaphysics than grammar. Still, in her fumbling way she made me aware that certain nouns have a dual nature: They take a singular or a plural verb depending on their meaning, not their form.

Over the years, I've developed a set of mental pigeonholes for these nouns and collected some rules of thumb to guide me in using them. The nouns fall roughly into three groups:

1. Collective nouns or, more specifically, a subset of them that Fowler, in *A Dictionary of Modern English Usage*, calls "nouns of multitude"

2. Nouns expressing number or quantity

3. Nouns ending in *-ics*

This discussion primarily treats collective nouns, but questions of subject-verb agreement commonly arise with all three types; the final arbiter is common sense.

1. Nouns of multitude

Fowler defines a noun of multitude as "a whole made up of similar parts." Words such as *company, government, family*, and *committee* generally take a singular verb but sometimes take a plural one. The general rule is to treat these nouns as singular if they refer to the group as a whole and plural if they refer more to the individual members than to the group.

> As the defeated crew rows back to the boathouse, the crowd straggle back to their cars.

The crew is acting as a unit, but the members of the crowd are dispersing separately; the reference to *their cars* reinforces the plural sense.

Adding "members of" to emphasize the individuals in the crowd would make the sentence less jarring.

> As the defeated crew rows back to the boathouse, members of the crowd straggle back to their cars.

Loose usages. The words *number, total,* and *variety* are often used in a loose sense to mean "some" or "many." These words are governed by two easy rules of thumb:

- When preceded by the indefinite article *a*, these words are being used loosely and take a plural verb.

> A variety of spicy dishes were served. A number of guests have complained of heartburn.

Here, the emphasis is placed on the plural noun in the prepositional phrase rather than on the collective noun that is the grammatical subject.*

- When preceded by the word *the*, these words are being used more specifically and take a singular verb.

> The number of guests complaining of heartburn has embarrassed the hostess.

Here, the emphasis is placed on the collective noun *number* rather than on the plural object of the preposition ("guests").

Similarly, *majority* can be used both specifically and loosely.

- When *majority* refers to the number of votes cast or to a party or group acting as a body (usually in an electoral sense), *majority* takes a singular verb.

> Her majority was a slim 2 percent. The majority has swung its support to Carrington.

- When *majority* refers to members of a group acting individually, the verb is plural.

> The majority of residents of this neighborhood attend St. Michael's Church.

Churchgoing is something they do individually. *Majority* is being used loosely here to mean *most.*

A simple way around these sometimes delicate distinctions is to avoid using *majority, number,* and the like loosely and to substitute modifiers such as *most, many,* and *some.* Not only are they more specific in meaning but, as adjectives, they leave no doubt that the verb should be plural.

> Most residents of this neighborhood attend St. Michael's Church.

Duos, trios, and quartets. Words such as *couple, pair,* and *trio* follow the general rule for nouns of multitude. Where people are concerned, however, the rule is not always easy to apply. *Is the couple married* or *are the couple married?* Opinion is divided, but most authorities favor the plural. "It is difficult to see how a writer can go wrong by treating *couple* as a plural," Theodore Bernstein notes in *The Careful Writer,* but adds that "treatment as a singular could be defensible sometimes." Roy Copperud, in *American Usage and Style,* states flatly that both *couple* and *pair,* used "in reference to people," should take a plural verb.

Whatever the usage, it should be consistent throughout the sentence; pronoun referents must agree with noun and verb. No one should accept split formulations such as *The couple is on their way to a honeymoon in St. Croix and Disney World.* (This sentence can be fixed by changing "is" to "are.")

2. Nouns of number and quantity

Like collective nouns, numbers or quantitative expressions pose questions of subject-verb agreement that sometimes require making fine distinctions. Again, rules of thumb will help.

Less than a whole. With fractional numbers and percentages the rule is this:

- The noun in the prepositional phrase that follows the fractional number, or is understood to follow it, determines the verb.*

  One-fourth of the members have already left, one-fourth are still debating, and the rest are milling about the hall.

  Members determines the number for all three verbs.

  Ninety percent of the vines have been picked clean.

  Vines determines the number for the verb. The sense of number resides in the prepositional phrase—what has been "picked"—rather than in the grammatical subject—the percentage of "pickedness."

- What if the noun following the fractional number is collective? In that case the complement may determine the verb. Edward D. Johnson provides this example in *The Handbook of Good English*: "About 50 percent of the population is rural. About 50 percent of the population are farmers."

- Quantitative expressions such as *some of, most of,* and *all of* follow the same rules as fractional numbers.

  Some of the children are getting impatient. Most of the baked goods were made from scratch.

Whole numbers. Sums of money, weights, and distances, though plural in form, are generally considered as a unit and given a singular verb.

Is thirty dollars too much to pay for this shirt?

Here, the total is more important than the dollars. But in another example, the individual units are more important than the total.

Thirty parkway miles cut through the heart of a hardwood forest.

Usage is divided on how to treat abstract numbers used in arithmetic. In the following examples, either is correct, although the singular is preferred:

Three plus three is six.

Three plus three are six.

3. Nouns ending in -ics

Nouns such as *politics, economics,* and *athletics,* though plural in form, take a singular verb when referring to a body of knowledge or a profession.

Though economics is his major, politics is his real love.

These nouns take a plural verb when referring to separate activities, facts, or attitudes.

The economics of the proposal don't support your assertion.

His politics stink.

What about the wages of sin?

Where does "the wages of sin" belong in all this? Ninety-nine percent of the time, *wages* behaves like any ordinary plural noun. Only when it is used in the sense of recompense ("getting one's just desserts") does it take the singular. That usage is now so rare as to be an endangered species. (Even my old stomping ground on Broadway no longer has its biblical admonition. Is there no one left to redeem?)

In that sense, my sophomore friend was right. *Wages* is singular because it's the wages of sin. I reserve judgment, however, on whether sin in New York is collective.

—Dianne Snyder

---

*Readers should understand that in no other case is the subject's number "determined" grammatically by the noun that follows it in a prepositional phrase. Such nouns that come between the subject and verb should, in fact, normally be ignored when determining subject-verb agreement. Loosely used collective nouns and fractional numbers are special cases where you can use the more readily discernible number of the modifying prepositional object as a reliable clue to get at the sense—the logic—of whether the collective noun subject should be treated as singular or plural.

Making Verbs Agree
with Fractions and Percentages

Which governs, the subject or the nearest noun?

Problem: Our problem is verb agreement with fractions and percentages. In fact, I have seen this problem before but always as one or two instances that I could rewrite or otherwise slip around. Now I am editing a 60-page report that is full of unavoidable sentences such as "By 1992, 47 percent of the population was (were) living in urban centers" or "One-third of the respondents was (were) employed in the formal sector." Obviously the subjects of those sentences are "47 percent" and "one-third," not "population" and "respondents," which just happen to be next to the verbs but are objects of prepositions.

Do you make the verb agree with the word next to it because it sounds better, or do you make it agree with the subject regardless of how it sounds? And isn't there another principle at work here: that a percentage or fraction can represent a single mass that's part of a larger mass (three-fourths cup of sugar) or a number of units that are part of a larger number of units (three-fourths of the school children)?

A lengthy search through *The Chicago Manual of Style* and several other style guides has been fruitless. Can you help us, please?

Solution: *Chicago* is the wrong place to look for answers to questions like this; it doesn't address word usage or grammar at all. For questions about subject-verb agreement you need a book like *Words Into Type, Webster's Dictionary of English Usage,* or *The New York Public Library Writer's Guide to Style and Usage*. All three say that a verb following a fraction or percentage—like a verb following *all of, any of,* or *some of*—should agree in number with the noun following *of*. The *NYPL Writer's Guide* gives the following examples:

> *Three-quarters* of the apple *was* left uneaten.

> *Three-quarters* of the employees *are* at a seminar today.

The same principle applies to the percentages in your examples. Your second example is straightforward: "One-third of the respondents *were* employed in the formal sector." The first is trickier. Does "population" take a singular or a plural verb? According to the *NYPL Writer's Guide,* "Collective nouns require singular verbs when the group is functioning as a unit and plural verbs when the individual members of the group are considered to be acting independently." The idea of individuals within the population is not strong in this sentence, so I'd write, "By 1992,

47 percent of the population *was* living in urban centers." But for some similar sentences I'd use *were:* "By 1992, 47 percent of the population *were* city dwellers" (or change *population* to *people*).

It's important to understand that the rule about fractions and percentages is not based on making the verb agree with the preceding word—what *Webster's Dictionary of English Usage* calls *proximity agreement*. That would lead to sentences like "Traffic on the streets are increasing" (which is clearly wrong). Your other idea is the correct one: The distinction is between "a single mass that's part of a larger mass" and "a number of units that are part of a larger number of units." Such distinctions are important in *notional agreement*, in which the number of a verb depends on the meaning, not just the grammatical form, of its subject.

The *$6,000 is* to be used as a down payment on the house.

(But: *Thousands* of dollars *have been spent* on the renovation.)

Usage guides should be a part of every editor's library. Others include Fowler's *Modern English Usage*, Bernstein's *The Careful Writer*, Follett's *Modern American Usage*, and Copperud's *American Usage and Style: The Consensus*. Take their advice with a grain of salt, however; it often represents no more than the author's pet peeves and prejudices (for example, Follett thinks that "the nation's capital" is an incorrect use of the possessive case). It's good to have several books on usage around to help you decide which issues are settled and which are controversial.

For some usage questions there is no consensus to be found. If the guides disagree, you'll have to read their discussions and then use your own judgment. That's one reason grammar-checking software isn't likely to replace human editors any time soon.

—*Keith C. Ivey*

Subject-Verb Agreement

In theory, subject-verb agreement is simple: A singular subject requires a singular verb, and a plural subject, a plural verb. In reality, two problems complicate the matter: locating the subject and determining whether it is singular or plural. Underline the subject and circle the correct verb in each sentence.

1. What if none of our district's students (wins, win) the $5,000 scholarship?

2. The jury (was, were) finally excused by the judge and left the courthouse.

3. She is one of the few contributors who not only (donates, donate) money but also (offers, offer) time.

4. Some of the sailboats (was, were) destroyed by the hurricane.

5. Two-thirds of the correspondence (has, have) yet to be answered.

6. Two-thirds of the freshmen (lives, live) in dormitories.

7. A small percentage of our employees (works, work) in this state but (lives, live) in another state.

8. The prime concern (is, are) better health care policies.

9. Preparing income tax returns (takes, take) all my time during tax season.

10. What our client wants to know and what we want our client to know (conflicts, conflict) with what our attorney wants our client to know.

ANSWERS

1. The pronoun *none* can be either singular or plural. In this sentence the singular is appropriate because there is only one scholarship to be won.

> What if none of our district's students **wins** the $5,000 scholarship?

2. A collective noun takes a singular verb if the group is working together as a unit. A collective noun requires a plural verb if the members of the group are working individually rather than as a group. If the plural verb bothers your ear, insert the words *the members of* before the collective noun.

> The jury **was** finally excused by the judge and left the courthouse.

The members of the jury **were** finally excused by the judge and left the courthouse.

3. As the subject of a dependent clause, the pronouns *who, that,* and *which* can be either singular or plural, depending on the antecedent. Because the antecedent of *who* is *contributors,* a plural noun, plural verbs are required. The sense of the sentence also indicates that there is more than one contributor.

She is one of the few contributors who not only **donate** money but also **offer** time.

4. The pronoun *some* is nearly always plural, with a plural antecedent or a plural noun in a following *of* phrase.

Some of the sailboats **were** destroyed by the hurricane.

Explanation for sentences 5-7: These sentences contain quantitative expressions. When the subject of the sentence is the term *a percentage* or a fractional number such as *two-thirds,* the noun in the prepositional phrase that follows the subject, or is understood to follow it, determines the verb.

5. In this example, *correspondence* follows *of,* so the subject *two-thirds* requires a singular verb.

Two-thirds of the correspondence **has** yet to be answered.

6. In this example, *freshmen* follows *of,* so the subject *two-thirds* requires a plural verb.

Two-thirds of the freshmen **live** in dormitories.

7. In this example, *employees* follows *of,* so the subject *a small percentage* requires a plural verb.

A small percentage of our employees **work** in this state but **live** in another state.

8. A sentence with a linking verb may have a singular subject and a plural complement or a plural subject and a singular complement. The verb should agree with the subject.

The prime concern **is** better health care policies.

9. A singular verb is required when a phrase or clause functions as the subject of a sentence.

Preparing income tax returns **takes** all my time during tax season.

10. Two singular subjects connected by the coordinate conjunction *and* require a plural verb. Because the subject of this sentence is two noun clauses, the verb must be plural.

What our client wants to know and what we want our client to know **conflict** with what our attorney wants our client to know.

—*Ellie Abrams*

Split Infinitives: Yes or No?

Old rules never die, they just keep trying to apply themselves

A technical editor asked: "When was it decreed that an adverb must precede the verb that it modifies? There was no such rule when I went to school.... But a large fraction of the cases of split infinitives that I have seen in over 30 years of editing seem to result from imposition of that rule. If it is given up, there is a much more graceful (in my opinion) way of handling the error in this sentence:

> Republicans plan drastically to revise the $30-billion crime bill so laboriously passed last summer.

"I'd make it read:

> Republicans plan to revise drastically the $30-billion crime bill....

"If a preceding sentence had described the laborious passage, so that the last few words were not needed, one could speak of their plan 'to revise the bill drastically.'"

The Editorial Eye **responds:** I know of no decree that an adverb should precede the verb it modifies; I just find *plan to drastically revise* sounds clearer and more natural than any other solution to the problem, though I have no objection if you prefer *plan to revise drastically*. Both solutions are certainly better than the original.

I think a lot of us have some old conflicting rules rattling around in our heads. On one side, they tell us not to separate the parts of any verb, but on the other to place adverbs near the important word. Maybe this quote from *The New York Public Library Writer's Guide to Style and Usage* will help clarify one of the so-called rules that is regularly broken:

> Editors...try to put words where they sound the most natural to the ear of a native speaker; for that reason, editors will sometimes "break" those inflexible rules learned in high school—"Never split an infinitive with an adverb...." Not splitting the infinitive leads to constructions like *to go boldly where no man has gone before* instead of *to boldly go*. Which sounds more natural? Today, only the most rigid grammarians do not allow split infinitives at least once in a while.

—Priscilla S. Taylor

Using the Correct Tense with Infinitives

Hard-core grammar is the only way to show correct sequence of action

A reader asked *The Editorial Eye* a devilishly good question: Which of the following sentences use the correct tense for the infinitives? According to an old edition of the *Prentice-Hall Handbook for Writers*, "Use a present infinitive after a verb in a perfect tense. A perfect infinitive may sometimes be used after a verb not in a perfect tense."

1. **I would like to have gone.** It's correct (perfect infinitive with the governing verb not in a perfect tense).

2. **I would have liked to have gone.** It's faulty. Revise it in one of these two ways:

Revised: I would have liked to go.

or

Revised: I would like to have gone.

Guidebooks differ in their approach to the question, however. My *Harbrace College Handbook* (sixth edition) says to "use the present infinitive to express action contemporaneous with, or later than, that of the governing verb; use the perfect infinitive for action prior to that of the governing verb."

Example A: I would have liked *to live* (not *to have lived*) in Shakespeare's time (present infinitive for action contemporaneous with that of the governing verb).

Example B: I would like *to have lived* in Shakespeare's time (the perfect infinitive for action prior to that of the governing verb).

Even simpler: I wish I had lived in Shakespeare's time.

3. **I would have liked to go.** It's correct (present infinitive for action contemporaneous with that of the governing verb).

Even simpler: I wish I had gone.

—Mary Stoughton

Feeling Tense and Moody

The confidence of a fellow toiler in the vineyard of verbiage has been shaken to the point of considering looking for a real job (I'd hate to see that happen):

> My problem concerns the use of *would* and *will* in conditional sentences. Much of our writing involves future conditional sentences (*If X happens, Y will result*). But many of our writers are wary of sounding too sure about an outcome, so they use *would* rather than *will*.

> My ear tells me that when the main clause contains *would*, the subordinate clause needs to be in the past tense (*If X happened, Y would result*).... The problem is that this rule—if it exists—is so often broken that I'm beginning to have deep doubts about it. I see reports at their final stage, so I don't want to waste time chasing a chimera. Is there anything wrong with the sequence of tenses in the following sentences, which I recently encountered?

1. The rules would require that the Congress adjust tax schedules so that overall growth in real incomes *does* not push people into higher income tax brackets.

2. Everyone now alive would contribute at some time if benefits for Social Security or Medicare *fall.*

3. If discretionary spending *is* frozen, the deficit would rise in 1997 and 1998 but would then begin to decline.

4. The accounts rely on the theory that existing capital would suffer a drop in value when an investment incentive *rises*, in the same way that a bond would if the interest rate rises.

5. The size of the future problem is so great that eliminating the deficit by 2002 would not alone ensure that future deficits *remain* at an acceptable level without additional changes in spending and taxes.

6. Even if such consumers could repay a loan out of their prospective earnings, lenders *may* not extend one because it could not be secured by a real asset.

ANSWERS

Like our correspondent, I found relatively few reference books that addressed the topic in any detail. My first thought was to check the old reliable *Words Into Type*, and sure enough, it offered counsel:

> Always consider the tense of a dependent verb form in relation to the time expressed in the verb upon which it depends.
>
> *Wrong:* How would natural conditions be affected if water continued to contract until it freezes?
>
> *Right:* ...until it froze?

Would be affected, the governing main verb, is in the past subjunctive tense; in the dependent clause that begins with *if*, water *continued to contract* correctly uses past tense—so, too, *froze* should follow. I think this example takes care of three of the problem sentences:

> 2. Everyone now alive would contribute at some time if benefits for Social Security or Medicare *fell*.
>
> 4. The accounts rely on the theory that existing capital would suffer a drop in value when an investment incentive *rose*, in the same way that a bond would if the interest rate *rose*.
>
> 6. Even if such consumers could repay a loan out of their prospective earnings, lenders *might* not extend one because it could not be secured by a real asset.

Words Into Type goes on to say,

> Sometimes the subordinate verb fixes the time and the principal verb requires correction....
>
> *Wrong:* If the unexpired subscriptions had amounted to $80,000, instead of $20,000, the adjusting entry would take the following form.
>
> *Right:* ...would have taken the following form.

In sentence 3, the principal verb could be made subjunctive to match the subordinate verbs:

> 3. If discretionary spending *were* frozen, the deficit would rise in 1997 and 1998 but would then begin to decline.

An alternative would be to leave *is* in the indicative mood and change the subordinate verbs:

> 3. If discretionary spending is frozen, the deficit *will* rise in 1997 and 1998 but *will* then begin to decline.

The choice depends on the context. The author may consider a freeze in spending unlikely, in which case the principal verb should be in the subjunctive. If the author is presenting the spending freeze as one of several alternatives, all equally likely, the indicative/future version of the sentence is a better choice. By that logic, sentence 2 could be written like this:

> 2. Everyone now alive *will* contribute at some time if benefits for Social Security or Medicare *fall*.

It's relatively simple to match the sequence of tenses when you're sure what the mood of the sentence should be. A thornier problem is deciding whether to use the subjunctive. *The Handbook of Good English*, by Edward D. Johnson, has a useful discussion of this point:

> Clauses that begin with *if* or *as if* are not always subjunctive. *If he is rich he will be welcome* is indicative; the *if* clause presents a condition that may be true. *He acts as if his life is in danger* and *He acts as if his life were in danger* are both correct; the indicative *as if* clause in the first sentence implies that his life may well be in danger, and the subjunctive *as if* clause in the second sentence implies that it is unlikely that his life is in danger....

Johnson's *Handbook* also zeros in on the very situation that our correspondent confronts. As an example, it quotes a sentence from a 1981 speech by President Reagan: "If there were some kind of international crisis, we would correct that with new legislation." Johnson notes that Reagan was

> ...using the...subjunctive for a conditional sentence about the future, which cannot logically be a condition contrary to fact. This use of the subjunctive is one of those that grammarians have been waving farewell to

for decades, but it has remained alive and seems to be becoming more common....

> Use of the distinctive *were* forms for the future conditional is defensible; it permits expression of a special degree of doubt about the future condition. It has always been common among the well-educated. It is perhaps a bit fussy, but it does not invite derision the way *It is I* and *Whom do you want to invite?* may.

Thank goodness for that! Back when I wrote a grammar column, I never worried about inviting derision (in fact, you might say it was what I was paid to do), but I'm sure most *Editorial Eye* readers, including our correspondent, would just as soon avoid it, while still counting themselves well educated. We can tweak sentences 1 and 5 to make both clauses conditional:

> 1. The rules would require that the Congress adjust tax schedules so that overall growth in real incomes *would* not push people into higher income tax brackets.

> 5. The size of the future problem is so great that eliminating the deficit by 2002 would not alone ensure that future deficits *remained* at an acceptable level without additional changes in spending and taxes.

—*Lee Mickle*

Bite-Size Morsels
and Long-Horned Cattle

When everything's an exception,
usage becomes a matter of preference

John DeRoo of Missoula, Montana, asks: "*Medium-size* house or *medium-sized* house—which do you prefer?" He has used the right word in his query: *prefer.* As Theodore Bernstein (*The Careful Writer*) says in his discussion of nouns that are made into the main components of compound adjectives: "No answer is possible because in this field the language submits to no rules. You can scrutinize whole categories of words and sometimes imagine you have hit upon a principle, but as soon as you do, the next word you can think of constitutes an exception."

Bernstein notes that although dictionaries indicate that the *-ed* used to make adjectives out of nouns means "possessing or provided with or characterized by," this does not explain when the *-ed* is used. The modern tendency, he says, is not to use *-ed* when the meaning of the adjective is "consisting in whole or in overwhelmingly predominant part," as in *three-room* apartment, *loose-leaf* notebook, *twelve-tone* scale, *three-ring* circus, *white-wall* tires, and *paperback* book.

The closest Bernstein comes to enunciating a rule is a suggestion that when the "nounal adjective" applies to an animate creature it takes the *-ed*: *four-legged* animal as opposed to *gate-leg* table. Others: *two-headed* calf, *cross-eyed* girl, *red-winged* blackbird, *yellow-bellied* sapsucker, *left-handed* pitcher. (But the *-ed* also is used with lots of objects, including *three-legged* stools, *two-pronged* approaches, *long-stemmed* glasses.)

At the same time, Bernstein mentions quite a few words that may be written with or without the *-ed*: *teen-age(d)* boy, *two-tone(d)* car, *hard-surface(d)* road, *long-sleeve(d)* shirt, *horn-rim(med)* glasses, and *honey-color(ed)* dress. He concludes that it's "simply a matter of idiom and sound."

Still, many style guides have weighed in on the side of *-size* rather than *-sized*, without attempting to give a reason. For example:

- *Washington Post Deskbook on Style* (1989). *-size.* In compound adjectives, use *-size*, not *sized*: *Olympic-size* pool, *king-size* bed.

- *U.S. News and World Report Stylebook for Writers and Editors,* seventh edition (1994). *(-)size.* Hyphenate combinations except those with a prefix that normally forms one word: *whale-size, midsize.* Follow the dictionary on spelling: *oversize, middle-sized, undersized.* For words not in the dictionary, use *-size*; *full-size, family-size.*

- *American Heritage Dictionary of the English Language*, third edition (1992). *-size* adj., *-sized*. Often used in combination: *bite-size* appetizers; an *economy-size* package.
- *Words Into Type* (1974). *Adjectives.* A compound adjective made up of an adjective and a noun in combination should usually be hyphenated: *cold-storage* vaults, *short-term* loan, *hot-air* heating, *small-size* edition, *toy-repair* shop, *different-size* prisms (some prefer *different-sized*).

  Compounds with noun plus "-d" or "-ed." Ordinarily hyphenate compound adjectives of which one component is an adjective and the other a noun to which *-d* or *-ed* has been added: *able-bodied, old-fashioned, blue-eyed, dull-witted, middle-aged, dimple-cheeked, acute-angled, freckle-faced, ripple-edged.*

In summary, look it up, and be prepared for things like *long-horned cattle*, but *Texas longhorn*, and *long-horned beetle* or just *longhorn*. And if you can't find a particular term in the dictionary and it doesn't sound right to you, revise awkward constructions like *different-size(d)* constituencies: say instead, *constituencies of different sizes.*

—*Priscilla S. Taylor*

comprise/compose

For centuries respected writers and speakers have used the passive constructions *comprised of* and *composed of* interchangeably to mean "to be made up of." But this is still a point of contention for those who adhere to the dictum: "The whole *comprises* the parts; the whole is not *comprised of* its parts."

To complicate matters, *comprise* is widely used as an active verb with a plural noun subject in a reversal of that part-whole relationship: "Her critical remarks were worded with such tact that they *comprised* a painless rebuke."

Substitute *compose* or *make up* if you wish to avoid the difficulties of using *comprise*. "An adventure series that *comprises* more than 200 titles" is *composed of* or *made up of* the titles. Writing either that the titles *comprise* the series or that the series *is comprised of* the titles may be generally accepted but will make some editors and readers very unhappy.

Not Enough of *That*

This simple relative conjunction contributes to meaning as well as euphony

The venerable Theodore Bernstein said, "It is difficult to give precise guidance on when the conjunction *that* may be omitted and when it should be used." But I think I can safely say that there's too little of *that* around. Here's an example:

> An EPA scientist in Triangle Park, N.C., told me how consumers drive and inflate their tires is critical.

When I skimmed this statement on the op-ed page in our local paper, my reaction was confusion followed closely by annoyance. The columnist first seemed to be saying that the EPA scientist told him something about "how"—the way—consumers drive and inflate their tires. Then when I came to "is critical," I realized that I was on the wrong track and I had to reread the whole sentence. The meaning would have been unmistakable if the columnist had written

> An EPA scientist in Triangle Park, N.C., told me that how consumers drive and inflate their tires is critical.

It's a bad idea to play syntax games with readers in this way. The conjunction *that*, as it's used in the example, introduces something that Latin teachers call "indirect discourse" and others call "indirect quote" or "implied quote." An indirect quote expresses someone's words or thoughts or feelings without using quotation marks. This construction can be introduced with *say, think*, or a word for one of many other related activities such as *believe, tell, feel, know, understand*, or *hear*.

The omission of *that* often represents an effort to write informally that is especially common in reporting. The columnist violated an important principle of writing, journalistic or otherwise: Be as clear as you can, as soon as you can. The English language is ambiguous enough without throwing in mixed signals. Skipping *that* may work well in speech, but in writing the absence of *that* where it's needed for clarity is a reminder that the spoken and the written word make different demands on us.

It is often possible to omit *that* in speech because listeners can take their cues from the speaker's intonation and pace. If you read the first EPA sentence out loud, you'll find that once you understand the meaning and repeat the sentence with that meaning in mind, you'll pause slightly after "told me" and perhaps even lower your voice somewhat on "how." But in written quotes that are implied or indirect, *that* is a modest but necessary part of the infrastructure, like a traffic sign: It tells us what to expect or what to do next. It's essential in the absence of auditory cues.

We can generally omit *that* in writing without sacrificing clarity when the lead-in word is *say* or *think,* or when the first word of the indirect quote is obviously the subject of the clause. Statements like the following pose no problem:

We think she'll be able to finish the project in two weeks.

She said she wouldn't accept any new projects until then.

In more complicated sentences, however, when *and that* or *but that* introduces a second clause, Bernstein says that the first clause should also include a *that:* "A matter of balance."

Not: I think this is a promising entry-level job and that you will be promoted quickly.

But: I think that this is a promising entry-level job and that you will be promoted quickly.

But sprinkling *thats* where not absolutely necessary for clarity, though not incorrect, can sometimes sound stilted or clumsy, as in this sentence:

One point that I don't address here is the mixing of *that* and *which* clauses.

Not all expressions are so straightforward, however. Unthinking writers who omit *that* force readers to backtrack with sentences like this:

They believed the salesman, who spoke to them at length and quite sincerely, was concealing the faults of the used car.

or this:

Those who understand the AIDS virus cannot be transmitted casually are less likely to shun co-workers who test positive for the virus.

or this:

The committee held his plan was the best way to encourage reinvestment.

Without the bracing conjunction *that,* the hapless reader follows the writer's misleading directions until the sentence stops making sense or the syntax suddenly takes a different tack—sometimes a ludicrous one. Readers don't appreciate being led astray in this manner.

Bernstein says that knowing when to include *that* and when to omit it comes with experience. Editors can develop an ear for potentially confusing indirect quotations by reading questionable sentences out loud. Could the proper meaning be lost without *that*? Will you be forcing your reader to stop and start over? The written page gives few clues about inflection, but *that* provides a simple clue that's often overlooked. And that's enough of *that.*

—*Karen Feinberg*

That vs. *Which*:
Is the Distinction Useful?

It can be the only way to interpret restrictive information

L anguage changes constantly, and change is usually good because it provides new opportunities for expression. However, change that results as the language evolves differs from change that results from oversight, ignorance, or expedience. The former enhances language; the latter restricts it and limits expression.

One example of language changing is the lessening distinction between *that* and *which* as "gatekeepers" of restrictive and nonrestrictive clauses, respectively.

Several months ago I spoke with a technical editor who insisted that a distinction is no longer being made in the use of *that* and *which*—even by the most discriminating writers, editors, and readers. According to that editor, "Whichever you choose is fine, commas or no. Moreover, there's no reason for a distinction. Few people know the rule anyway."

I beg to differ. Although a change *has* begun to occur in the use of these words to introduce restrictive and nonrestrictive clauses, there hasn't yet been a large-scale abandonment of this perfectly valid and useful grammatical convention.

Let's review the traditional guidelines for the use of *that* and *which*.

- Use *that* to introduce clauses that are restrictive (or essential), for example, clauses containing information that is *necessary* to understand the main idea of the sentence. Commas *do not* precede or follow such clauses or other restrictive information. *Example: The sales meeting that was held in Peoria was not well attended.*

- Use *which* to introduce clauses that are nonrestrictive (or nonessential), for example, clauses containing information that is *not necessary* to understand the main idea of the sentence. Commas *do* surround these and other nonrestrictive clauses and information. *Example: The original 1989 budget, which reduced spending in many areas, has been modified by the new administration.*

- A memory device to help distinguish between *that* and *which* is "*that* defines, *which* describes."

These guidelines are easy to learn but not always easy to follow; determining whether information is restrictive or nonrestrictive can be difficult. Editors should make this determination for readers, who may not have sufficient expertise or information to do so. An editor who cannot

163

determine whether the information in the clause is essential should query the author.

Consider the following two sentences:

Nicotine that is addictive is a major ingredient in tobacco.

Nicotine, which is addictive, is a major ingredient in tobacco.

The first sentence implies that some nicotine is nonaddictive and that only addictive nicotine is an ingredient in tobacco. The use of *that* and no commas tells readers that all the information is essential and therefore

The choice of *that* or *which* sets expectations for the reader

necessary. The second sentence indicates that all nicotine is addictive. The use of *which* and commas tells readers that the information surrounded by commas is nonessential (even if enlightening)—it can be deleted with little or no effect on clear communication.

An easy way to decide whether information is restrictive or nonrestrictive is to determine whether the information in the clause applies to *all* people or things defined or described in the clause. If the information does apply to all, the clause is nonrestrictive (it does not set limits and adds no needed information) and requires commas. If the information does *not* apply to all, the clause is restrictive (it sets limits and adds needed information) and does not require commas. Using this technique, decide which of the following sentences is correctly worded and punctuated:

Rules of grammar, which are purposeless, should not be followed.

Rules of grammar that are purposeless should not be followed.

Are all rules of grammar purposeless? If you answer *yes*, the first sentence is correct and you are probably reading this newsletter by mistake, because *which* (with commas) used to introduce the clause in this sentence indicates that *all* rules of grammar are purposeless. If you answer *no*, the second sentence is correct, because the restrictive clause introduced by *that* (no commas) signals the reader that *not all* rules of grammar—only the kind noted—are purposeless.

These two sentences convey markedly different messages. The first advocates total abandonment of rules of grammar; the second, judicious use of them. Obviously, the second sentence is correct and conveys the generally accepted view.

The choice of *that* or *which* with the attendant punctuation sets expectations for the reader. In making a choice, the editor distinguishes for the reader between necessary and unnecessary information.

Even if it's true that few people know the rule for using *that* and *which*, as the editor mentioned earlier contended, the suggested "cure" (to encourage or be guided by ignorance) is inappropriate. Some people do not know and therefore cannot follow the rules of subject-verb agreement, but "they is" is not about to come into vogue in formal, written communication. An appropriate remedy for a lack of knowledge is to educate readers through consistent usage.

English isn't a throwaway language; it's an evolving, growing entity that is so rich in variations that the use of grammatical standards and conventions is essential for clear communication. The important consideration here is not tradition but standard usage, the reader's expectations resulting from long-established practice, and chiefly the usefulness of the form.

In some publications, it's already becoming acceptable to use *which* to introduce both types of clauses and to let the punctuation signal the distinction. In such cases, commas are omitted around restrictive clauses introduced by *which* and included around nonrestrictive ones. The distinction is still being made, but made differently. This movement away from the traditional guidelines is an example of how language can evolve and still maintain useful and necessary distinctions. This form of linguistic evolution accommodates the need for distinctions and standards by developing new treatments before abandoning existing ones.

We can change the signals to readers only with caution and good cause—and neither expedience nor ignorance is good cause.

—*Mary J. Scroggins*

Rules for Using
That vs. *Which* and *Who*

Yes, it still matters

Here are the rules for using *that*, *which*, and *who*:

1. *Who* is usually used with persons and *that* and *which* with things. If you're referring to a combination of people and things, use *that*.

2. "Restrictive" and "essential" describe phrases and clauses that contribute information essential to the meaning of the sentence. In other words, they restrict the meaning of the sentence. If an essential phrase or clause is dropped, the sentence no longer means the same thing. Restrictive clauses are preceded by *who* or *that*, or an understood *that*, and are not preceded by a comma.

3. "Nonrestrictive" and "nonessential" describe phrases and clauses that contribute information extraneous to the meaning of the sentence. Nonessential in this context doesn't mean "worthless"; rather, it means "extra" or "subordinate." Nonrestrictive clauses are preceded by a comma and begin with *which* or *who*.

4. Once you determine whether a phrase or clause is restrictive or nonrestrictive, you can then edit it. In the interest of brevity or clarity, you sometimes may delete *which* or *that*, but commas—or the lack of them—tell the reader that the phrase or clause is restrictive or nonrestrictive.

—Mary Stoughton

That vs. *Which* and *Who*

Change *which* to *that* or *who* in these sentences and indicate whether the phrase is restrictive or nonrestrictive. Be able to explain why—inquiring writers want to know why their editors do these things.

1. The team which is responsible for drafting the Strategic Alignment Policy Summary reports directly to the president.

2. The SAPS team which has been working overtime on the policy manual which is overdue sent out for pizza.

3. "Strategic alignment" which is a plan for a 50 percent reduction in force is key to doubling corporate income which has been steadily declining.

4. Corporate communicators often can't combat the rumors which circulate in the wake of management transitions.

5. Positions which are not key which are left open by disgruntled employees that retire early will not be filled.

6. Documents which were published by the Office of Technology Assessment which has been abolished are still available through the Superintendent of Documents, P.O. Box 371954, Pittsburgh, PA 15250-7974.

7. Portable Document Format (PDF) which is an almost exact replica of the printed product is one way a database of documents can be made available on the Internet.

8. The Institute for Federal Printing and Publishing is offering a service to its customers which elect to receive reminders of upcoming classes by fax.

9. A thorough procedure guide which has been prepared by Conference Call USA which is a provider of teleconferencing services explained to participants which wanted to retrieve printed materials how to use fax-on-demand.

10. Memories of people, places, and things which meant a lot to my parents were carefully preserved in scrapbooks which we showed to the children on our last visit.

11. Downsizing the workforce which grew in the 1980s is a task which no company undertakes gladly.

ANSWERS

1. Restrictive.

   The team responsible for drafting the Strategic Alignment Policy Summary reports directly to the president.

2. I read the first clause as restrictive (although several other *Editorial Eye* editors think it's much more likely to be nonrestrictive) and the second as nonrestrictive.

   The SAPS team *that* has been working overtime on the policy manual, *which* is overdue, sent out for pizza.

3. Both are nonrestrictive. I think the adverb carries more force if it's moved to the end of the sentence, though some might leave it before *declining*.

   "Strategic alignment," a plan for a 50 percent reduction in force, is key to doubling corporate income, *which* has been declining steadily.

4. Definitely restrictive.

   Corporate communicators often can't combat the rumors *that* circulate in the wake of management transitions.

5. All restrictive. The relative pronoun doesn't need repeating in the first clause and the pronoun in the second should be changed from *that* to *who*.

   Positions *that* are not key and are left open by disgruntled employees *who* retire early will not be filled.

6. Restrictive, nonrestrictive.

   Documents published by the Office of Technology Assessment, *which* has been abolished, are still available....

7. Nonrestrictive, restrictive.

   Portable Document Format (PDF), *which* is an almost exact replica of the printed product, is one way *that* a database of documents can be made available on the Internet.

8. Restrictive.

   The Institute for Federal Printing and Publishing is offering a service to its customers *who* elect to receive reminders of upcoming classes by fax.

9. Restrictive, nonrestrictive, restrictive.

   A thorough procedure guide prepared by Conference Call USA, *which* is a provider of teleconferencing services, explained to participants *who* wanted to retrieve printed materials how to use fax-on-demand.

10. Restrictive, nonrestrictive.

    Memories of people, places, and things *that* meant a lot to my parents were carefully preserved in scrapbooks, *which* we showed to the children on our last visit.

11. I chose to view the first clause as nonrestrictive, but the point is arguable. The second clause is definitely restrictive.

    Downsizing the workforce, *which* grew in the 1980s, is a task no company undertakes gladly.

    —*Mary Stoughton*

Two Possessive Constructions in Search of Approval

The black sheep of the apostrophe family

Strictly speaking, the *double genitive* and *possessive with gerunds* are more a matter of syntax than of punctuation—there's more going on than simply adding *'s*. Usage authorities have long sparred over the "correctness" of these constructions, but there's nothing wrong with them.

Double genitives

That moth-eaten old coat of my father's has got to go! Sentences that show possession in two ways are termed double genitives. In this sort of construction, the *'s* is redundant since the *of* already implies possession. Nevertheless, most authorities accept the usage as idiomatic.

Follett, in *Modern American Usage*, points out that the *'s*, redundant or not, is often needed for clarity. Without it, for example, we cannot differentiate *a portrait of Mary Cassatt's* (a painting done by her or possibly a painting owned by her) from *a portrait of Mary Cassatt* (a painting of her done by someone else). Of course, we can write around the ambiguity by using *a portrait by Mary Cassatt* for one she painted.

Possession with a gerund

The church bell's tolling interfered with his hearing our song. Using the possessive with a verbal noun (or gerund) is standard practice, and some authorities view it as the only acceptable construction to use with gerunds. But, in fact, the usage has been disputed among grammarians for more than three hundred years. Should it be *the bell's tolling* or *the bell tolling*? And does the clamor interfere with *his hearing* or *him hearing*?

Webster's Dictionary of English Usage points out that for centuries good writers have used either construction depending on what they want to emphasize. Among many contrasting examples cited are two from Flannery O'Connor's letters:

> She approves of this one's being a girl.

> ...I can't see me letting Harold C. condense it.

In the second example, *Webster's* notes, the use of *me* instead of *my* emphasizes the pronoun by making it the object of the verb, whereas in the first example the whole phrase "this one's being a girl" is the object of the verb and "one" needs no emphasis.

Webster's accepts both constructions and provides these general observations:

1. Personal pronouns used with a gerund are usually possessive but may be objective if the writer intends special emphasis. (*I wouldn't mind your seeing; without me knowing it.*) (*The pediatrician frowns on my rocking the baby to sleep nightly. The deadline passed without us realizing it.*)

2. The possessive is less frequent with nouns. Writers often drop the possessive if the noun ends in an *s* sound: *The twins shouting woke us up.*

3. The possessive may be dropped if the noun or pronoun is followed by a modifier: *I worried about Sebastian perhaps not having enough to eat.*

4. Some nouns and pronouns simply resist the possessive form: *The odds of that occurring are one in ten.*

"The possessive," Webster's concludes, "will almost always be safe for pronouns and will probably work most of the time with nouns."

—*Dianne Snyder*

prolific/prodigious

P*rolific* describes a person, animal, or thing showing "abundant inventiveness or productivity" or "occurring in great numbers." The writer Joyce Carol Oates (for her decades of nonstop fiction), flying foxes (for their progeny), and cereal manufacturers (for their daunting array of similar products) can all be called *prolific*.

Prodigious means "inspiring amazement or wonder" or "extraordinary in bulk, quantity, or degree," and so describes the body of work, litter, or output produced in the examples above, not the producer itself.

If you called Joyce Carol Oates a *prodigious* writer, you would be wrong on two counts: She's physically as slight as your chance of spotting a flying fox.

The Right Preposition

Decide whether the italicized prepositions and the words preceding them are used correctly. If not, correct the prepositions.

1. Because George was *careless about* his editing, he lost his job.

2. The manager was so *disgusted with* her supervisor's swearing that she asked for a transfer to another department.

3. The antique furniture presented a *contrast with* the high-tech architecture of the office building.

4. *Ranging between* 230 and 250 degrees, the oil bath was preferred to the water bath for the experiment.

5. Mr. Jacobs was unable to hide his *resentment at* his supervisor, Ms. Simmons, when she rejected his reorganization plan.

6. A substantive editor must be *attentive about* tone and readability, as well as *about* organization and content.

7. Being *well educated in* the field of civil engineering, Ms. Hogan was an excellent candidate for the position of department manager.

8. A believer in saving the environment, David was willing *to labor at* the recycling movement in his community.

9. The writer was *wary about* the inexperienced editor's being responsible for reorganizing the manuscript.

10. As an *advocate for* free enterprise, the banker wrote a weekly editorial.

ANSWERS

1. Careless *about* dress; *in* one's work; *of* the feelings of others.

Because George was **careless in** his editing, he lost his job.

2. Disgusted *at* an action; *by* a quality or habit of a person or animal; *with* a person.

The manager was so **disgusted by** her supervisor's swearing....

3. Contrast *between* this and that; this presents a contrast *to* that; this is in contrast *with* that.

The antique furniture presented a **contrast to** the high-tech architecture....

4. Ranging *between* boundaries; *from* x *to* y degrees; *within* a territory.

Ranging from 230 **to** 250 degrees, the oil bath was preferred....

5. Resentment *against* a person; *at* (or *for*) a wrong.

Mr. Jacobs was unable to hide his **resentment against** his supervisor....

6. Attentive *to*.

A substantive editor must be **attentive to** tone and readability, as well as **to** organization and content.

7. Educated *about* (or *concerning*) the needs of life; *for* living; *in* a field of study. The sentence is correct as is.

8. Labor *at* a task; *for* (or *in*) a cause; *under* a taskmaster; *with* tools.

A believer in saving the environment, David was willing to **labor for** the recycling movement....

9. Wary *of*.

The writer was **wary of** the inexperienced editor's....

10. Advocate *of*.

As an **advocate of** free enterprise, the banker wrote....

—*Ellie Abrams*

classic/classical; historic/historical

The distinctions between these adjectives are often overlooked. *Classical* is preferred for things pertaining specifically to Roman and Greek culture or to an established, authoritarian method (a classical education). *Classic* is commonly used both as noun and adjective to denote an attribute that *classical* only implies: being of enduring importance or excellence (a classic model).

Historic means important in the framework of history (a historic landmark or occasion). *Historical* means based on a particular period of history or events that happened in the past (a historical novel). For example: The *historical* documentary recreated the *classic* speech studded with *classical* analogies that the president made in a *historic* appeal for unity.

By the way, the article *a* is correct before *historic* and *historical*, no matter what your local TV news anchor says.

Two Views on Usage and Why Each Needs the Other

The middle ground is only for the brave

At the extremes of perspectives on usage are the restrictive "rules approach," which pronounces judgment on how people express themselves, and the point of view that says usage should not be judged at all because, in the end, all "correctness" is relative to time and space—what native speakers say is automatically good usage.

The rules approach grew from the 18th-century literary view that English should conform to the rules of classical Greek and Latin, which were quite regular in their grammars (a feature strongly reinforced by the fact that people had stopped speaking them more than 1,500 years before).

Many educated Europeans took the view that the grammatical rules of classical languages should be normative for all languages. Thus, "It is I," not "It is me," became grammatically correct English, because in Latin, forms of the verb *to be* are followed by the nominative case, not the accusative. Unfortunately, not all languages agreed to follow the rules, even languages directly descended from Latin. In French, for example, the expression is *c'est moi*; *c'est je* is never said.

Nonetheless, a critical attitude about English usage developed, and there was a great interest in "improving" the language. Before 1700, for example, there were few books devoted to English language criticism; in the first half of the 18th century, some 50 such books appeared; in the succeeding half-century, more than 200 were published.

Aside from becoming a breeding ground for pedantry, a rule-bound approach to usage doesn't seem to work well for two important reasons: (1) rules can never keep up with language change because they are necessarily generated from past usage, and (2) the "logic" of grammar, which the rules supposedly reflect, is not embedded in eternal reason but, like usage, is historically, socially, and culturally conditioned.

Moreover, as is well known, the best writers break the rules from time to time. Thus Elizabeth Barrett Browning can, for poetic effect, use *gift* as a verb ("The world must love and fear him / Whom I gift with heart and mind"—"Swan's Nest"); this usage can, in fact, be traced back to 1619. When it comes to the strictures of logic, *decimate*, originally (and quite logically) meant "to reduce by a tenth," but it was used rhetorically by Charlotte Brontë to mean "destroy a large part of" in 1828, and it has been so used ever since.

At the other end of the spectrum is the school of thought, sprung from the brow of modern linguistics, that insists that usage should not be judged at all. The argument runs roughly as follows:

1. Language changes constantly.
2. Change is normal.
3. Spoken language *is* the language.
4. All correctness ultimately rests on usage.
5. "Correct" usage is relative to the time, place, and user group.

The credo of this school thus becomes: If you are a native speaker you cannot make a mistake, because you don't know how; grammar is what you say.

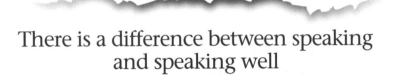

There is a difference between speaking and speaking well

This view of usage has the important advantages of taking seriously the dictum that usage is king and of sloughing off the dead skin of rule-ism. But there is also another problem here. If grammar is simply what speakers say and what writers write, how can we trust that language reflects accurately our world and experience?

There is, in Ben Johnson's phrase, "a difference between speaking and speaking well," *and the difference is profoundly important.* How, then, do we decide on the nature of the difference and sustain it?

Even if usage is king, we are bound to say that language arises from a shared process of constructing meanings. That process, for better or worse, *is* ordered by rules, but we should not be imprisoned by them. Thus usage may be king, but he is not an absolute monarch. Rules are the guardians of communication, and the order they impose cannot be abandoned without paying a price, usually in the form of some meaning getting mangled somewhere. For example, English speakers, over centuries, have continuously shaped verbs into singular and plural forms, and their choice has not been arbitrary. They have done so, at least in part, because reality presents itself as both singular and plural, and human beings need some way to speak about that fact.

Being rule-correct is not the point, and neither, in the end, is simply being understood. Somewhere between the lockstep of hard-and-fast rules and the chaos of "spoken language is the language" lies a commonsense approach to usage that takes quality of expression seriously. We need rules because without them we sooner or later risk unsound and unreliable communication. But we have to be careful because when we are too rigid, we risk choking off English's considerable plasticity, flexibility, and creativity—ultimately to the impoverishment of useful communication.

In sum, deciding on what constitutes "good" usage is important because quality and grace are important in both oral and written communications, because exactitude and nuance are important, and because, in the end, language is the most precise instrument available to any culture for engaging, manufacturing, and disseminating the ideas by which it lives or dies.

—Bruce O. Boston

Style and Punctuation Perennials

How (and Why) to Create an In-House Style Manual

Clear standards help us produce professional-looking documents

Writing or revising an in-house style guide is one of those dreaded jobs that are easier to put off than to start. The reasons for delay are practically universal: no time, little enthusiasm for the job, and no good plan for getting it done. In most publications departments, the task is saved for those "slow periods" that never seem to come. With the right approach, however, you can quickly create a guide that will help you and your colleagues work more efficiently and professionally.

How can a style guide help?

Most organizations understand the benefits of an in-house style guide, but in case you need to convince upper management of the need to devote time to creating or revising one, you can cite these advantages:

- A style guide saves time (i.e., money) by addressing often-asked questions of style, grammar, punctuation, format, and policy. It's always cheaper and faster to do something right the first time than to redo it. (Not catching problems at all is not an option.)

- A style guide provides clear standards for producing documents—printed or electronic—that have a consistently professional look. Upper-level managers may not care about commas or hyphens, but they do realize that the public consciously or subconsciously forms opinions about an organization based on the quality of its written products. Lasting impressions are often made by a corporate brochure, proposal, or annual report.

- A style guide saves time spent settling arguments, both within the publications department and with others in the organization—as long as users understand that many of a style guide's points are arbitrary and the goal is consistency, not editorial absolutes.

You don't have to reinvent the wheel

Before the writing starts, decide on a common format and unified approach. This step is crucial to any group writing effort and will save time and strain now as well as editing time later. Most in-house style guides are based on one of the larger, painstakingly produced guides.

If your department hasn't decided on a primary style guide as the basis for its editorial style, or is looking for a more appropriate model for your publications, you may want to consider the following:

- *Associated Press Stylebook and Libel Manual* (1994). Known as AP style, this guide is used by many newspapers, newsletters, and magazines. It's arranged alphabetically and covers word usage, style, and some grammar and punctuation problems.
- *Chicago Manual of Style*, 14th edition (1993). The classic reference for writers and editors, this guide is widely used by book publishers and scholarly organizations in the social sciences and humanities. Chicago style emphasizes matters of style and punctuation, with extensive chapters on reference citations and documentation.

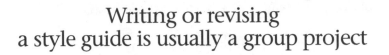

Writing or revising
a style guide is usually a group project

- *New York Public Library Writer's Guide to Style and Usage* (1994). This relatively new entry in the primary style guide market is geared toward general interest, business, and technical publications not as well served by more specialized guides. It covers word usage and grammar and punctuation problems as well as all the traditional style points.
- *Publication Manual of the American Psychological Association*, fourth edition (1994). Known as APA style, this guide is used by publishers in the social sciences and contains useful sections on tables and reference citations.
- *Scientific Style and Format: The CBE* (Council of Biology Editors) *Manual for Authors and Editors* (1994). Known as CBE, this guide is used by many scientific journals and publications, especially those in the life sciences.
- *U.S. Government Printing Office Style Manual* (1984). Known as GPO, this book is strictly a style manual—grammar and usage issues are not covered. It is used by government agencies and many government contractors, especially in technical fields.

With the exception of GPO, all of these books can be found at or ordered through most large bookstores. GPO is available through the GPO Bookstore at (202) 512-1800. More specialized guides may be harder to find on the shelf, so we've provided addresses:

- *The ACS Style Guide: A Manual for Authors and Editors* edited by Janet S. Dodd (1986). American Chemical Society, 1155 16th St. N.W., Washington, DC 20036.

- *American Medical Association Manual of Style,* eighth edition (1989) by Cheryl Iverson et al., edited by William Hensyl. Williams & Wilkins/American Medical Association, 515 N. Dearborn St., Chicago, IL 60610.
- *Mathematics into Type: Copy Editing and Proofreading of Mathematics for Editorial Assistants and Authors* by Ellen Swanson, revised edition (1986). American Mathematical Society, P.O. Box 6248, Providence, RI 02940.

Why waste time and effort on topics that are already covered well elsewhere? In your guide, you can discuss your exceptions, adaptations, or additions to a topic, while giving users the page or section number of the primary style guide to refer to for more background if they need it.

First, map the trouble spots

Writing or revising a style guide is usually a group project. At a kickoff meeting, decide which topics and areas should be included. Ask everyone to contribute examples of problems and questions that come up time and time again. These trouble spots will form the heart of your style guide. Keep a list of all these concerns, then organize the items into a few general sections. For example, you may want sections for word usage, grammar, punctuation, number style, capitalization, and format.

Next, prepare section outlines

Once you've decided on these sections, divide the work among your staff and ask them to prepare fairly detailed outlines of what their section should include. Then set a date to regroup and review the outlines. This approach lets people delay the actual writing, a task many editors hate, while they become invested in the planning—and you gain the benefit of being able to review the scope of the content before the writing starts. This step helps limit the time and agony spent rewriting and reorganizing later on. After everyone has approved the section outlines, set a date for completion of first drafts.

Use lots of lists

Lists are easy to write and much easier to read than narrative text. A style guide is basically an instruction manual that lends itself well to brief, clearly stated sentences or items. If all writers agree to use lists whenever possible and to begin each list item with a verb, the writing will go much faster.

Use lots of examples

Think about how you actually use a style guide like Chicago: If you're like me, you'll scan pages of examples before you finally resort to reading the text for an explanation. Don't spend a lot of time creating original examples—borrow liberally from the documents that cross your desk (as long as you're not reprinting text as your own that is proprietary, or copyrighted material, like *The Editorial Eye*'s Test Yourself columns). This approach saves writing time and has the added benefit of providing real-life examples for your users.

Keep formatting rules to a minimum

Don't waste a lot of words describing format specifications. Instead, insert actual examples, such as cover and title pages, tables of contents, tables and charts, bibliographies, lists, and other standard formats. Mark up these pages to show typefaces and sizes, spacing, and other typographic treatments, as well as notes about page content. You'll save time now and allow for quick referencing later.

Include flexible troubleshooting lists

Some parts of your style guide will need updating more frequently. To simplify making additions to the changing style issues particular to your profession or industry, keep several helpful checklists in a separate section. You might include

- troublesome words that trip people up with tricky spelling, usage, compounding, and hyphenation;
- frequently used abbreviations; and
- terms and special treatments specific to your organization.

You may also want a directory of names and titles of the people, departments, products, and services you frequently need to refer to. Consider printing the lists on colored paper to make them easy to spot for quick reference.

To create these lists, ask each writer or editor to contribute copies of the personal "cheat sheets" they keep. Also check with your equivalent of the marketing, public affairs, corporate communications, and human resources offices.

If your organization has a legal office or corporate attorney, ask for the latest guidance on trademark and proprietary information issues. How do you indicate trademarks in running copy? in your own sales brochures? That could end up being one of your most helpful lists.

Make updating easy

For ease of updating, you'll probably want to use standard 8½-by-11-inch paper and three-ring binders. Be sure to include a table of contents, and tabbed divider pages would be a real favor to users. Put the date of issue of every edition in a header or footer on each page; as you make changes, simply distribute new pages with a notation that they supersede the earlier pages. Once every year or so, reissue the entire guide to ensure that everyone is using the most current version. (You can't force people to add the inserts!)

Help people follow your style guidelines

If you count on others in your organization to follow certain standards and conventions when preparing submissions to your publications department, they'll need a brief, friendly set of instructions to follow. Don't just hand them a copy of your main style guide and expect them to fall in line.

Summarize the points you're most concerned about on a single sheet of paper and call them something nonthreatening like *The Top 10 Most Frequent Errors in [your company's name] Documents*. Error-prevention guidelines can cover everything from file-naming conventions to common capitalization problems.

Getting buy-in

Most publications departments serve several internal "customers"—sales and marketing groups, technical and engineering departments, and human resources. How can you get them to recognize the value of your style guide—and use it?

From the start, try to get feedback from representatives of other in-house groups that will be using the guide, and ask them to review the final draft. Try to incorporate their comments and find solutions for the problems they encounter. If your colleagues seem to feel that having a style guide will just mean more work and rules for them to follow, make it clear that you don't expect people to become editors. That's what you are there for: to see that standards are met. It's just easier all around when the team is playing with the same set of rules.

—Andrea J. Sutcliffe

Who Said That?
On Handling Quotations

Accurate quoting is like truth-in-lending. The fine points are important

Did Virginia Woolf write that James Joyce's *Ulysses* has genius, but of an inferior kind? Yes, she did. But did Virginia Woolf write *"Ulysses* has genius, but of an inferior kind?" No, she didn't. To be precise, she wrote, "Genius it has, I think; but of the inferior water."

That is the difference between a **paraphrase** and a **true quotation**.

If we use quotation marks, we are promising our readers that we are reporting Woolf's words exactly as printed. If we don't use them, we are not making that promise. In both cases, however, there is an implicit promise that we are reporting the *meaning* accurately.

In nonfiction, indentation (that is, block quotation) usually replaces quotation marks for quotations of more than a few lines. A block quotation makes the same promise of strict accuracy that quotation marks do.

The following block quotation is a larger slice of Woolf's diary entry for September 6, 1922, which I will use to illustrate some of the fine points of fair quotation.

> I finished *Ulysses* and think it a mis-fire. Genius it has, I think; but of the inferior water. The book is diffuse. It is brackish. It is pretentious. It is underbred, not only in the obvious sense, but in the literary sense. A first-rate writer, I mean, respects writing too much to be tricky; startling; doing stunts. I'm reminded all the time of some callow board-school boy, full of wits and powers, but so self-conscious and egotistical that he loses his head, becomes extravagant, mannered, uproarious, ill at ease, makes kindly people feel sorry for him and stern ones merely annoyed; and one hopes he'll grow out of it; but as Joyce is 40 this scarcely seems likely.

Quoting fairly

"Genius it has," said Woolf of Joyce's novel is obviously an unfair use of quotation; it gives a false impression of Woolf's opinion. It is also more casual in form than it should be, especially if the context is a scholarly study of Woolf's writing, because it gives no indication that Woolf's sentence continues. Adding points of ellipsis to the quote—

"Genius it has..." said Woolf

—would at least provide the information that Woolf had more to say on the matter, but the quote would still be misleading.

Note that including Woolf's comma in the original (*"Genius it has,..." said Woolf*) is correct but fussier than necessary in most contexts; punctuation within a quoted passage should not be changed or omitted, but punctuation at the end can usually be dropped or changed to suit the enclosing sentence. Note also that if words are omitted not at the beginning of a quotation but in the middle, points of ellipsis are not optional—they *must* be used:

> Wolfe commented, "Genius it has...but of the inferior water."

The entire extract here is a fair use of quotation, although even it does not communicate everything Woolf had to say about *Ulysses*—the passage goes on to admit that she has spent little time so far on the book, and she takes the subject up again in subsequent diary entries.

But we can be fair without quoting the whole thing. Perhaps all we want from Woolf is the gist of her opinion, in which case the freest paraphrase would suffice:

> Woolf reported in her journal that she considered *Ulysses* a pretentious failure.

Or perhaps we want to report only a specific comment, in which case a short quotation and straightforward attribution may be best:

> Woolf wrote, "The book is diffuse."

Often, though, rather than rely on bland paraphrases or simple attributed quotations, we want to work quoted material into our own sentences, enlivening our text and giving our readers direct contact with our source. That's fair—but it should be done properly.

Extracting only the words we want

What about compiling a direct quotation from several sentences? To write

> Woolf considered *Ulysses* "diffuse, brackish, pretentious, and underbred"

might be fair enough as far as the meaning goes, but it is not true to the actual words. Those four damning adjectives have been extracted from their separate sentences and put into a series, and the quotation marks promise the reader falsely that Woolf had them all in a single sentence.

A trivial lie? Maybe, but still a lie. Misreporting the sentence structure of the source is as irresponsible as misreporting the words. The quotation could be rendered truthfully this way:

> Woolf considered *Ulysses* "diffuse," "brackish," "pretentious," and "underbred."

That may look fussy, but it doesn't really bother readers—and it doesn't lie to them. If we really want to avoid the multiple quotation marks, we could use points of ellipsis:

> Woolf considered *Ulysses* "diffuse...brackish...pretentious...underbred."

Note that neither way of extracting words tells readers the whole truth that the four adjectives come from separate sentences—they just let it be a possibility. The conventions of quotation have their limitations, but we at least can make sure we don't tell lies.

Making just a tiny change

How literally must a quotation be rendered? The sentence

> Woolf wrote that she "finished *Ulysses* and thought it a misfire"

is, again, fair to the meaning but not a proper direct quotation. By changing *think* to *thought*, the writer has made it an indirect quotation—a kind of paraphrase in which the choice of words remains pretty much the same, but person and tense are changed to suit the enclosing sentence. Indirect quotations should not be in quotation marks.

In addition to changing *think* to *thought*, the example in the preceding paragraph changes Woolf's hyphenated *mis-fire* to *misfire*. In principle, closing up *mis-fire* corrupts the quotation, and no corruption is permissible in some kinds of writing, such as scholarly studies of literary texts. But trivial changes like this one are defensible much of the time.

Variant spellings are distracting, and a writer or editor who judges such a variation to be of no possible significance to the reader—in this case, for instance, *mis-fire* is just a quirky spelling, not a British variant—may rightly decide to eliminate the distraction. I myself would hesitate to change Woolf, but in another case—for example, a modern writer published in a poorly edited periodical—I would certainly correct such a variant and might change number style, capitalization, and even some punctuation to suit my own conventions.

Quotation vs. paraphrase

A direct quotation often has a punch that an indirect quotation or a free paraphrase does not, but it may take some effort to fit the borrowed words into good sentences of our own. Paraphrase is sometimes a better choice. Here is a passage from a later diary entry, after Woolf had discussed Joyce with T.S. Eliot:

> Tom said, "He is a purely literary writer. He is founded upon Walter Pater with a touch of Newman." I said he was virile—a he-goat; but didn't expect Tom to agree. Tom did, though; and said he left out many things that were important. The book would be a landmark, because it destroyed the whole of the nineteenth century. It left Joyce himself with nothing to write another book on. It showed the futility of all the English styles. He thought some of the writing was beautiful. But there was no "great conception"; that was not Joyce's intention.

Woolf makes skillful use of direct quotation *(Tom said, "He is...")*, of standard indirect quotation *(I said he was virile.... [Eliot] said he left out many things that were important)*, and of a looser indirect quotation that probably departs considerably from Eliot's diction but is doubtless an accurate paraphrase (*The book would be a landmark.... It left Joyce himself with nothing to write another book on*).

The last sentence of the passage, although itself a paraphrase, has *great conception* in quotation marks. Perhaps they indicate that the phrase was Eliot's, but more likely they are "raised eyebrow" quotation marks—suggesting irony or some insinuating qualification, just as we do with voice

Often, we want to work quoted material into our own sentences

and facial expression when we say something scornful like *I suppose you think this piece of yours is "great literature."* Like scorn itself, this use of quotation marks can be unpretty; often it seems jeering and mean-spirited. But Woolf, of course, is showing scorn of her own expectations as a reader and critic, if anything. Her criticism of Joyce is not insinuated with raised eyebrows but stated bluntly.

Common quotation errors

Suppose a writer wants to give a brief account of Woolf's reaction to *Ulysses*, using Woolf's own words as much as can gracefully be done. Here is a beginning that makes two common errors:

> When she first read *Ulysses,* Woolf wrote in her diary that "The book is diffuse," that it "reminded her all the time of some callow board-school boy."

The first quotation is a complete sentence, initial capital and all, and it should not be introduced by *that* but by a comma or colon:

> ...Woolf wrote in her diary, "The book is diffuse."

or

> ...Woolf wrote in her diary: "The book is diffuse."

The *that* should alert readers to an indirect quotation or to a direct quotation of a sentence fragment that has been incorporated into the writer's own grammar. (The indirect quotation can, of course, go on to include a direct quotation, just as Woolf included the raised eyebrow quotation *"great conception"* in her paraphrase of Eliot.)

The writer could, however, retain the *that* and simply lowercase Woolf's *The* to make it clear that even though the quotation is a grammatically complete sentence, it is not being presented as one but included as part of the writer's own sentence. If the writer considers it important to indicate any change that has been made to the capitalization of the first word of a quotation to fit the context, the lowercase letter that is supplied can be put in brackets:

> Woolf wrote that "[t]he book is diffuse."

Just as points of ellipsis are mandatory to indicate the omission of words in the middle of a quotation, brackets are mandatory to mark any additions or changes to a direct quotation beyond capitalizing or lower-casing an initial letter.

The phrasing *Woolf wrote...that it "reminded her..."* is a giveaway; obviously the writer has taken some liberty with Woolf's words, because she would not have referred to herself in the third person. This error could be repaired by putting *her* in brackets to indicate that the writer is supplying the word, but it would be smoother either to move the opening quotation mark to *all* or to change the enclosing words to accommodate the grammar of Woolf's words. Here is a corrected version:

> When she first read *Ulysses*, Woolf wrote in her diary that the book was "diffuse," that she was "reminded all the time of some callow board-school boy."

The cost of truth-in-borrowing

An editor can't always do much about inaccurate quoting, which may be neither intentional nor apparent, or clumsy quoting, which may be impossible to improve without complete rewriting or extensive research. But it's an editor's specific responsibility to understand the mechanics and to make sure the accepted rules are properly applied. For their part, writers who are careful to quote fairly will agree with Ralph Waldo Emerson's judgment: "In fact, it is as difficult to appropriate the thoughts of others as it is to invent."

—Edward D. Johnson

Can You Edit a Direct Quotation?

This point/counterpoint sums up the controversy

No. Imagine watching President Clinton on CNN. There he is, in a speech taped earlier that day, offering his thoughts on the Oklahoma City bombing. Suddenly, you still see Clinton's lips moving but the voice you hear is no longer his—for half a sentence, the voice of the President is portrayed by CNN's Bernard Shaw.

A TV network would never put words in a person's mouth, of course, but print journalists take this liberty all the time. They call it "cleaning up quotes," and the excuse is that people make mistakes in speech that they would never make in writing and therefore reproducing such mistakes in print would "make them look stupid."

Nonsense. To change a person's exact words once you've put them inside the "these are a person's exact words" punctuation marks is lying. It makes you look stupid.

Extending this courtesy might have had a tinge of validity before radio, when few people heard public officials speak, but in the age of 24-hour TV news, fiddling with people's words to make them look superior to you and me is irresponsible. Not only that—the electronic age means that print journalists who do this risk being caught. It's pretty likely that someone somewhere is watching a clip of somebody yelling, "I ain't saying nothing to nobody, dumb-ass," while reading a printed account of the same statement that says, "I respectfully decline to comment, my good man." (Or whatever. The degree to which a quote is changed isn't the issue; once a quote is changed, it's no longer a quote.) Can a reader who witnesses such deception be blamed for doubting everything in that publication in the future?

Of course, if the above quote came from a condemned murderer and not, say, the secretary of state, it likely would have been printed verbatim (we now need this additional qualifier to let people know that a particular quote is real and not made up). Once you get into the quote-changing business, you put yourself in a position of having to decide which people are "good enough" to get the full cleanup treatment. If William Safire failed to use the subjunctive when he should have, you'd probably correct that, but would you do the same for an inarticulate football player? You have to decide on a "correct but not too correct" version of your stylebook to ensure that smart people don't look stupid but stupid people don't look too smart. Once you've gone this far, why not just make up all your quotes? (What a tangled web we weave....)

And then there are cases where an editor might want to make people look stupid, or at least colorful. In a feature story on a Southern sheriff's down-home ways, do we want to impose sequence-of-tenses restrictions on his yarn about a possum over yonder by the woodpile? Or how about this: If a big story about a public official who made a hilarious goof in a speech were to break, wouldn't it be a little unfair to report this in a publication that essentially pretends nobody else in the world ever misspeaks?

Now, when I say quotes shouldn't be changed, that doesn't mean that we need to reproduce every "um," "er," or cough, it doesn't mean that a reporter's transcription errors can't be corrected, and it certainly doesn't mean that stories should routinely attempt to re-create dialect (everybody pronounces "should have" as "should of"). But it does mean that a reader should expect the writer to stop and the speaker to take over once an open-quote mark appears. If a "problem" quote is the best one to tell the story, ellipses, bracketed inserts, and the partial-quote device are always available. A good editor using these tools can "fix" almost any slip of the tongue without being dishonest to the reader.

The answer is simple: "Quote" means "quote." Writers have word after word after word at their disposal outside quotation marks; they have no business inserting their own prose inside them.

—*Bill Walsh, copy desk chief,* The Washington Times

Yes. A "saving" edit on a quote doesn't depend on how important the person is or how bad the quote is. We should have a good reason for editing a quote, and we should have an equally good reason for using one unedited if it might be embarrassing.

Quotes draw readers in, giving human warmth and an approachable tone to abstract news. They crystallize a story's focal point. As transitional devices, they carry a story forward. But if people unwittingly say (as people will, including you and me) something that sounds ignorant or buffoonish, it's usually unfair to print it verbatim. Both Associated Press and United Press International style guides acknowledge circumstances in which editing a quote is not just appropriate but recommended. In fact, UPI strongly advises writers to remember the difference between spoken and printed language.

I've heard writers at a Society of Professional Journalists workshop insist heatedly and loftily that a quote must never, ever be "altered," but strict adherence to such j-school cant is, ultimately, a kind of cynical defaulting. News writing isn't a transcript of reality. It's a creative and analytical enterprise fueled by the exercise of selective judgment.

Quotes are, in fact, an artifice. Even literally rendered, they take on certain implications, depending on the context of the article. When quotes are paraphrased for transition and copy flow, they are further isolated from the direct quotes they once were linked to (reality) and the original emphasis is skewed, however benignly (story). What the speaker may have meant often becomes secondary to the writer's focus—quotes are used as a way to force news into a pattern. None of this is unusual; textbooks recommend these discretionary techniques. But it's ridiculous to try to hold that writers must honor a sacrosanct rule of literalness because anything less is not "genuine."

Journalists need to get over the idea that they're models of ethical probity and beacons of objectivity if they never touch a quote. Why repeat the halting, broken speech patterns of a young woman who has already been identified in stark detail as a destitute, uneducated, battered single mother in a homeless shelter? But a major newspaper did it. That's doubly manipulative and condescending—to the speaker and the reader.

Direct quotes have clarity and force on the page out of realistic proportion to the spontaneous rush or sputter of the spoken word. Nobody's arguing for homogenizing colorful vocabulary that gives readers a sense of someone's personality. But in very, very few cases is it necessary to quote someone's fractured or halting English to prove a point, set a scene, or identify a personality.

My colleague Bill Walsh says that our only choices are to quote verbatim or to paraphrase. However, putting uncharacteristic words in someone else's mouth or changing the speaker's meaning are not the inevitable results of editing quotes. It takes creativity and integrity, but to lightly edit what was said while preserving the essence of what was meant is possible. An edited quote is no more of a violation than a partial quote Superglued to a paraphrase of the spoken words (two removes from the first source) or, worse, blended into the writer's own analysis.

As the UPI style guide says, short of a face-to-face conversation from someone's mouth to your ear, all quotes are edited. Putting those words judiciously on the page is the difference between a conversation and a news story—the telling difference. All but the most unregenerate reporters avoid using quotes, edited or unedited, that caricature someone merely for effect.

—Linda B. Jorgensen

Punctuation with Quotation Marks

Here are the three basic rules for closing quotation marks. They apply to full and single quotation marks alike.

1. Commas and periods are placed inside closing quotation marks.
2. Colons and semicolons are placed outside closing quotation marks.
3. Question marks and exclamation points can be placed inside or outside closing quotation marks, depending on the sentence.

In the sentences below, the parts that do *not* involve quotation marks are punctuated correctly, but I have left to you the placement of the quotes themselves and related punctuation. Some of the capitalization should help you.

1. My accountant said, The best information on this topic can be found in the article Everything You Need to Know About Property Taxes

2. The economics professor asked, Have you read the article The Intelligent Consumer Demands More

3. I know only one way to sing The Star Spangled Banner lip-synching.

4. On Monday I will conduct the seminar WordPerfect for DOS on Tuesday I will conduct WordPerfect for Windows

5. Who yelled, Look out

6. Can you believe old Scrooge said, We'll have a party next week

7. When you saw your boss at the restaurant, did you actually say When will I get a raise

8. The checks we need are the ones marked Insufficient Funds the bank teller told the manager

ANSWERS

1. Follow rule 1. A quote that falls within a quote is set off with single quotation marks. No space is placed between single and double quotations. The placement of the period within the closing quotation marks is an American usage, although in commands the period might be placed outside the closing quotation mark depending on the meaning—as in this example: *In sentence three of paragraph two change "Monday" to "Thursday".* The period is not part of the

change or the command. In British usage, the period may be placed outside the closing quotation mark, depending on the meaning.

> My accountant said, "The best information on this topic can be found in the article 'Everything You Need to Know About Property Taxes.'"

2. Because the quoted information is a question, place the question mark inside the closing quotation mark. The title of the article is a statement, so place the question mark outside the closing single quotation mark.

> The economics professor asked, "Have you read the article 'The Intelligent Consumer Demands More'?"

3. Rule 2 requires that the colon be placed outside the closing quotation mark.

> I know only one way to sing "The Star Spangled Banner": lip-synching.

4. Rule 2 requires that the semicolon be placed outside the closing quotation mark, but rule 1 requires that the period be placed inside the closing quotation mark. This is a good example of a case where it does not make much sense to place the period inside the closing quotation mark, but American usage punctuates this way.

> On Monday I will conduct the seminar "WordPerfect for DOS"; on Tuesday I will conduct "WordPerfect for Windows."

5. According to *Words Into Type*, "If a question or exclamation occurs within a question, both ending at the same time, retain the stronger mark. It is often hard to say which is the stronger mark...." Here the exclamation is stronger.

> Who yelled, "Look out!"

6. The entire sentence is a question, and the quoted information is a statement; the question mark is placed outside the closing quotation mark. According to *Words Into Type*, if an exclamatory or an interrogative sentence ends at the same time as a statement, retain the exclamation point or the question mark and omit the period.

> Can you believe old Scrooge said, "We'll have a party next week"?

7. Both the sentence and the quoted information are questions. According to *The Gregg Reference Manual*, a sentence cannot end with two terminal marks of punctuation; the one used first is retained. Therefore, the question mark is placed inside the closing quotation mark.

> When you saw your boss at the restaurant, did you actually say, "When will I get a raise?"

8. Follow rule 1 above; place a comma inside the closing quotation marks.

> "The checks we need are the ones marked 'Insufficient Funds,'" the bank teller told the manager.

—Ellie Abrams

Numbers: To Spell Out or Not?

A modest proposal for reforming clumsy conventions

I recently read a book by Roger A. Caras—*A Dog Is Listening* (Summit Books)—that contains the following eye-catching passages replete with long strings of spelled out numbers:

> Their two-thousand-five-hundred-year history kicked in like a giant engine.

> We have about five million such [olfactory] cells working for us while the dog has anywhere from one hundred and twenty-five to two hundred and twenty million.

The same week, my eye stopped at the following passages in two national newspapers. The first is from the *Washington Post*:

> American political ideas and social and cultural values, expressed in American cadences (often those of the third and 16th presidents)....

The second is from the *Wall Street Journal*:

> They had first hoped for three million or more subscribing homes, then trimmed it to 2.8 million, then reduced even that projection to perhaps two million homes....

Enough! This article is an unabashed appeal for a simplified number style, not just for technical and scientific writing but for almost all writing. Why on earth should we readers have to put up with trying to grasp numbers like these? And why should newspapers continue to mix numbers like "10 dogs, six cats and 97 hamsters" (the advice given in the *Associated Press Stylebook*)?

As the world becomes increasingly technical, writers are devising number styles that make it easier to read their work. Fewer people are willing to spell out large numbers at all, because figures are easier to understand in the first place and easier to compare than words.

Author William Zinsser has struck a blow for freedom in his new book *American Places* by using numerals for all numbers starting with 10 except in quotations. In a recent letter to me he commented:

> I'm sick of having to translate words into numbers, especially in *The New Yorker*: sentences like "in the mid-nineteen-seventies a thirty-seven-thousand-ton tanker carrying forty-two million gallons of oil would take seventeen or eighteen days to, etc." Numbers were invented to create an instant picture of a numerical amount, and as I wrote my book I found myself typing out what I thought were unusually interesting numbers. I wanted my readers to have the same pleasure without struggling to decipher them because of a stylistic convention.

Zinsser admitted to being a little apprehensive that, in the book, the numbers "might look a little cheap," but when he saw them in print he decided they looked "wonderful." He added, "When my long-time copy-editor at HarperCollins called to ask if I *insisted* on doing something so 'journalistic,' I said, 'I've been expecting your call.' No blood was lost. Maybe next time, with another author, she'll even insist on doing it herself."

All the standard style manuals recognize the problems that number style poses.

As the *Chicago Manual of Style* (14th edition) puts it:

> It is difficult if not impossible to be entirely consistent in the use of numbers in textual matter. As soon as one thinks one has arrived at a simple rule for handling some category of numbers, exceptions begin to appear, and one realizes that the rule has to be made more complicated.... Several factors work together to govern the choice between spelling out and using numerals for any particular number. Among them are whether the number is large or small, whether it is an approximation or an exact quantity, what kind of entity it enumerates, and what kind of text it appears in—scientific or technological on the one hand, humanistic on the other.

Similarly, *Words Into Type* comments:

> In deciding whether to use numerals or spell out numbers, the nature of the writing should be considered and literary style distinguished from technical and scientific style....

> As a very broad rule, numbers under 101, round numbers (for example, *about two hundred years ago*), and isolated numbers are expressed in words in general text matter; in scientific and technical writing the rule is to use numerals for all physical measures and for most quantities and qualities of 11 and over. Another rule of thumb is that when several large numbers appear in the same context the style for the larger numbers governs that for the smaller.

Journalistic style often defies logic. The *Washington Post Deskbook on Style* says:

> Use figures in ages of people and animals: *A 4-year-old horse; a four-year-old building;*...[and] in a series of three or more numbers any one of which is larger than 10. [Note that this means that when only two numbers are used, one may be spelled out while the other is not: *He had six goats and 12 chickens.*]

I believe that many of these complications could be eliminated if writers will forget about spelling out numbers between 10 and 100 except in special circumstances (explained later) or approximate numbers, and stop trying to decide whether the text is mainly technical or humanistic. Further, let's use numerals for *all* numbers whenever numerals make more sense—particularly for at least two numbers, one of which is higher than nine. Let's abandon long-winded number styles.

We do not, however, have to reinvent the wheel. The general rule of the *Publication Manual of the American Psychological Association* (*APA*) makes the most sense to me. *APA*'s general rule is to "use figures to express numbers 10 and above and words to express numbers below 10"—except for numbers that

...are grouped for comparison with numbers 10 and above (in the same paragraph)—*3 of 21 analyses; in the 2nd and 11th grades;*

...immediately precede a unit of measurement—*a 5-mg dose;*

...represent statistical or decimal quantities, percentages, ratios, and percentiles and quartiles—*the 1st quartile; more than 5% of the sample* [I'd spell out *percent* except in tables, however];

...represent time; dates; ages; sample, subsample, or population size; specific numbers of subjects in an experiment; scores and points on a scale; exact sums of money; and numerals as numerals—*2 weeks ago, 2-year-olds, $5*; or

...denote a specific place in a numbered series, parts of books and tables, each number in a list of four or more numbers—*Grade 8, chapter 5, row 5* [*APA*'s capitalization style is another matter altogether].

APA style does recommend using words to express numbers below 10 that do not represent precise measurements and that are grouped for comparison with numbers below 10—*eight items, three-way interaction*—and with *zero* and *one* when words are easier to comprehend than the figure—*zero-base budgeting, one-line sentence.*

Along with most other style guides, *APA* spells out any number that begins a sentence, title, or heading, but suggests rewording of a sentence to avoid beginning with a large spelled-out number. Common fractions are spelled out (*APA* doesn't hyphenate the fraction as a noun—"one fifth of the class"—but most other styles do), and *APA* doesn't tamper with universally accepted usage (the Fourth of July).

Like *Chicago* and *Words Into Type*, *APA* also recommends a combination of figures and words to clarify back-to-back modifiers—*2 two-way interactions, twenty 6-year-olds.* This last rule makes far more sense than the *Associated Press Stylebook*'s slavish adherence to its rules for numbers in a series, which results in such mind-boggling constructions as this: "They had four four-room houses, 10 three-room houses and 12 10-room houses."

What are we waiting for? Writers of the world, unite.

—*Priscilla S. Taylor*

Punctuating Restrictive/Nonrestrictive Elements

When trying to decide whether information is restrictive or nonrestrictive in these sentences, try thinking of a pair of commas around nonrestrictive elements as handles that can be used to lift the phrase or clause out of the sentence. If the sentence does not make sense when the phrase is removed, then the information is *necessary,* or *restrictive* (essential, definitive). Commas should *not* be used to set off restrictive information.

If the meaning of the sentence is clear and complete when the information is lifted out, then the information is *not necessary;* it is *nonrestrictive* (nonessential, extraneous). Set off nonrestrictive information with commas.

Often, the key to deciding whether to use commas is deciding whether an element is a restrictive *appositive*—a noun that means the same as another noun or creates an identity—or merely adds information.

Remember that an element can be a word, a phrase, or a clause that describes, explains, or defines another element. A restrictive clause is usually introduced by *that* and is not set off by commas, whereas a nonrestrictive clause is introduced by *which* and does have commas.

1. Until recently, the modern Olympic Games that were begun in Athens, Greece, in 1896 were held during the last year of each Olympiad—a period of four years ending in a leap year.

2. During the Golden Age of Greece, the great poet, Pindar, wrote odes in honor of the winners, who were presented with a laurel or wild olive wreath.

3. *Stadium* is derived from the Greek word, *stadion,* which is a unit of measure equal to about 190 meters, the length of the first footraces.

4. Only free male citizens were permitted to participate in the games; women were forbidden on penalty of death to even see them.

5. Milo, a wrestler in the sixth century B.C., who won the wrestling crown six times, has often been considered the greatest athlete of ancient times.

6. The competition, added in 1924, included cold-weather sports and became known as the Winter Games.

7. At the 1936 Olympic Games, the dictator, Adolf Hitler, refused to acknowledge the

triumphs of Jesse Owens, a black American sprinter and long jumper.

8. The movie, *Cool Runnings,* that co-stars John Candy recounts the tale of the Jamaican four-man bobsled team.

9. The International Olympic Committee organized in 1894 by Baron de Coubertin governs the Games and works with the national committees that must avoid any commercial, religious, or political interference.

10. The spectator, who was shooting a video of Nancy Kerrigan, an Olympic hopeful, caught on tape a man, holding a club while watching Kerrigan skate.

ANSWERS

Boldface has been used to show the nonrestrictive or restrictive element discussed in the answer.

1. In this sentence, the information in the clause is nonessential (extra) information; therefore, *that* should be replaced with *which* and commas should be used.

> Until recently, the modern Olympic Games, **which were begun in Athens, Greece, in 1896,** were held during the last year of each Olympiad—a period of four years ending in a leap year.

2. The name *Pindar* is a restrictive appositive and should not be set off with commas, but because all winners received wreaths, the *who* clause is nonrestrictive.

> During the Golden Age of Greece, the great poet **Pindar** wrote odes in honor of the winners, **who were presented with a laurel or wild olive wreath.**

3. *Stadion* is the restrictive appositive for *Greek word.* The clause *which...meters* is the nonrestrictive modifier of *stadion,* and the appositive phrase *the length...footraces* is the nonrestrictive modifier of *190 meters.*

> *Stadium* is derived from the Greek word *stadion,* **which is a unit of measure equal to about 190 meters, the length of the first footraces.**

4. A quick survey of *Editorial Eye* editors on this one shows the difficulty that can arise when deciding what "essential" information is. One editor says that the phrase *on penalty of death* is essential information; women weren't just sent home, they were executed. Two other editors say that understanding the concept of being "forbidden" does not hinge on knowing the penalty for disobedience. I also consider the phrase to be nonrestrictive. Extraneous information that makes important qualifications can still be considered nonrestrictive—that's what makes it hard to decide.

Only free male citizens were permitted to participate in the games; women were forbidden, **on penalty of death**, to even see them.

5. No commas should set off the clause *who...times* because it restricts the meaning to a specific 6th century wrestler. (But set off the entire nonessential phrase *a wrestler...times*.)

> Milo, **a wrestler in the sixth century B.C. who won the wrestling crown six times**, has often been considered the greatest athlete of ancient times.

6. The participial phrase *added in 1924* restricts the meaning to a particular competition, so no commas.

> The competition **added in 1924** included cold-weather sports and became known as the Winter Games.

7. *Adolf Hitler* is immediately preceded by the restrictive appositive *the dictator* so no commas. In 1936, the world had more than one dictator. Although the phrase after *Jesse Owens* might seem to be essential information, an appositive (*a black American...*) following a proper name is almost always set off by commas, or in this case by a single comma.

> At the 1936 Olympic Games, the dictator **Adolf Hitler** refused to acknowledge the triumphs of Jesse Owens, **a black American sprinter and long jumper**.

8. The movie title should not be set off with commas because it defines *the movie*. Change *that* to *which* because it introduces the nonrestrictive clause *which... Candy,* and set it off.

> The movie *Cool Runnings,* **which co-stars John Candy**, recounts the tale of the Jamaican four-man bobsled team.

9. Set off the participial phrase *organized...Coubertin* because there is only one international Olympic committee. Change *that* to *which* because it introduces a nonrestrictive clause.

> The International Olympic Committee, **organized in 1894 by Baron de Coubertin**, governs the Games and works with the national committees, **which must avoid any commercial, religious, or political interference**.

10. The clause *who...Kerrigan* defines the noun *spectator*, and the participial phrase *holding...skate* defines the noun *man*. The nonrestrictive appositive *an Olympic hopeful* is set off with commas.

> The spectator **who was shooting a video of Nancy Kerrigan, an Olympic hopeful**, caught on tape a man **holding a club while watching Kerrigan skate**.

Note: Some of these sentences were adapted from *The New Book of Knowledge,* Vol. 14, 1989, Grolier Inc., Danbury, CT.

—*Ellie Abrams*

The Acrobatic Apostrophe

The boundary between possessives and plurals remains uncertain

"**Y**ou find not the apostrophes and so miss the accent"—thus the schoolmaster in *Love's Labour's Lost* criticizes a curate who has just read aloud a love letter intended for someone else. The schoolmaster's concern with apostrophes should come as no surprise in a Shakespearean play whose very title contains two of them. Those of us who work with words know whereof he speaks.

With the possible exception of the comma, no mark of punctuation is more misunderstood. And none provokes the level of editorial consternation that a wrongly used apostrophe does: "The company went broke, in 1995, it's fifth year in business." Readers might forgive the unnecessary comma skulking on the baseline but not the errant apostrophe bold as a flagpole-sitter or a high-wire artist.

The source of apostrophic conventions

The conventions governing the apostrophe distinguish three usages:

- To show possession (*her mother-in-law's house*)
- To show omission and elision of letters or numbers (*isn't, o'clock, the '90s*)
- To denote certain plurals (*1960's, learn your ABC's*)

The last is a matter of style; some style guides prescribe the apostrophe while others omit it except when needed for clarity, as in "dot your i's." The second usage is uniformly accepted and rarely misused. The first usage—to show possession—is where most questions arise.

Scholars believe that these conventions all emerged from one primordial bog. When the apostrophe was originally introduced into English in the 16th century, it was used simply to show omission. As English began to drop its inflected endings, the apostrophe was used to mark the omission of *e* from *es*, the Old English genitive (possessive) singular ending (*scipes = ship's*). It was later similarly used with certain nominative plural nouns (*foxes = fox's*) and more commonly with words ending in a vowel (*comma's*). Shakespeare would have been familiar with both usages, though neither was consistently applied until the 18th century.

Gradually, the use of the apostrophe to mark the possessive spread to include all possessive nouns (with or without an *s*), while the plural usage ceased with the few exceptions noted earlier. Perhaps a remnant of that ancestral apostrophe remains imprinted on our genes and causes some of our present-day confusion.

A comprehensive discussion of the apostrophe could end up back at the bog. Although usage to show possession is now clearly differentiated from usage to show omission, the boundary between possessives and plurals remains uncertain. The main areas of dispute, along with some guidelines and caveats for sorting them out, follow.

Strunk and White's rule number one updated

Form the possessive of singular nouns by adding 's, said Strunk and White's first rule of usage. "Follow this rule whatever the final consonant," they advised, although, like most rule givers, they granted a few exemptions (*for conscience' sake, in Jesus' name*). The trend today, however, is to exempt many more.

Increasingly, the *s* is being dropped after all multisyllabic nouns ending in an *s* or *z* sound (*Horowitz' piano*). Some styles drop the *s* even after monosyllabic words where speakers normally pronounce it (*my boss' husband*). Fortunately, the question of *s* or no *s* is easily resolved by recourse to a style guide or one's ear. The main thing is to be consistent.

The more thought-provoking part of the Strunk and White rule comes at the beginning: "Form the possessive...." In a world populated by the likes of *Teachers College* and *users manual*, what in fact constitutes a possessive noun?

Can false possessives be forgiven?

"I sank back on the Cadillac's plush seat for an hour's nap." If possessive nouns are defined as nouns that show ownership—the standard definition—a fair percentage of them are what Wilson Follett, in *Modern American Usage*, calls "false possessives." Inanimate objects used as possessives are the main offenders; strictly speaking, inanimate objects can't own things.

According to Follett, constructions such as *the Cadillac's plush seat* or *Florida's governor* are false because they're descriptive, not possessive. "The error...is to assume that Florida's governor means the same thing as the governor of Florida," Follett states, ruling that the possessive apostrophe should be reserved for "ownership by a person." (It's not clear where that leaves either the cat's whiskers or its pajamas.)

Other authorities are more indulgent. Theodore Bernstein, in *The Careful Writer*, dismisses Follett's reasoning as pedantry. "If the purists are going to insist on their rule, perhaps we shall have to rewrite our national anthem to get rid of 'dawn's early light'...." Bernstein observes that "we seem to be approaching a stage where genitives with lifeless things are acceptable except when they sound unusual enough...to call attention to themselves."

Another group of false possessives comprises expressions of duration (*one week's vacation, two hours' rest*). The usage is idiomatic; no real ownership is involved. Some authorities, including Fowler, note that these expressions could also be regarded as attributive nouns (nouns used as adjectives preceding another noun), in which case the apostrophe would be omitted. The consensus, though, is to treat expressions of duration as possessive.

Attributive nouns come with strings

Nouns used to modify other nouns have a long history in the English language, but their proliferation in recent years has been striking on two counts: Many of these newer descriptive nouns have been pluralized (funds solicitation), and often the nouns they modify are themselves used attributively (*funds solicitation planning committee*). In a rush to condense that would do the *Reader's Digest* proud, nouns, phrases, and even clauses piggyback and fuse into dense strings.

One effect of this proliferation, aside from raising editors' eyebrows, has been to diminish the supply of inanimate possessives. Thus, *Florida's governor Lawton Chiles* has become *Florida governor Lawton Chiles*. If you object to the idea of possessive inanimate objects, the missing apostrophe may count as progress, but clarity is frequently traded for brevity, particularly when a long noun string is formed. Is a *young adult fiction writers workshop* (a) a workshop for people who write fiction for young adults or (b) a workshop for young adults who write fiction?

Writer's Center? Writers' Center? Writers Center? The distinction between a possessive noun ("a center created by or belonging to writers") and a descriptive one ("a center created for writers") is often so fine that the question becomes one of nuance. Do we want to encourage an individual sense of belonging or a collective sense (*'s* or *s'*)?

Do pluralized attributive nouns have a place in good writing? Most authorities, while conceding that they do, voice concern about ambiguity or unholy combinations of sounds. *Weapons systems* may be defensible on military grounds, but on grounds of euphony it deserves execution.

Whither the apostrophe?

Did the fortune cookie saying "You are the center of every groups attention" portend the future of the apostrophe? It is omitted with many attributive nouns, but educated writers and editors are unlikely to relinquish it as a routine sign of possession. Perhaps it will come full circle and be used simply to mark omission and elision. More likely, the apostrophe will continue to be used and flagrantly abused, in all its variety.

—*Dianne Snyder*

Commas, Colons, and Semicolons

When to use colons and semicolons instead of commas is often a problem even for proficient writers. The "comma splice" (independent clauses joined by a comma) and overuse of the colon are frequent errors. Correct the punctuation in the following sentences by replacing commas with colons or semicolons or by deleting unnecessary colons.

1. You'll have to forgive my delay in replying, I've been working under a tight deadline this week.

2. He has only one ambition, to produce a Broadway musical.

3. Blue jeans are fashionable all over the world, however, Americans, the creators of this style, still wear jeans more often than citizens of any other nation.

4. On my wish list to visit are Nashville, Mt. Kisco and Pound Ridge, New York, San Francisco, and Santa Fe.

5. If you drop by the medical center without an appointment, you can be sure of one thing, an icy reception.

6. Present at the meeting were Mr. Connel, the president of ABC Company, Ms. Michaels and Ms. Roberts, the coordinators of the advertising campaign, Ms. Becker, the client, and Mr. Lupo, Ms. Becker's assistant.

7. The weather report predicted high winds, freezing rain, and snow, the highway patrol advised caution when driving, yet the storm blew out to sea.

8. The winner had a choice of one of three prizes, a trip around the world, a vacation home in the Bahamas, or a new car.

9. The governor issued this statement, "I have done nothing wrong, the IRS will find that my returns are all in order."

10. Many scientists share a similar view of our future, they believe that we have all the necessary technology to clean up the earth and restore nature's cycles.

11. Our order included: printer paper, mouse pads, monitor covers, and diskettes.

12. The cover design was created by: Matthew, Susan, and Fay, our graphic artists.

ANSWERS

Here are general rules for using the semicolon and the colon:

(a) Use a semicolon to separate two main clauses when a coordinating conjunction is not used.

(b) Use a semicolon to separate main clauses that are connected by a conjunctive adverb (*however, therefore, thus, nevertheless, moreover,* and so on).

(c) Use semicolons to separate a series of complex clauses or a series of grammatically equal items if the series is long or contains internal commas. Use semicolons in these cases even if the clauses or items are joined by a coordinating conjunction.

(d) Use a colon to introduce a concluding explanation, a long or formal quotation, a series following a complete sentence, or an appositive (a noun or noun phrase placed beside another that it equals and explains). A colon should never be placed between a verb or a preposition and its object.

(e) Use a colon to separate two main clauses when the second explains or amplifies the first.

1. Rule (a) or (e). This is a good example of a case where either a semicolon or a colon would be acceptable. Because the two main clauses are closely related, the semicolon is correct. If the writer intended to emphasize that the second sentence explains the first, the colon is correct.

> You'll have to forgive my delay in replying; I've been working under a tight deadline this week.

2. Rule (d).

> He has only one ambition: to produce a Broadway musical.

3. Rule (b).

> Blue jeans are fashionable all over the world; however, Americans, the creators of this style, still wear jeans more often than citizens of any other nation.

4. Rule (c). Note that if a city name is very well-known, you can omit the state name, even if the series includes other city-state pairs.

> On my wish list to visit are Nashville; Mt. Kisco and Pound Ridge, New York; San Francisco; and Santa Fe.

5. Rule (d).

> If you drop by the medical center without an appointment, you can be sure of one thing: an icy reception.

6. Rule (c).

> Present at the meeting were Mr. Connel, the president of ABC Company; Ms. Michaels and Ms. Roberts, the coordinators of the advertising campaign; Ms. Becker, the client; and Mr. Lupo, Ms. Becker's assistant.

7. Rule (c).

> The weather report predicted high winds, freezing rain, and snow; the highway patrol

advised caution when driving; yet the storm blew out to sea.

8. Rule (d).

The winner had a choice of one of three prizes: a trip around the world, a vacation home in the Bahamas, or a new car.

9. Rules (d) and (a).

The governor issued this statement: "I have done nothing wrong; the IRS will find that my returns are all in order."

10. Rule (e). Whether or not to capitalize the first word after a colon is a style issue. Some styles say that if the group of words following the colon is not a complete sentence, do not capitalize the first word; however, if the group of words following the colon is a complete sentence, do capitalize the first word.

Many scientists share a similar view of our future: They believe that we have all the necessary technology to clean up the earth and restore nature's cycles.

11. Rule (d). Most authorities will not allow the colon to be placed after the verb even if the information following the verb is broken out into a list. However, *The Gregg Reference Manual* does allow a colon in displayed lists.

Our order included printer paper, mouse pads, monitor covers, and diskettes.

12. Rule (d). Neither a comma nor a colon should be used to separate a preposition from its object; therefore, deleting the comma after *by* makes this sentence correct. (*The Editorial Eye* endorses the use of the serial comma.)

The cover design was created by Matthew, Susan, and Fay, our graphic artists.

—*Ellie Abrams*

TEST
Yourself
Help Stop Comma Litter

Many *Editorial Eye* readers have requested a column on the mighty comma. As you insert commas in the following sentences, keep in mind that some commas are necessary while others are litter. Do you add commas uncertainly, thinking, "I think a comma should go there, but I'm not sure why"? It pays to have a reason for every comma you use.

1. The seminars will be conducted every Saturday from August 1 1994 until November 30 1994 at the town hall; certificates will be mailed in January 1995.

2. Because we must meet our Friday deadline we have hired temporary employees to get us through the "crunch."

3. My father Robert Smith III and my grandfather Robert Smith Jr. have both decided to toss their hats into the political arena.

4. The wisecrack "Men don't make passes at girls who wear glasses" is attributed to Dorothy Parker.

5. Traffic in the area is usually congested but since the new construction work has begun on the bridge into the city rush hour has become a nightmare.

6. Although I was offered a good position at a small newly created privately owned company I chose to accept an offer from a well-known well-established large nonprofit organization.

7. The candidates who received last-minute funds from local PACs for a media blitz plan to saturate the airwaves before election day.

8. The bicycle which was left in the driveway was stolen last night.

9. The bicycle that was left in the driveway was stolen last night.

10. Recognizing your own weaknesses as well as your strengths will help you advance in your career.

ANSWERS

1. Commas should be placed before and after the year in a three-part date, but not between the month and year in a two-part date. When European or military style is used, no commas are needed: *1 June 1994.*

> The seminars will be conducted every Saturday from August 1, 1994, until November 30, 1994, at the town hall; certificates will be mailed in January 1995.

2. This sentence begins with a dependent clause (*Because...deadline*) and ends with an independent clause *(we...crunch).* A comma follows the dependent clause; if these two clauses were reversed, no comma would be needed because the dependent clause is restrictive. However, some dependent clauses—for example, those beginning with *although*—are always parenthetical and thus are always preceded by a comma.

> Because we must meet our Friday deadline, we have hired temporary employees to get us through the "crunch."

3. Traditionally, commas set off *Jr.* and *Sr., II* and *III,* and so on. Journalistic styles long ago abandoned this sort of comma, and the *Chicago Manual of Style* (14th edition) has done so as well. The important point to remember is, if you decide to set off *Jr., Sr., II,* or *III,* don't forget the second comma.

My father, Robert Smith III, and my grandfather, Robert Smith Jr., have both decided to toss their hats into the political arena.

or

My father, Robert Smith, III, and my grandfather, Robert Smith, Jr., have both decided to toss their hats into the political arena.

4. No commas are used before and after the quotation because it is an appositive (that is, the same as the subject, *the wisecrack*). A quotation that is used as a subject, predicate noun, or restrictive appositive is not set off with commas. (Commas would signify that the quotation was not essential to the sentence and could be lifted out.)

> The wisecrack "Men don't make passes at girls who wear glasses" is attributed to Dorothy Parker.

5. Commas are used after an introductory dependent clause and between long independent clauses that are joined by a coordinate conjunction *(and, but, for, nor, or, yet).* A comma may be omitted between short independent clauses.

> Traffic in the area is usually congested, but since the new construction work has begun on the bridge into the city, rush hour has become a nightmare.

6. Commas are used between coordinate adjectives (adjectives that are of equal weight), but a comma is not placed after *large* because the

entire phrase *nonprofit organization* is being modified. To test whether a comma is necessary between two adjectives, reverse the adjectives or place *and* between them. If the sentence still makes sense, a comma is needed.

> Although I was offered a good position at a small, newly created, privately owned company, I chose to accept an offer from a well-known, well-established, large nonprofit organization.

7. Commas are used to set off clauses that are nonrestrictive (parenthetical or nonessential to the meaning of the sentence). Sometimes only the writer knows whether a clause is restrictive; when in doubt, an editor should query the author. In this sentence, a query is definitely in order. If all the candidates have indeed received funds from local PACs, commas are needed because the information is parenthetical. If only some candidates have received PAC funds and they alone plan to saturate the airwaves, the commas should be omitted because the information is essential.

> The candidates, who received last-minute funds from local PACs for a media blitz, plan to saturate the airwaves before election day.
> or

> The candidates who received last-minute funds from local PACs for a media blitz plan to saturate the airwaves before election day.

8. The pronoun *which* usually introduces a nonrestrictive clause, which must be set off with commas. There was only one bicycle and it was stolen from the driveway where it had been left.

> The bicycle, which was left in the driveway, was stolen last night.

9. The pronoun *that* introduces a restrictive clause; therefore, a comma should not be used. More than one bicycle was on the premises, but only the one left in the driveway was stolen.

> The bicycle that was left in the driveway was stolen last night.

10. A comma is never placed between a subject (*recognizing your own weaknesses as well as your strengths*) and its verb (*will help*).

> Recognizing your own weaknesses as well as your strengths will help you advance in your career.

> —*Ellie Abrams*

Compound Adjectives:
To Glue or Not to Glue?

Taking hyphens too seriously can be hazardous to your health

A colleague has asked why *well-known* and other compounds listed with hyphens in *Merriam-Webster's Collegiate Dictionary* should not be treated as permanent compounds (always requiring the hyphen)—in contradiction to the conventional wisdom that the hyphen is not needed in compound adjectives that come after the noun in a sentence (e.g., *The method is not well known*).

Despite my adherence to John Benbow's famous maxim ("If you take hyphens seriously you will surely go mad"), I will take up that challenge.

I have to admit that I often do not remove hyphens that authors have used in compounds appearing after the noun they modify (e.g., *The project, though time-consuming, was found to be cost-effective, and the participants, all of whom worked part-time, remained drug-free.*).

In general, though, I approach this subject from the opposite end of the spectrum: Instead of seeking justification for inserting a hyphen, I generally seek justification for leaving one out. The reason is that hyphens exist primarily to avoid ambiguity and to speed the reader along. Where there is no ambiguity, theoretically there should be no hyphen. It's impossible to misinterpret a statement such as *The method is not well known.* Hence why add a hyphen? To be consistent with the way you treat the compound when it precedes the verb (*The well-known method saved time*) is not reason enough.

I once reviewed an editing job by an otherwise good editor who had only one obvious flaw—she never saw a unit modifier she didn't want to add a hyphen to. It's a slippery slope. She sprinkled hyphens throughout the text: high-school graduates, real-estate sales, social-security laws— nothing was safe—and the manuscript was a nightmare.

All other things being equal, I tend to give authorities like the *Chicago Manual of Style* the benefit of the doubt. Most authorities do not consider *well-known* a permanent compound. In fact, although there may be much confusion about other compounds, most authorities specifically exempt *well-* words from permanent hyphenation.

Roy Copperud, who synthesizes the views of numerous authorities in *American Usage and Style: The Consensus*, writes, "Compound modifiers do not require the hyphen when they occur in the predicate position (that is, standing after the element modified). These often are combinations with *well: A well-educated man;* but *The man was well educated.*"

But Copperud also addresses the problem of *well* compounds:

Fowler says flatly that the combination of *well* with a participle (*well-read, well-tuned*, etc.) is hyphened [*sic*] only when used attributively and not when used predicatively. That is, it may be hyphened, but not necessarily, when it stands before the noun modified (*A well-tuned piano*) but not after (*The piano was well tuned.*). American usage, however, as is indicated by Random House and Webster, is inconsistent in the use of the hyphen in the predicate construction; American Heritage omits it.

Hyphens exist primarily to avoid ambiguity and speed readers along

And to illustrate how confusing and contradictory the authorities are on this subject, consider Copperud's parting advice:

The best advice perhaps is to follow the dictionary for such *well-* terms as may be found there. Fowler is right, however, when he says that the hyphen grammatically serves no purpose in the predicate construction, and so it may well be omitted; in such instances, *well* can modify nothing but the verb form following it.

The *New York Times* style manual says this:

The usefulness of the hyphen in forming compounds that serve as adjectives before nouns is demonstrated in the entries *ill-* and *well-*. An example: *He wore a well-tailored gray suit.* But the hyphen is omitted when the words follow the noun they modify: *The suit was well tailored.*

The *Washington Post* manual says this:

5. Modifiers may be hyphenated, run together or not compounded, depending on their use.

a. Generally hyphenate a compound modifier preceding the word modified.

far-reaching program,...well-known teacher....

b. Generally do not hyphenate a compound modifier used in the predicate if its last element is a participle.

The program was far reaching. The area was drought stricken.

My colleague's "strongest card" in support of her attempt to persuade us to consider *well-known* as a permanent compound is *Words Into Type*'s advice ("When [a unit modifier] follows the noun, it may be set as two words unless it has been used so commonly that it has become established as a hyphenated compound."). But she didn't look far enough. *Words Into Type* specifically answers her question about whether *well-known* fits this category of permanent compounds: "Compounds with *well* and *ill* need not be hyphenated when they follow the noun modified, although the hyphenated form is often seen."

Incidentally, although some editors seem to take it for granted that compounds such as *well-known* are always hyphenated before the noun they modify, it's easy to think of several instances when they need not be:

- When the compound adjective is preceded by an adverb modifying only the first word of the compound: *a very well informed source; a reasonably well fitting suit;*

- When quotation marks surround the unit modifier: *a "well informed" source;* and

- When both parts of a compound used as an adjective are capped: *the Open Door policy, Old World countries.*

Having said all this to shoot down the proposition to glue *well-* compounds together wherever they appear, however, let me add a qualification. Everyone agrees it's better to use a hyphen where it's *not* needed than to leave it out where it's essential for sense, as in *small-business owner, rare-book dealer, little-used car.* Among the examples Copperud cites of ambiguity caused by lack of a hyphen is this headline, "Man eating / piranha sold / as pet fish," which prompted the comment, "Did he *look* like a fish?"

—Priscilla S. Taylor

Hyphenated Compounds

Would you hyphenate the following compounds? Justify your decision.

1. carbon dioxide emissions, sodium chloride solution

2. pro rata assessment, per diem allowance, per capita income, per pupil expenses

3. large scale project, short term loan, high quality product, low income neighborhood

4. bluish green sea, sky blue truck, blue green algae

5. secretary treasurer, city state, soldier statesman

6. Spanish American War, French Canadian ancestry, Latin American region

7. 20 mile hike, six year old child

8. fifth floor apartment, Twentieth Century Limited

9. $20 million project, 50 percent increase

10. grand jury decision, stock exchange building, bubonic plague outbreak

11. eye catching decor, interest bearing account

12. poverty stricken family, hard boiled eggs, poorly equipped kitchen

ANSWERS

1. Most compound chemical or scientific terms require no hyphen as unit modifiers, hence *carbon dioxide emissions, sodium chloride solution.*

2. The first three terms—*pro rata, per diem, per capita*—are Latin and require no hyphens; the last term is not and usually takes a hyphen: *per-pupil expenses.*

3. A compound adjective consisting of an adjective and a noun usually requires a hyphen before the noun it modifies: *large-scale project, short-term loan, high-quality product, low-income neighborhood.* Authorities are divided on whether to hyphenate compounds with comparatives or superlatives; for example, the *Washington Post Deskbook* and the *U.S. Government Printing Office Style Manual* (GPO) do not hyphenate *lower income neighborhood* or *best loved books,* whereas most other styles do. Style guides agree that no hyphen should be used when the expression carries a modifier: *a very well intentioned deed.*

4. Authorities give contradictory advice on handling these terms. *Words Into Type* says "a compound adjective denoting color whose first element ends in *-ish* should be hyphenated when it precedes a noun, but it need not...when it follows the noun it modifies. When a noun is compounded with a color, or two colors are combined, they should always be hyphenated." Hence *bluish-green sea, sky-blue truck,* and *blue-green algae.* Conversely, the *Chicago Manual of Style* hyphenates only *blue-green algae* ("If the color terms are of equal importance in the compound and do not denote a blend of colors, the compound is hyphenated"). *Bluish green paint* and *coal black* are listed as "color term[s] in which the first element modifies the second." Take your choice.

5. Two joined nouns of equal value require a hyphen: *secretary-treasurer, city-state, soldier-statesman.*

6. Although rules for hyphenation with countries and references to ancestry are somewhat idiosyncratic, the *Chicago* manual says that compound adjectives formed from the unhyphenated proper names of Central European countries are always open. Thus, *Spanish-American War* (Spanish does not modify American), but *French Canadian ancestry* (a Canadian of French ancestry) and *Latin American region* (a region in the Americas with Latin ancestry).

7. A compound modifier consisting of a cardinal number and a unit of measurement is hyphenated when it precedes the noun; hence, *20-mile hike, six-year-old child.*

8. A compound modifier consisting of an ordinal number and a noun is normally hyphenated when it precedes the noun: *fifth-floor apartment.* No hyphen is needed when the compound is capitalized: *Twentieth Century Limited.*

9. Both terms are clear without hyphens: *$20 million project, 50 percent increase.* (GPO says to hyphenate *50-percent increase,* but this rule is not often observed.)

10. *Grand jury decision, stock exchange building,* and *bubonic plague outbreak* are all clear without hyphens.

11. Almost all compound modifiers consisting of an object and a present participle are hyphenated if they precede the noun: Hence, *eye-catching decor, interest-bearing account.* One exception is a well-established compound: *word processing equipment.*

12. Compound adjectives consisting of a past participle and a noun or adverb are hyphenated when they precede the noun they modify (*poverty-stricken family, hard-boiled eggs*) and often when they don't (*The eggs were hard-boiled*), unless the adverb ends in *-ly* or the term otherwise could not be misread: *poorly equipped kitchen.*

—*Priscilla S. Taylor*

Self-ishness:
Capitalization with Compounds

Editorial Eye editors respond to a reader wrestling with style

Paula Glitman, director, Department of Editorial Processing, Specialty Journals, for the American Medical Association, asked the kind of style question that can drive strong editors to distraction:

Is *self-* considered the first element of a whole term or is it considered a prefix? If it is a prefix, the second part of the term should be capitalized in titles; if it is the first part of a whole term, the second part should not be capitalized. Our house style considers *self-* to be a prefix, but *Webster's Tenth* lists many *self-* words that can be interpreted as being whole terms like the adjective *long-term*. Some of us consider all *self-* words to be whole terms. We would appreciate your thoughts since we are thinking of changing our style.

Two EEI editors respond from slightly different angles

• It sounds as though your editors are on the eternal quest to transcend ambiguity in rules of style and usage, to increase the odds that everyone will apply the rules the same way. We're on the same quest, although in this instance we may be taking a different path.

Self- can be used as a prefix with reflexive meaning, in various relations with the second element of the compound. It can also be used as the first part of a permanently hyphenated compound (a whole term). In the *Chicago Manual of Style*, 13th edition, the rule for hyphenated compounds was to "...capitalize the second element if it is a noun or proper adjective or if it has equal force with the first element" and *not* to capitalize "if (*a*) it is a participle modifying the first element or (*b*) both elements constitute a single word."

The 14th edition of *Chicago* no longer asks us to make decisions about "equal force"; it says simply:

> Subsequent elements [in hyphenated compounds] are capitalized unless they are articles, prepositions, coordinating conjunctions, or such modifiers as *flat, sharp,* and *natural* following musical key symbols; second elements attached to prefixes are not capitalized unless they are proper nouns or adjectives....

We've opted to consider *self-* words hyphenated compounds, to capitalize the second element, and to hope this issue can be a thing of the past.

—*Judy Cleary*

- Unfortunately, as in the 13th edition of *Chicago*, the rules for capitalization of words with hyphens in *The New York Public Library Writer's Guide to Style and Usage* (written by EEI) can lead to the appearance of inconsistency. The distinction between temporary and permanent compounds is the heart of the problem. The *Guide* capitalizes the second part in temporary compounds but not in permanent ones (defined as those "found in an up-to-date dictionary"). But suppose my up-to-date dictionary is *Webster's Tenth,* which lists *high-pressure* and *low-pressure* as hyphenated adjectives but does not list *medium-pressure* or *high-temperature*. If I follow the rules, I will write "High-pressure and Medium-Pressure Systems" or "High-Temperature and High-pressure Systems" in heads and titles.

I contend that the distinction between permanent and temporary compounds is arbitrary and should not be part of the rules for capitalizing hyphenated words. The new *Chicago* rule (7.128), cited from the 14th edition by Judy Cleary, doesn't rely on hairsplitting and seems the most helpful to follow. The only fuzzy area becomes deciding what constitutes a prefix. Do *self-* and *cross-* count as prefixes or just as nouns stuck on the beginning? One of *Chicago's* examples muddies the waters further with "Post-Modern"; surely *post-* is a prefix, but perhaps "Modern" is being interpreted as a proper noun.

I'd *like* to advise just capitalizing all parts of hyphenated combinations as if they were separate words, but I can't quite bring myself to like "E-Mail," though "Multi-Family" wouldn't bother me. Perhaps the length of the prefix is a factor?

—Keith C. Ivey

The Editorial Eye editor attempts a summary, settles for a sop

There's always a sneaky exception to any rule about hyphenated compounds—we once failed to agree around here about the word *unselfconscious*. I just couldn't accept either *un-self-* or *unself-* as a prefix, believing as I do with James Thurber that in matters of style, "You might as well fall flat on your face as lean over too far backward" (from *The Bear Who Let It Alone*). Now, about that distraction we were driving toward—are we there yet?

Rules for Commas with Modifiers

Does the phrase make sense with *and*?

A standard approach for deciding whether to use a comma between compound adjectives is this: If the phrase would make sense with *and*, insert a comma. Using that test on the phrase *high-interest short-term bank bonds*, the term *high-interest and short-term* clearly makes sense, but *short-term and bank* doesn't, thus *high-interest, short-term bank bonds*.

There's also a second standard test: Change the order of the adjectives. If the switched version would have the same meaning and "sounds" like something someone would say, use a comma. Testing, *short-term high-interest bank bonds* sounded fine; *short-term bank high-interest bonds* seemed libelous; and *bank short-term high-interest bonds* was patently foolish. I could rearrange the hyphenated adjectives without harm, but *bank* had to stay where it was. Thus, again, *high-interest, short-term bank bonds*.

Both tests rely on editorial judgment to interpret the results, and that's not such a bad thing. Still, neither test explained why to add the comma or why not to use two. I dug into my reference books and found several guidelines:

- First and foremost, distinguish between coordinate, cumulative, and attributive modifiers:
  - **Coordinate modifiers** are of roughly equal weight; they can be joined by *and* or by a comma and can usually be switched around without damage to meaning.
  - **Cumulative modifiers** build up to the noun; rearranging the words or adding *and* or a comma yields nonsense.
  - **Attributive modifiers** (nouns that modify other nouns) are so closely linked to the modified noun that they are treated as being part of a compound; they are not preceded by a comma.
- A number (cardinal or ordinal) goes at the beginning of the adjectival phrase and is virtually never followed by a comma.
- Regardless of the number or type of adjectives, the noun is never preceded by a comma. This is true for simple nouns and for compound nouns, such as vice president.
- If there are only two simple adjectives, the phrase is often fine without a comma.

—Diane Ullius

Commas with Compound Adjectives

Years ago, there was a popular song about a "one-eyed, one-horned, flying purple people-eater." (If you're old enough to remember the song, you're probably humming it already.) I recalled it recently when faced with the phrase *high-interest short-term bank bonds*. To comma or not? Even with simple adjectives, deciding when to use a comma is sometimes a puzzle. With compound adjectives, the puzzle often seems more challenging.

Ready to try your hand? Add commas as appropriate.

1. Somehow, Sandy was not persuaded by the widely held childhood belief in a beautiful open-handed tooth fairy; that first little incisor never did get put under the pillow.

2. Lee, a hard-working interior designer with a talented long-suffering staff, had to make the best of a bad situation while dealing with three work-related disasters in one exhausting week.

3. The project managers relied on a well-known cost-free data source as they outlined the report for their most important new client.

4. The question is this: Should less-productive agricultural land in played-out marginal areas be taxed at the same high rate as fields that yield bumper crops?

5. Go ahead and eat your nice juicy steak, darling; I'll be perfectly happy with a cool crisp salad.

ANSWERS

Most editors would probably add one comma in each sentence.

1. Here, *childhood* is an attributive, so it stays where it is and is not preceded by a comma. In the next phrase, however, the tooth fairy could just as well be described as *beautiful and open-handed* or as *open-handed and beautiful,* so the modifiers are coordinate adjectives

and take a comma. In the final clause, *first* is a number and so is not followed by a comma.

> Somehow, Sandy was not persuaded by the widely held childhood belief in a beautiful, open-handed tooth fairy; that first little incisor never did get put under the pillow.

2. Here, you can construe *interior* as an attributive or look at *interior designer* as a compound noun. In neither case is a comma appropriate. Lee's staff, however, can be seen as *talented and long-suffering,* so this pair of modifiers deserves a comma. In the final part of the sentence, both adjectival phrases have numbers and they receive no commas.

> Lee, a hard-working interior designer with a talented, long-suffering staff, had to make the best of a bad situation while dealing with three work-related disasters in one exhausting week.

3. In this sentence, *well-known* and *cost-free* could be interchanged or joined by *and,* so they can take a comma; but *data* is an attributive, inseparable from *source*—no comma. *Most important,* a superlative, can't be switched with *new*; cumulative modifiers take no comma.

> The project managers relied on a well-known, cost-free data source as they outlined the report for their most important new client.

4. This comparative form needs a hyphen for clarity, but it takes no comma because the modifiers are cumulative: What kind of land? *Agricultural.* What kind of agricultural land? *Less-productive. Played-out* and *marginal* could be switched or joined by *and*, so they can take a comma. (Some editors might omit this one.) *Same* and *high* could not be switched or

joined by *and,* so they get no comma.

> The question is this: Should less-productive agricultural land in played-out, marginal areas be taxed at the same high rate as fields that yield bumper crops?

5. Remember that two simple adjectives are often fine without a comma; if in doubt, try one or both of the tests. Either way, the *salad* phrase calls out for a comma. But *nice juicy steak,* while it passes the *and* test, falls apart when we try to change the order. Some editors might add the comma anyway, for consistency within the sentence; others might leave it out, especially considering the comma necessary before *darling.*

> Go ahead and eat your nice juicy steak, darling; I'll be perfectly happy with a cool, crisp salad.

> OR

> Go ahead and eat your nice, juicy steak, darling; I'll be perfectly happy with a cool, crisp salad.

All of this brings us to the moral of the story: Judgment is essential. Some cases are clear-cut and some aren't; some matter and some don't. Being an editor means making decisions on behalf of your readers, but it doesn't mean obsessing over commas. It's perfectly fine to say occasionally, "This one is okay either way. I'm not going to worry about it." That's not shirking; it's keeping your perspective.

—*Diane Ullius*

Spelling Out Abbreviations

They don't all stand for proper names

Here's a simple rule from the *New York Public Library Writer's Guide to Style and Usage (NYPL)* (HarperCollins, 1994) for giving the spelled-out counterparts of abbreviations:

> The spelled-out expression of an abbreviation is *not* capitalized unless it is a proper name.

This little rule is often ignored. For example, *GNP, AIDS, IRA*, and *APR* don't stand for proper nouns, but it's common to find *gross national product, acquired immunodeficiency syndrome, individual retirement account*, and *annual percentage rate* capitalized when they precede the abbreviation in text.

To some people, such terms may seem to require capitalization to "match" the capital letters of the abbreviation. This error is understandable: So many abbreviations stand for organizations and institutions that are proper names.

There's a flip side to this error. Examples of terms seen more often as abbreviations than spelled out are *chief executive officer, standard error of the mean*, and *cardiopulmonary resuscitation* (abbreviated *CEO, SEM*, and *CPR*). *NYPL* says this:

> In cases where the abbreviation is the more familiar term, the spelled-out form may, if necessary, follow in parentheses.

Where the counterpart follows in parentheses, it may be uppercased in error precisely because it is less familiar than the abbreviation. When in doubt, check your dictionary or a book like the *Proper Noun Speller* (Quick Ref Publishing) rather than making assumptions. Technical or professional abbreviations may "sound" as if they stand for proper names when they are merely shorthand for formal terminology.

—*Linda B. Jorgensen*

Em Dashes, Parentheses, or Commas—
How to Choose?

Many of my students have asked me the following questions when we were punctuating material that had to be specially set off:

- Why did you use em dashes? I would have put that stuff in parentheses because it doesn't seem essential to the sentence.

- Commas? You've got to be kidding! My supervisor would make me use em dashes. The trend is away from commas, isn't it?

- Isn't there a rule saying that em dashes should never be used in formal writing? We're not allowed to use them in our office.

Students are disappointed that I don't have one right—or simple—answer to these questions. But as editors, we have to be careful when we change em dashes to commas or parentheses because we might be changing the author's meaning or intended emphasis. The following three basic rules can be helpful in judging whether material has been set off appropriately.

1. Use em dashes to emphasize information. Em dashes tell the reader, "Stop! Read this; it's really important." Also use em dashes to set off a series that already has internal commas.

2. Use parentheses to deemphasize information. Parentheses tell the reader, "If you want to skip this stuff, go ahead; it's not all that important."

3. Use commas to show that information goes with the flow of the sentence. Commas tell the reader, "This information is as important as everything else in this sentence."

In many cases, emphasis is a matter of opinion, but sometimes one form of punctuation is preferable because of the flow or complexity of the sentence. Add em dashes, parentheses, or commas to help the reader understand the following sentences.

1. By overcoming the seven devils that ruin success false success, fear of change, guilt, vanity, impatience, habit, and the clock author James Dillehay turned his life on a new path.

2. James Dillehay's father had painstakingly built the business an accomplishment that reflected a steady vision of success.

3. Adnan Sarhan the man who became Dillehay's teacher was born with a heritage of Sufi experiential knowledge and grew up in a cultural tradition where everyday life and spiritual development were interwoven.

4. The work of Sufi Master Adnan Sarhan director of the Sufi Foundation of America develops higher intelligence and awareness through a wide range of techniques exercises, meditation, drumming, movement, dancing, and whirling that heighten concentration.

5. Conflicting desires one for financial security, the other to study with Adnan often waged war in Dillehay's troubled brain.

6. Dillehay chose to follow the path of the Sufi the path that

7. Dillehay claims that the second devil fear of change can be overcome only when someone's desire to change is stronger than the desire to stay stuck.

8. Impatience rushing to complete an activity before its natural time creates stress which in turn creates more impatience.

9. Sometimes we get so wrapped up in something our job, our family, a relationship that we forget about ourselves.

10. After the first day of the workshop December 4, 1994, the participants cleared their thoughts and felt a sense of readiness.

ANSWERS

Remember that "setting aside" something can either highlight it or relegate it to secondary importance. I could support using a pair of em dashes, commas, or parentheses in almost all these sentences, but I tried to objectively follow the rules delineated at the beginning of the test. You may not agree with me—and you do not have to. The punctuation I've used reflects my judgment about how the elements in each sentence are weighted.

1. By overcoming the seven devils that ruin success—false success, fear of change, guilt, vanity, impatience, habit, and the clock—author James Dillehay turned his life on a new path.

2. James Dillehay's father had painstakingly built the business—an accomplishment that reflected a steady vision of success.

3. Adnan Sarhan, the man who became Dillehay's teacher, was born with a heritage of Sufi experiential

offered no promises the path that would force Dillehay to be the maker of his own destiny.

knowledge and grew up in a cultural tradition where everyday life and spiritual development were interwoven.

4. The work of Sufi Master Adnan Sarhan, director of the Sufi Foundation of America, develops higher intelligence and awareness through a wide range of techniques (exercises, meditation, drumming, movement, dancing, and whirling) that heighten concentration.

5. Conflicting desires—one for financial security, the other to study with Adnan—often waged war in Dillehay's troubled brain.

6. Dillehay chose to follow the path of the Sufi, the path that offered no promises, the path that would force Dillehay to be the maker of his own destiny.

7. Dillehay claims that the second devil, fear of change, can be overcome only when someone's desire to change is stronger than the desire to stay stuck.

8. Impatience (rushing to complete an activity before its natural time) creates stress, which in turn creates more impatience.

9. Sometimes we get so wrapped up in something (our job, our family, a relationship) that we forget about ourselves.

10. After the first day of the workshop (December 4, 1994), the participants cleared their thoughts and felt a sense of readiness.

Note: Sentences were adapted from *Overcoming the 7 Devils That Ruin Success*, by James Dillehay (Warm Snow Publishers, Torreon, NM).

—*Ellie Abrams*

Punctuation with Conjunctions

My seminar participants doggedly cite these "rules": "My grad school teacher told me to always put a comma before *and.*" "I was taught never to use a comma in a compound sentence." "I know a comma should always be placed after *but.*" "I think *but* should be preceded and followed by a comma." "The word *however* is always preceded by a semicolon, but the word *but* never follows a semicolon."

This test is designed to debunk some of these myths and set the record straight. Although the rules for semicolons are fairly straightforward, comma usage is complex and in flux. Many people use commas where a speaker would normally pause, and in some cases this usage is correct. The rules for commas are sometimes based on grammar and sometimes on style. Use of commas can be optional, especially for compound sentences.

Some sentences are compound-complex, a sentence form used sparingly in the real world for good reason: It's hard to write well and can be hard to understand. Rewrite them if you can.

With all this in mind, add or delete punctuation as necessary for the following coordinate, correlative, and subordinate conjunctions and conjunctive adverbs. (If your mythical memory is short, cheat and check the list of conjunctive adverbs in item 3 of the answers.)

1. As a young writer, Bella ghosted for several mystery writers, and she now feels that this "ghosting" was more valuable than anything she learned in the classroom.

2. Bella ghosted for several mystery writers, and has always felt that this "ghosting" was more valuable than anything she learned in the classroom.

3. A private investigation novel, by its very nature, requires some violence, however, the trick is to make the violence rational, and thus, advance the plot.

4. Medical research oddities, political trivia or reports of unusual psychic, or extraterrestrial events can trigger the beginning of an idea.

5. Sometimes an amateur sleuth becomes involved in a case at the request of a friend. Or, maybe the sleuth is just naturally curious.

6. Orient your reader to the locale and use background to your advantage.

7. Avoid creating a villain who is more interesting than the protagonist because the plot will be lopsided.

8. When we speak of something that did not exist before we are referring to an *invention* but when we speak of something that did exist before but was not known we are referring to a *discovery.*

9. We requested information on patent attorneys qualifications for applying for a patent and the length of time for which a patent is valid but information on royalties patents in other countries and the history of the United States Patent Office was sent instead.

10. After you are granted a patent you may sell the rights to a manufacturer or you may license your rights—that is you may allow a company to make or sell your invention in return for royalties.

11. It is legal not only to patent an invention but also to patent an improvement on an already existing device or machine.

12. A modern jet with its hundreds of comfortable seats and movies and lavatories and kitchens hardly compares with the Wright brothers' biplane, in which a single pilot lay on his stomach with the wind gusting all around him.

ANSWERS

1. In compound sentences, a comma is used between two main clauses—that is, clauses that are complete sentences—joined by a coordinating conjunction (*and, but, for, or, nor,* and *yet*), unless the clause before the conjunction is very short. The example sentence is correctly punctuated.

2. No comma is needed to separate the parts of the compound predicate *ghosted* and *has always felt.*

> Bella ghosted for several mystery writers and has always felt that this "ghosting" was more valuable than anything she learned in the classroom.

3. A semicolon is placed before a conjunctive adverb that connects two main clauses, and a comma usually follows conjunctive adverbs like *furthermore, therefore, moreover, nevertheless, consequently, still, otherwise, besides, also, however,* or *accordingly.* A comma isn't needed after the conjunctive adverbs *hence, nor, then, thus,* and *so.* No comma is needed between the two parts of the compound predicate.

> A private investigation novel, by its very nature, requires some violence; however, the trick is to make the violence rational and thus advance the plot.

4. To ensure clarity in a series of three or more elements, *The Editorial Eye* endorses the placement of a comma (called the "serial comma") before the conjunction that connects words, phrases, or clauses. No comma is used before the conjunction *or* that connects the adjectives *psychic* and *extraterrestrial,* however.

Newspaper publishers generally view the serial comma as an unnecessary and costly (space-eating) form of punctuation, except when confusion would result without it, as in cases where one element in the series already contains a conjunction. Regardless of the style, editors and writers should be careful to use—or not use—serial commas consistently throughout a manuscript or publication.

> Medical research oddities, political trivia, or reports of unusual psychic or extraterrestrial events can trigger the beginning of an idea.

5. Commas are never placed *after* coordinating conjunctions, even when the conjunction appears at the beginning of a sentence.

> Sometimes an amateur sleuth becomes involved in a case at the request of a friend. Or maybe the sleuth is just naturally curious.

6. When one or both verbs in two independent clauses are imperative, a comma is usually placed between the clauses for clarity. If the clauses (especially the first one) are very short, however, the comma is optional. Determining what is short can be a matter of opinion, but the second sentence below does not need a comma.

> Orient your reader to the locale, and use background to your advantage.

BUT

> Orient your reader and use background to your advantage.

7. A comma should follow an introductory dependent clause. However, a comma is optional before a dependent clause at the end of the sentence. We use it in the example because the two clauses are relatively long, but the second sentence below does not need it.

> Avoid creating a villain who is more interesting than the protagonist, because the plot will be lopsided.

BUT

> Avoid creating a convoluted plot because the reader will be left behind.

8. A compound-complex sentence usually consists of two main (independent) clauses that are joined by a coordinate conjunction (*and, but, or*) and one or more subordinate (dependent) clauses. To punctuate this kind of sentence, place a comma before the coordinate junction (here, the first *but*) and then punctuate each clause separately. Both halves of this sentence have the same pattern: a subordinate clause that begins with the subordinate conjunction *when* followed by a main clause. A comma is needed after each clause.

> When we speak of something that did not exist before, we are referring to an *invention,* but when we speak of something that did exist before but was not known, we are referring to a *discovery.*

9. If the internal punctuation of either of two main clauses joined by a coordinate conjunction causes confusion, use a semicolon between the two sentences instead and either delete the conjunction or keep it, depending on the flow. If you keep it, do not use a comma after the conjunction. Using the serial comma can often make such a construction clearer, as in the second example.

> We requested information on patent attorneys, qualifications for applying for a patent and the length of time for which a patent is valid; but information on royalties, patents in other countries and the history of the United States Patent Office was sent instead.
>
> OR
>
> We requested information on patent attorneys, qualifications for applying for a patent, and the length of time for which a patent is valid, but information on royalties, patents in other countries, and the history of the United States Patent Office was sent instead.

10. When an introductory subordinate clause modifies both main clauses of a compound-complex sentence, no comma is necessary between the two main clauses. It's iffy whether a comma should be placed after the relatively short introductory clause because individual definitions of "short" are, in fact, relative. Here, we prefer it for clarity. Also, *that is,* in the sense of *for example,* is always followed by a comma.

> After you are granted a patent, you may sell the rights to a manufacturer or you may license your rights—that is, you may allow a company to make or sell your invention in return for royalties.

11. No commas are necessary to separate phrases joined with correlative conjunctions (*either...or, neither...nor, not only...but also*).

> It is legal not only to patent an invention but also to patent an improvement on an already existing device or machine.

12. Don't automatically delete the *and*s and insert commas in their place when a writer has used repetition deliberately for emphasis. Items in a series with reiterated *and*s do not require separation by commas. In this example, however, *hundreds* might be read as modifying the other nouns that follow *seats.* In addition, the comparison between hundreds of people aboard in comfort and a solitary windblown pilot is obscured by the ungainly string of *and*s. *Editorial Eye* editors had different solutions; among them were the following edits:

> A modern jet, with its hundreds of comfortable seats (and movies and lavatories and

kitchens), hardly compares with the Wright brothers' biplane, in which a single pilot lay on his stomach with the wind gusting all around him.

OR

A modern jet—which has hundreds of comfortable seats and movies and lavatories and kitchens—hardly compares with the Wright brothers' biplane, in which a single pilot lay on his stomach with the wind gusting all around him.

Note: Many of the example sentences were borrowed from *Writing Mysteries: A Handbook by the Mystery Writers of America* (Writer's Digest Books).

—*Ellie Abrams*

The Right WORD

anyone...their/anybody...their

Although grammatically singular, *anyone* and *anybody* are sometimes followed by plural references: "Anyone who makes a reservation is shown to their table as soon as they arrive." Strict grammarians try to enforce the use of singular pronoun referents with these and similar collective pronouns, but the fact is that for the past 400 years people have used *they, their,* and *them* to refer to *everyone* and *everybody*. Such usage is analogous with *any* in the sense of meaning "all."

Them and *their* are sanctioned with *any* by those who dislike the awkwardness of mouthfuls like *his or her*. Many also favor the utility of third-person plural to convey gender-free inclusiveness. These authorities include Val Dumond's *Elements of Nonsexist Usage* and *Webster's Dictionary of English Usage*, which cites Copperud, Flesch, and the *American Heritage Dictionary of the English Language*.

But Theodore Bernstein (*The Careful Writer*) gets the last word. He is characteristically pragmatic in suggesting that the best solution is often "to recognize the imperfections of the language and modify the wording" when being grammatical means sounding odd. Amen.

Dashes

If you're an editor or desktop publisher, you probably know the differences between hyphens and em dashes; maybe you even remember how to produce an em dash in your software without having to check your help screen. But what about en dashes? Where do they fit into the mix?

Standard stylebooks offer differing opinions on such questions. To maintain consistency and appropriate style in your publications, be sure to check your stylebook and expand on it if necessary to meet the needs of your particular environment.

These general guidelines are based on University of Chicago style:

- Use em dashes to mark an abrupt change in thought or construction or to replace parentheses.

- Use hyphens to break words at the ends of lines or to link the parts of ordinary compound words or unit modifiers when necessary for style or sense.

- Use en dashes to link ranges of continuous numbers, to join prefixes or suffixes to open compounds, to link a pair of open compounds, or to join two or more hyphenated compounds.

Mark hyphens, em dashes, and en dashes. (End-of-line word breaks don't count.)

1. The researchers-if I understand correctly-are working with laboratory-adapted strains of HIV-1.

2. The Arlington Street People's Assistance Network (A-SPAN) operates an emergency winter shelter, which serves 40-50 homeless persons a night.

3. Los Angeles-based writer Bebe Moore Campbell-author of *Your Blues Ain't Like Mine,* among other works-will be the featured speaker.

4. Why so many errors? It's because some careless writers fin-ish a story-or think they have finished it-and never look back.

5. Domestic violence, drug abuse, and budget shortfalls-these are some of the areas that the mayor-elect will face.

6. In the Fort Lauderdale-Pompano Beach market, real estate prices should be skyrocketing-or so I'm hoping.

7. A five-year-old tradition, the library's read-aloud programs are extremely popular. Call 555-1234 for information.

8. To close out the 1995-96 program year, the board will hold its annual meeting June 12-15, 1996. Be sure to complete both sides of the registration form on pages 7-8.

9. The 4,940-ton *Triton* boasted two water-cooled-nuclear-fueled reactors in her 450-foot hull.

10. For our non-CD-ROM users-you know who you are-other options are still available at prices ranging from $39.95-$289.95.

ANSWERS

1. Em, em, hyphen, hyphen.

   The researchers—if I understand correctly—are working with laboratory-adapted strains of HIV-1.

2. Hyphen, rewrite. Many people wouldn't use an en dash for what is really an approximation, not a true range.

   The Arlington Street People's Assistance Network (A-SPAN) operates an emergency winter shelter, which serves 40 or 50 homeless persons a night.

   or

   ...which serves from 40 to 50 homeless persons a night.

3. En, em, em.

   Los Angeles–based writer Bebe Moore Campbell—author of *Your Blues Ain't Like Mine*, among other works—will be the featured speaker.

4. Em, em.

   Why so many errors? It's because some careless writers finish a story—or think they have finished it—and never look back.

5. Em, hyphen.

   Domestic violence, drug abuse, and budget shortfalls—these are some of the areas that the mayor-elect will face.

6. En, em.

   In the Fort Lauderdale–Pompano Beach market, real estate prices should be skyrocketing— or so I'm hoping.

7. Hyphen, hyphen, hyphen, hyphen. (Since telephone numbers are not ranges of continuous numbers, Chicago style uses a hyphen; some other styles use an en dash instead.)

   A five-year-old tradition, the library's read-aloud programs are extremely popular. Call 555-1234 for information.

8. En, en, en.

   To close out the 1995–96 program year, the board will hold its annual meeting June 12–15, 1996. Be sure to complete both sides of the registration form on pages 7–8.

9. Hyphen, hyphen, comma, hyphen, hyphen. Yes, the en dash is in this case less preferable. Trick question.

> The 4,940-ton *Triton* boasted two water-cooled, nuclear-fueled reactors in her 450-foot hull.

10. En, hyphen (or en, in some styles), em, em, the word *to*. Another trick question! Although the en dash in a range of numbers or dates does mean *to*, careful editors avoid using the en dash with the word *from*—and, of course, they also use words in combinations such as *between 1992 and 1994* (Note: never *between...to*).

> For our non–CD-ROM users— you know who you are—other options are still available at prices ranging from $39.95 to $289.95.

—*Diane Ullius*

The Right WORD

more than/over

Despite a long and illustrious battle by grammarians to preserve what is in effect the "fewer, less" distinction—between countable numbers and gross amounts, respectively—all dictionaries, most commentators, and many excellent writers make no difference in the use of *more than* and *over*.

Copperud tells us that Ambrose Bierce, in *Write It Right*, "an extremely idiosyncratic guide" (they don't make them any more), was the first to attempt to impose a rule on these terms. In cases where the distinction is logical and obvious, writers will, of course, be perfectly correct to use the "fewer, less" rule, as for such statements as "I have waited more than three days for you to return my phone message" and "It's been over a year since I heard from my niece in Louisiana."

But someone who happens to say "I waited over two hours for the doctor" or "We've lived here for more than a year" is also correct, by most lights, and not to be frowned on merely from ambrosial habit.

Design and Typography

The Music Is Not in the Violin

And good design is not a default in the computer

Untrained designers are mistaken in thinking that the music is in the violin. The gap between good and bad design has grown because the person sitting at the computer is often not trained to be a designer. Persuasive, communicative design is difficult enough for trained professionals to achieve. Given the array of potential missteps the computer provides, what possibility of success does a design newcomer have?

It's tempting to change text size, mix several display typefaces, or alter the line spacing to stretch or compress type to fit the column, simply because the software makes it so easy to do. But the work of design is to compose elements so that they are maximally interesting and comprehensible to the reader. "Maximally interesting" does not mean *Hey! Wow! Pow! Zoom!* It means revealing the content of the story instantly and efficiently.

If your writing and editing result in publication, you are a *visual* communicator, just as a designer is, and your job is to make sure the message is read and absorbed, not just to fill in all the space. Editors, writers, and designers, regardless of title, can contribute to the effectiveness of the visual material presented to the reader. In short, if you lay out pages, you are a designer, and designers should

- create hierarchies,
- align similar elements,
- differentiate elements based on true differences, and
- select images based on their expository content.

What is good design?

> [Design] is the efficient means to an essentially utilitarian and only accidentally aesthetic end, for enjoyment of patterns is rarely the reader's chief aim.
>
> —*Stanley Morrison*

Good design is communicative design: the presentation of information in a clear, unselfconscious way. Design has evolved to reveal the relative importance of text elements and can affect a reader's first impression of whether the content is valuable—which is why bad design matters: People *do* judge a book by its cover (and a newsletter by its typeface, and an annual report by its graphs). The reader must not be aware of the act of reading or absorbing information.

To produce communicative design, you must put yourself in the reader's place. What will make someone want to read? Use well-written, informative headlines and subheads and select pictures that invite attention—not necessarily the prettiest ones. Don't go overboard with variety in an attempt to make the page look more interesting (in this regard, self-discipline is vital). Consider these four conventions:

- **Good design requires sharply defined visual relationships.** It requires the self-discipline to make similar elements consistently similar; after all, you can't make something pop out with importance if the surroundings are all busy being special. Good design requires breaking long blocks of copy into smaller, nonthreatening, undemanding segments. It requires different ways for the eye to enter copy easily, not just a linear path that begins with a title or a headline and abandons the reader to gray pages.

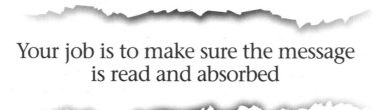

Your job is to make sure the message is read and absorbed

- **Good design requires a clear page structure.** Readers expect to glean information quickly, so scanning the page to find entrances must be effortless. Because the hierarchy of information must be neon bright, the designer must understand the material. Too much design is done without the designer's having read the material.

- **Organic design is achieved by listening to the material.** Beyond page structure, how can design support the substance of the message? Paying attention to the nature of the message allows pattern and shape to grow out of it and correspond in a seamless way to the content. Developing sensitivity to the way graphic elements can create sophisticated visual analogies requires a great deal of experience in handling type and imagery. It's a highly subjective learning process, but that's what makes visual communication rewarding and so much fun.

- **Use an external format, or grid, to organize material.** A grid is simply a plan that gives starting points for the placement of elements. Unfortunately, a relentless grid may be substituted for thinking, and the result is a suffocating sameness throughout a publication. Knowing when to break the grid is an essential aspect of having one in the first place.

The organic approach and the external format are different approaches that will yield different results. Driving on an interstate highway and driving on a parallel two-lane road are qualitatively different, yet both may lead to more or less the same destination. Neither route is intrinsically better, but at certain times one may be easier, faster, or more convenient. It's useful to remember that there is always an alternate design route.

Design is the cumulative effect of many decisions

It is interesting to discover [design] rules which are in use only because of tradition. It is also interesting to ponder the practical reasons for their perpetuation and to suggest remedies.

—Bradbury Thompson

Messages that require minimal exertion by the reader require design decisions that lead to a balanced, ordered page. Each decision may not be mightily significant by itself, but if two or three out of ten decisions made for a single page are bad—for example, too many characters per line, misalignment of headline and subhead, and too narrow an outside margin—the page will be sufficiently disturbed to slightly repel readers. Design must take into account the *cumulative* effect, for that is what the reader perceives.

The human eye looks for relationships and contrasts (similarities and differences); they are flip sides of the same coin. To create a relationship, all you need to do is have two or more elements—typographic, photographic, or illustrative—in agreement. They may be the same size, shape, color, or position, but their shared characteristics cause them to be perceived as related. An editor or designer who fully understands the importance of this idea will be able to make *any* group of closely connected elements function effectively. Establishing relationships requires making tough decisions so that *almost* similar elements appear to *be* similar—thus reducing visual conflict that distracts or confuses readers. A simplified page is an inviting one.

For **contrast**, one element must dominate another. To be an effective communicator, you must pay as much attention to each element as you do to its surroundings. When two or more elements exist in the same space, a relationship between them is created, and relationships perforce create hierarchy. Good design organizes information in a hierarchical fashion: Elements are organized to be seen in a specific order. The element that is seen first, called a focal point, dominates the page.

A basic contrast exists between type and imagery. Because type and imagery and, of course, space are the elements at a designer's disposal, designs are said to be either **type dominant** or **image dominant**. The topic will often suggest its own treatment. Great visual material lends itself to an image-dominant layout; a great headline or pull quote or a lot of copy suggests a type-dominant one.

Typography is the thread that binds

The typographer's one essential task is to interpret and communicate the text.

—*Robert Bringhurst*

Type holds a publication together. It's the constant, the thread leading from spread to spread. It's crucial to the life of your publication that type be presented consistently and in a way that makes sense to the reader. Steady use of a single typeface family unifies the pages of a publication. You'll tire of your typography long before your readers do. Develop a system that works for your particular needs and stick to it.

- **Restrict your use of typefaces.** Use the least possible number of typefaces, sizes, and weights to create clear differentiation and hierarchy, while still allowing for flexibility as unusual circumstances warrant. When in doubt, do *not* make a special change. Your readers are well served if you err on the side of typographic consistency. If your system is thoughtfully devised, the variations in your regular typographic arsenal will cover any situation. Making special changes or experimenting from page to page or issue to issue confuses and severely weakens the unity of your product. Minor typographic variations distract the reader from the content. And creating style exceptions takes a lot of time and invites formatting errors, as well.

- **Standardize columns and type specifications.** Column structure and text type together create a publication's personality. Taking a standard three-column format and shoving "interesting" display type at the tops of the columns results in **uninformed design**. Using a unique column structure so that all type looks distinctive to *this* publication is **informed design**.

  Flush-left/ragged-right type is an all-purpose setting in which word spacing is always consistent, regardless of the column width. Justified type, in contrast, achieves two smooth edges at the expense of even word spacing: Each line of type is sucked out to or shoved into the full measure, and word spacing is automatically inserted or deleted as needed. This is a minor distraction in lines that have at least 40 characters, but shorter justified lines can create horrible word spaces. You can avoid the problem by setting all type flush left/ragged right and allowing hyphenation. The idea that justified type looks more dignified is nonsense.

- **Catalog all essential typographic treatments** for the past year's worth of issues of your publication, and develop a system of text settings and column placements that can accommodate all those circumstances. It is extremely likely that future stories can be made to behave like one of those past articles.

- **Standardize type placement.** After you have decided on type specifications, determine exactly where every element will be placed, how far from the trim, how far from other type elements. Also decide how much space there will be between picture and caption, between headline and subhead, between subhead and text. This space management makes your publication look clear and well organized. It will make readers trust and value the content.

Take off the blinders and look around

Design is not the abundance of simplicity. It is the absence of complexity.

—Anonymous

Design choices are too often based on a narrow horizon of possibilities. They tend to be bounded by our past decisions, our second-guessing of what others involved with the project will allow or like, the level of our self-confidence in doing something new and risky, and, perhaps most important, our sense of what is possible. We visual communicators need to widen the horizon of typographic and page design possibilities.

Take off the blinders. Inspiration for interesting typography can be found in many places. Two of the best sources are books: Carl Dair's *Design with Type* and Erik Spiekermann's *Rhyme & Reason: A Typographic Novel.* But don't look at type alone for ideas. Look at other objects and try to imagine various kinds of visual relationships. Galleries and museums can help you see common things afresh. Experiment. Ideas that may not work at all now can be sifted and refined and lead to ones that work well later.

Good design is available to everyone, but no machine can produce it automatically, even with a big budget. There's music in the violin, all right, but it springs from the hands, the thought, and the imagination of the player.

—Alex White

Six Rules for Jumping Newsletter Stories

Take your readers with you

There's a journalistic trend toward printing longer stories, but careful writing and editing are wasted if the reader doesn't stay with a narrative that jumps pages (that is, continues after pages of intervening copy). Here are a few suggestions for making it less likely your readers will use the continuation as an excuse to jump ship:

- Run at least four column inches of a story before you jump it. Give the reader a chance to become interested before asking for a leap of faith to another page.

- Jump at least six column inches of a story to avoid a sense of letdown. The reader ought to feel it's been worth the trouble to make the jump.

- Jump stories once—twice at most—if at all possible. Cut copy or redo the layout until it *is* possible. Remember that browsers may start in the middle or at the end of a story; if you point them in conflicting directions to continue, you may lose them entirely.

- Handle jumps in a consistent manner from article to article within an issue with clear *continued on page...* and *continued from page...* lines.

- Avoid filling a page exclusively with several runovers—they'll look like the leftovers they are. That's not what the term "refrigerator journalism" means. (It means printing short items likely to be clipped and saved.)

- Avoid jumping pages backward into the publication from the back cover. It's a trendy technique found in magazines (and the *New York Post* sports section), but many readers say they hate it—it feels like the trick it is.

—Linda B. Jorgensen

On Breeding Hardy Hybrids

We just plain love this book

For those of you who don't want to read all of this review: Go buy *The Non-Designer's Design Book: Design and Typographic Principles for the Visual Novice* by Robin Williams. You'll love it and you'll learn from it.

Many designer-writers over the past few years have grappled with the problem posed by easy access to page layout and typography software, trying to stem the tide of undistinguished (and sometimes downright dreadful) pages pouring out of laser printers all over the world. Most of their books are helpful in pointing out and illustrating good and not-so-good design, but almost without exception, the reader picks up a distinct undertone: "If you're going to do design, darn it, act like a designer!" We are told to cultivate the "eye" of a visual artist, to seek inspiration, to experiment. This is something like asking a kid who just finished her first piano lesson to do an improvisation on a Thelonius Monk tune. You really can't operate on anything close to an abstract, creative level without a mastery of the basic tools. Even the length of some of these books assumes a level of commitment to learning design that, let's face it, a lot of people don't have.

In her little book, Robin Williams recognizes that many folks who work, maybe even every day, with powerful design tools *don't want to be designers*. What they do want is to be able to lay out a sensible, good-looking page, or brochure, or whatever. So Williams organizes her book around basic concepts that are the underpinning of all good design. She expresses them in clear, concrete terms. She demonstrates them with relevant, real-life examples. And she does it all with charming wit and consistent good humor.

One section of the book explores basic design principles. After a thoroughly illustrated discussion, each principle is encapsulated in a one-page summary that covers "The basic purpose," "How to get it," and "What to avoid."

Another section presents the underlying concepts that govern designing with type, with an emphasis on the issues involved in combining more than one typeface on a page (Williams's eight pages on that subject alone are worth the price of the book).

A special treat can be found in the examples of text layouts that, instead of the normal "greeking," use passages of "Anguish Languish"—a wonderful invention that I had forgotten—English-twisting versions of fairy tales and nursery rhymes with names like "Ladle Rat Rotten Hut" and "Guilty Looks Enter Three Bears." They just beg to be read and laughed at, aloud. Though I can't remember where I first read these stories, I learned from the credits that they were the creation of Howard L. Chace.

Scattered through the book are "Little Quizzes" that allow readers to test their understanding as they go along. Also included are a short annotated bibliography and a helpful list of all the typefaces used in the book, by categories that include the font vendor.

Underlying all this is an approach that sets Williams apart from most designer-writers. The concept, which will be dear to the hearts of word people foundering in the graphic world, is that things remain unknown to us until we give them a name. In Williams's words, "Once you can name something, you're conscious of it. You have power over it. You own it. You're in control."

Even with no aspirations to a career in graphic design, the average desktopper can communicate more effectively by cultivating "visual literacy." Rather than insisting that the visual and verbal remain two separate mental neighborhoods, Williams provides techniques that promote the integration of these sometimes very disparate modes of perception and expression, thereby allowing one to enhance the other. This is an important phase in the evolution of an all-around professional, rather than an editor or writer who is also a not-very-good designer.

Although there will always be a need for the highly developed skills and special genius of the trained graphic designer and the professional wordsmith, for most of us, cross training is the order of the day. The challenge of this era is in developing strong hybrids to respond to the specific needs of particular situations, rather than publishing mongrels with a motley assortment of generalized characteristics.

—*Jayne O. Sutton*

The Non-Designer's Design Book: Design and Typographic Principles for the Visual Novice by Robin Williams (ISBN 1-56609-159-4, 1994, $14.95, 144 pp.) is published by Peachpit Press, 2414 Sixth Street, Berkeley, CA 94710, 800-283-9444.

A Design Primer for Editors

Good design is far from being just decoration

Editors who are faced with the challenge of working without a designer to make text inviting to the reader need to shift gears in order to concentrate on the placement of words on the page—rather than on their meaning. Even editors who work with designers should know how to analyze how the text relates to graphic elements such as pictures, headings, columns, and margins. This interaction of design elements with words creates the distinctive personality of a page.

In the foreword to my do-it-yourself guide, *Book Design & Production for the Small Publisher,* award-winning designer Steve Renick makes the point that to impose style upon any manuscript without knowledge of the nature of the manuscript is a mistake. Style that denies or overshadows the content is at best decorative—and good design is definitely not decoration.

Ideally, authors and editors, who are most familiar with the content, should have a voice in judging whether a completed design serves the writing and intended audience well. In many cases, however, publishers make the final design decisions. But editors who develop an informed eye will be able to spot trouble early and carve a niche for themselves in the design process.

Uniformity of design reassures readers

Uniformity of design (not the same as monotony) contributes to an overall impression of excellence and tells readers, "We know what we're doing." Take your favorite reference book off the shelf and flip through it to check for the following signs of a unified design:

- An invisible line indicates that all top lines on a page of text begin at the same place.

- Margins are generous and the type is easy to read—not too tightly or too loosely spaced on the lines, or so black that the page appears heavy and forbidding.

- Illustrations are cropped to enhance their images and are positioned carefully, with captions as necessary, where they can complement the copy.

- The paper has been chosen with care—thick enough so that the ink does not show through, and not textured if photographs are used. The paper used for most fiction and nonfiction books is a warm, creamy white; a brighter white is often chosen for scholarly textbooks.

Editors should focus on design fundamentals

Learning to think of facing pages as a unit is a good place to start. A basic rule of design is to plan two facing pages as a single spread instead of as separate units. What happens visually on the right page should balance or complement what happens on the left. The same principle can be applied to a folded flier: When viewed open, all panels should create a harmonious whole, with the margins acting as a unifying factor. Here are some other basic design considerations.

Image area and margins. The two major elements on a page are the image area (total area occupied by headings, text blocks, illustrations, etc.) and the margins. Margins should not be thought of simply as the area where there is no text. They need to be carefully planned. A good balance is two-thirds text to one-third white space.

To figure your margins, first decide on a size for your text block. Readability tests indicate that the ideal length for a line of type is 60 to 70 characters (including punctuation marks and spaces). Although typefaces vary in thickness, this rule of thumb usually translates into a line about 4¼ to 4½ inches long.

For this reason, text on an 8½-by-11-inch page should be broken into two or more columns, unless you use large type with additional interline spacing, as many large-print and children's books do. Alternatively, the text column could be approximately 4¼ inches wide, with a column beside it for illustrations, subheads, or callouts.

Traditionally, the margins closest to the binding are narrower than the outer ones (though no smaller than ⅝ inch in a book of average size and more for thicker books), while the margin on the bottom of the page is deeper than the one at the top. Once the margins are established, they should not be violated—not even by a caption or footnote—except for page numbers and illustrations that bleed (that is, extend to the very edge of the page).

Baselines and subheads. Baselines (imaginary lines on which words of text sit) on one page should align with baselines on the opposite page, as well as on subsequent double-page spreads. Keep this in mind when determining your spacing above and below heads and subheads. Allowing your computer to align vertically (i.e., to stretch or shrink interline spacing so that the text fills the image area from top to bottom) may be a good choice for a single-page flier or a newsletter but not for a book.

Subheads should have more space above them than beneath them in order to emphasize their relationship with the paragraphs that follow.

When subheads have equal space above and below, they tend to float, with no apparent connection to the body text.

Justification. A major design consideration is whether to justify the text. Justified text (with all lines ending at the same sharp edge) creates one image, while ragged text (with uneven lines) creates a very different one. Unless great care is given to the spacing *within* these lines, however, either justified or ragged text can be visually disastrous and play havoc with a reader's pace.

Justified and ragged text create very different images

To justify text, computer software stretches and reduces spacing between letters and words. Sometimes the result is unnatural spacing. Check each line for extremes of too much or too little space, and adjust manually if necessary (and possible).

Ragged text is even more demanding. One way to achieve balance is to decide on a minimum line length—perhaps ½-inch shorter than the text area—and then to look at every line carefully. Add hyphenation where possible, or edit judiciously.

Color of type. If you look at a page of text through half-closed eyes or hold it upside down, you can see what traditional typesetters call *color of type,* that is, the overall effect created by a combination of type styles, type sizes, word spacing, and line spacing. A trained eye sees this combination as tones of gray. The more evenly balanced these tones are, the more harmonious the page.

End-of-line hyphenation. According to one school of thought, using ragged text means that you need not (or should not) hyphenate words at the ends of lines. Rather than accepting this dictum in blind faith, however, look at published examples through your newly awakened designer's eyes and decide for yourself how hyphenation (or the lack of it) affects the appearance of the page. What happens to the color of type? Nonhyphenated text is likely to be an ungainly mass of disparate gaps. By hyphenating line endings we are better able to control the balance of text and white space.

Keeping these guidelines in mind, study a variety of books and look at all the brochures and catalogs that arrive unbidden in the mail; develop your sense of design by using it. Soon you'll be able to distinguish good design from mediocre, and then you'll be better able to tell your designer what you're looking for. Perhaps you'll even be on your way to creating fine examples of your own, if that's within the scope of your job. Since form follows function, a strong case can be made that editors—by definition close to the content—should learn to be apt contributors to the design process.

—*Malcolm E. Barker*

if/whether

Is there really a distinction between *whether* and *if?* Most authorities say there is. Theodore Bernstein in *The Careful Writer* says that *whether* is generally "the normal word used to introduce a noun clause." *Whether* should always be used to introduce a noun clause serving as a subject: "Whether politicians can agree on a way to reduce crime is doubtful." But *if* can be and commonly is used interchangeably with *whether* to introduce noun clauses that follow verbs such as *ask, doubt, hear, learn*, and *know*. Either word is acceptable in this sentence: "Do researchers know (if/whether) a virus causes the common cold?"

A note of caution: To avoid confusion, reserve *if* for expressing conditional statements ("If this is true, then that...."). "Tell me if I have spinach between my teeth" can have a conditional sense—"Should that ever be the case, tell me"—as well as a true-or-false sense: "In case that is true now, tell me." *Whether*, which implies *or not*, is clearer in the true-or-false case.

By the way, saying *whether or not* is usually unnecessary, although it has been considered acceptable for more than 300 years. The one case where adding *or not* is required is with the use of *whether* to introduce a noun clause that functions as a sentence adverb: "Whether or not you agree with my opinions, I have the right to voice them."

Choosing a Designer

What should you look for when reviewing an artist's portfolio?

Question: I'm the manager of the publications department in a growing consulting firm. Until recently, we've never needed outside designers, but as our company's graphics needs become more sophisticated, I've felt the need to look beyond the skills of our in-house staff. I have no graphic arts or design training. How do I review a designer's portfolio and know which designer will do the type of work I need?

Answer: Reviewing a graphic artist's portfolio can be difficult for managers who aren't artists themselves and haven't had first-hand experience with the work. As you begin your search, first ask for recommendations from professional acquaintances whose publications you admire. Check with local chapters of graphic arts groups, or look for potential designers in regional directories like the *Creative Sourcebook*, a guide to graphic artists, photographers, printers, video production companies, media consultants, and related services in the Washington-Baltimore area. Then use the following tips to help you evaluate an applicant's portfolio and determine whether the designer's skills match your needs.

- Talk with the applicant before the interview and describe the types of work you will be looking for. For example, if you want to see only computer-generated samples, the designer may choose to leave watercolor renderings at home. If variety is important, give the applicant the opportunity to present a full range of samples. Accomplished graphic artists have more samples than they could possibly bring to an interview; give your applicant the chance to show you the samples most appropriate to your needs.

- Let the applicant tell you something about each piece, and then ask questions. When John Jones says, "I produced this brochure when I worked for the Smith Corporation," ask for details. Did he produce the entire piece from start to finish, or was he part of a team? Did he design the piece, or did he produce mechanicals from a designer's comprehensive layouts? Did he do the illustrations himself or use clip art? Did he manage the project? Did he meet with the client, or did someone else get the specifics and give him instructions? Did he work with the printer? Get a clear understanding of the applicant's role on the project for each piece you review.

- Ask questions to ensure that the applicant actually produced the presented samples. For example, you might ask, "How did you create that shading effect?" "What guidelines did the client give for that design?"

"I'm not familiar with that software package—what else can it do?" There is no way to determine conclusively whether the applicant is honestly representing his or her skills, but any hesitation about details should raise a red flag. Check references thoroughly to get a more complete picture.

- Find out how much latitude the applicant had on each project. If the colors of a particular piece seem like poor choices, remember that the client may have insisted on them. Applicants frequently offer disclaimers about some pieces in their portfolio: "I'm proud of this design, but unfortunately the printer didn't do a good job."

- Give the applicant feedback on the portfolio. Don't hesitate to comment on samples that are particularly impressive. If a sample is impressive but does not reflect your needs, say so: "Your illustrations are beautiful, but unfortunately we don't get to do much of that kind of work."

- Remember your goals as you look at the portfolio. If you are looking for a pasteup artist, don't hire a person solely because of his or her beautiful watercolor paintings. If you need a designer, don't hire a person solely because of his or her excellent technical illustrations. Look for samples that demonstrate the skills you need.

—*Robin A. Cormier*

Editors and Designers: Talking the Same Language

What to do when give-and-take becomes tug-of-war

Question: As a marketing specialist in my company's corporate communications department, I wear many hats. One of my responsibilities is to serve as editor/production coordinator on company publications such as direct mail packages, the in-house newsletter, and our annual report. On each piece, I work directly with a designer from our graphics department. I've worked with a number of different designers, and I have the same problem each time: I can't seem to get my ideas across about the look we're aiming for.

When we start a project, I usually have a mental picture of the finished piece, but I'm almost always disappointed with the comps I get back. I mark them up and send them back to the designer, but it usually takes several rounds of revisions before we close in on an appropriate design. This process is very time-consuming, and it's frustrating for everyone concerned.

From what I hear from others in my field, this is a common problem. I think it has to do with the fact that "word people" and designers just don't speak the same language. How can I ensure that my ideas are incorporated without alienating the designers in the process?

Answer: The age-old battle between the "word people" and the "picture people" continues, even though technology has blurred the distinction somewhat. Now more than ever, both editors and designers have to be "bilingual." Although there will always be some give-and-take in this process, there are several steps you can take to improve communication and thereby streamline your production process.

First, be sure that design is really what you want. Are you asking the designer to use your ideas as a starting point and apply creativity, or are you simply asking that your exact specifications be executed? If the idea you have is very specific, right down to typefaces and column widths, you're asking only for layout. Be sure the designer knows how much latitude you're allowing. Chances are you feel stronger about some of your ideas than others; be sure the designer knows which elements are "must haves" and which you intend simply as suggestions.

Before you meet with the designer, put instructions in writing. You may want to modify these instructions once you and the designer discuss the project, but writing down your initial thoughts will force you to think through the details of what you are asking for. Having a written list of what you and the designer agree to will give you both something to refer to when you review the comps.

In addition to giving specific instructions, be sure that the designer understands the overall goals of the product. To develop an appropriate design, the designer must know the purpose of the piece (for instance, to introduce a new product or service), the intended audience (existing clients, prospects, stockholders, and so on), and any other factors that affect the design (such as the fact that a brochure will be the first in a series, or that it will be used in conjunction with another piece and must be compatible in appearance).

To further illustrate what you believe to be an appropriate look for your department's publications, keep a collection of publications similar to those your department produces. When you meet with the designer to discuss your ideas, bring samples of the look you're after as well as those you think would be inappropriate. Point out the specific elements you like or dislike on each piece, and explain why you think they are effective or ineffective.

But even when editors and designers communicate well with one another, revisions are almost inevitable. When you review the designer's comp, go over it together; don't just send back a markup. Talk about the problems in a constructive, noncritical way. Remarks like "This layout just isn't working" don't tell a designer a thing. Instead, make your comments as specific as possible: "This boxed text is the most important element on the page, so it needs to stand out more. Can we try a different typeface, or maybe less shading in the box?" The more you tell the designer about what you want, the better the chances that you'll get what you have in mind. On occasion, you may get back exactly what you asked for and not like it at all. When this happens, be sure to acknowledge that you changed your mind.

Even after you've taken these steps to ensure clear communication, you may still experience some conflicts. There may be times when the designer doesn't feel that your ideas can be executed in a way that will yield a good design. When this happens, it is important to respect the designer's professional opinion. If design is indeed what you want, designers must have the freedom to propose alternatives rather than just to execute exactly what you specify. If the project is to be a true team effort, you have to be prepared to let go of your own visions occasionally and let the designer try other ideas instead.

As with any project that requires teamwork, good communication is the key to success when it comes to design. Word people and picture people can work well together when expectations and requirements are clear.

—Robin A. Cormier

'Doing Art' before You've Learned How

Pursue artful design and you'll find it

When I first read John Keats' "Ode on a Grecian Urn" in high school, I was struck by one of those thunderbolts of inspiration. Now I had the clues to the search for what I thought I had to find: "Beauty is truth, truth beauty." Years later, I've learned in my publications design corner of the "art" world that there is indeed an intimate relationship between the effectiveness of a message and the "beauty" of the design.

Those who take on the role of publications designer (by choice or necessity) without formal training in the "art part" may worry about their work being "beautiful" enough, but first they need to learn how to impose structure with appropriate enhancements. A well-structured book-length publication can communicate a complex message very effectively, but poor structure can make even a short sales brochure hard going. Here are some guidelines for new designers:

Simple type treatments work best. Playing with the gee-whiz tools that most desktop publishing and word processing programs offer is the first temptation of the inexperienced designer. But even experienced designers take the risk that bold treatments will call attention to themselves rather than to the message; the risk is greater for those just starting out. Splashy fireworks are fine for the Fourth of July, but not for an annual report—unless it's for a fireworks company.

Using elaborate fonts and special effects costs more and can get in the reader's way. Strikingly clean type gains a reader's attention better than overdesign every time, and consistent treatment for levels of structure keeps it. Typographical beauty creates a psychological link between the reader and the text: This may sound like poetry, but beauty has very real consequences in the brain of the beholder.

The look of the page affects the reader. Page design is a matter of forming a harmonious whole out of disparate graphic and text elements. You should try to create a work of graceful proportions that will be a pleasure to read, and resist the urge to use all the space on a page for "useful" information. A page crammed full betrays a determination—understandable but counterproductive—to cram the reader full of information. If the reader resists absorbing the "truth" of a message, your publication isn't effective, no matter how many words you fit on the page or how crafty your design.

Your job is to keep an eye on shape, space, and flow as well as function. Although it's an intangible thing, perhaps as much as 50 percent of the pleasing impact a page makes on first sight is due to the favorable proportion of margins to text. Look at books whose layout you admire to see how their designers used margins and other white space to good advantage. Look for what's not there!

Use graphics sparingly. Sidebars and illustrations should elucidate, not compete with the main text. Nor should they be shoehorned into the text. When you set them off, use text-on-tints and shaded boxes sparingly. Text over color or gray boxes can be harder to read. Black text on a lightly screened background effectively emphasizes short passages; text boxes featuring big blocks of colored text on a colored, screened background are cruel to readers.

Brochures and newsletters allow more freedom than other publications, but even for them you should balance artwork with text blocks and white space on a page. When designing with images, follow a few simple rules:

- For books or reports, keep graphics at the top of the page or at the bottom—avoid putting them in the middle of a large page with text flowing randomly on all sides.

- You can set images creatively, but follow an effective model (perhaps one from a graphic design idea book), and be sure to step back and review full spreads to see whether facing pages balance or complement each other.

I've learned as I've chased my way around the urn that Keats was right: Almost all we need to know is that beauty has a kind of truth all its own. Pursue artful design—the kind that directly unites readers with the message—no matter how new you are to the craft. That's the best way to learn artistry. It's certainly not a hopeless pursuit. Aristotle put it best: "For the things we have to learn before we can do them, we learn by doing them."

—Kathryn Hall

Can One Picture Be Worth More Than a Thousand Words?

Graphics can replace words, but they should
make the message clearer

It's no wonder that graphics have become an essential part of written communications. Today, with even the most basic PC or Mac, almost anyone can easily and inexpensively become a novice graphic artist. Graphics are everywhere—in newspapers, books, magazines, journals, newsletters, advertisements, and technical reports. The painstakingly edited manuscript, an endangered species, is being replaced by the quickly produced, concise documents demanded by economics and an entire generation raised on visual media.

The abundance of graphics is a mixed blessing. We are deluged with graphics of all kinds—accurate and inaccurate, attractive and ugly, helpful and useless, important and irrelevant. Good graphics are excellent tools for communication because readers often acquire and retain information more quickly from graphics than from text. At the same time, a poorly designed graphic can convey incorrect or distorted information.

Regardless of your job title, as a publications professional the probability is high that you will be asked to plan, create, or edit graphics, or at the least define which graphics should be included in a document. These days, the distinct identities of editorial professionals are irreversibly blurred. Just as writers are likely to find that they are also editors and desktop publishers, editors are likely to find that their responsibility has been broadened to include evaluating sophisticated graphics. Designers or desktop publishers not only lay out text and tables but are also expected to produce a wide variety of illustrations using one or several of the graphics software packages on the market. What principles should guide you as you strive to accommodate the demands for more and more graphics?

Planning for graphics

First, remember that graphics should enhance the written message. To be sure that they do, here are some questions to ask:

- Who are the potential readers?
- Why will they want or need to read the document?
- What information do you want them to get from the document?
- Is this a throw-away piece, a reference work, or something in between?

Once you know the audience and the content, you will have other questions about how a document should be presented or, more precisely, how specific data should be presented within the document. Should a graphic or graphics

- present a broad trend or a snapshot of more detailed data?
- replace text that contains the same data or supplement the text with more data?
- serve as the "grabber" or illustrate ideas within the document?

It can be a challenge to select appropriate graphics among the many kinds available: **tables**, **charts**, **maps**, **photos**, **drawings**, and **cartoons**. This discussion is illustrated with examples of graphics that are less than successful. They make the point that different kinds of relational data are served better by some graphics than others. Software cannot magically create useful graphics, although it readily creates handsome ones. In fact, some of the most impressive looking graphics are meaningless because they obscure the data. Even if you've determined that your readers are intractable information snackers who resist all but the catchiest "infographics," accuracy and ease of interpretation must be part of the picture.

Tables

Text tables can summarize or replace many pages of explanation; data tables can buttress the case presented in the text. Your word processing program probably contains a "tables" function that also allows you to create rows and columns and even do simple math. Or you can use a spreadsheet program to create a separate file containing tables; many systems will import spreadsheets into a word processing file. (See "Editing a Table," page 257, and "Editing a Word Table...," page 260.)

Charts

Tables of numbers are the basis for most charts. Spreadsheet programs have print-to-screen choices that allow you to preview various styles before making final decisions about the "look" of a chart. If you are producing a draft, simple charts without enhancements will suffice. However, if you must create camera-ready art, you will add design elements. There are many types of charts: **pie**, **bar**, **scatter point**, **line**, **organizational**, and **flow** charts are the basic ones.

To pick the best means of displaying your data graphically, keep clearly in mind the correlations you are trying to demonstrate, the relative emphasis you want to make on some elements of information rather than on others, and the need to limit extraneous variables that will make the graphic too complex.

Pie. A pie chart is used to show proportional relationships. Keep the number of segments to a minimum because the greater the number, the harder it is to compare the slices of the pie. Exploded pies show one element removed a bit from the circle to show emphasis. Three-dimensional (3-D) pies and pies showing perspective are interesting, but they can be misleading and difficult to read. (In fact, 3-D charts frequently are impossible to untangle.)

Bar. Bar charts show trends or compare quantities. Items being measured can be arranged alphabetically, in ascending or descending order, sequentially, or in other ways. Bars can contain a number of different elements distinguished by colors or shading. Adding a three-dimensional perspective can change the impact of these charts and distort data. Too many elements can reduce the readability and overall impact.

Scatter point. All data points are plotted on an x-y axis to show trends or patterns. Various elements can be shown by using different graphic shapes for the points.

Line. Line charts, also known as fever charts, are used to show change over time. Color or solid and broken lines can identify several categories of data. Axes should be clearly identified, and the labels should be clear and accurate. Too many lines or a background grid can make line charts impossible to interpret.

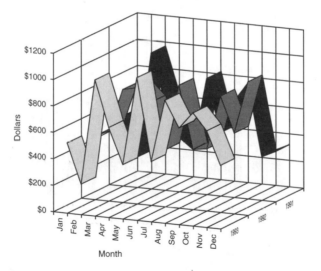

3-D Line Chart. Floating ribbons look very spiffy, no question. But because they are floating, the reader has a difficult time tying the plotted points on the ribbon to either axis. The 3-D view, too, distorts the depiction of the data—is the front or the back edge of the ribbon the plot point? Don't let your computer do this to you.

253

Organizational. These show the hierarchy of an organization or project. Elements are combined so that the relationships between people or departments are clear.

Flow. Movement from one point to another (for processes or steps) or over time (for milestones, like triangles in PERT charts) is shown.

Maps

Creating and producing useful, accurate maps requires specialized skills. People usually hire cartographers to produce maps, although programs exist for creating and modifying simple maps electronically.

Photos, drawings, and cartoons

Ideas need to be roughed out before you set up a photo shoot or ask someone to create original drawings and cartoons—this is subjective territory, and the graphic concept matters as much as technical execution. Remember that most all other art is copyrighted. The publishers of PhotoCD and stock photo books negotiate rights to use the images they have created. Electronic clip art is available, though it often ends up being picked and placed carelessly.

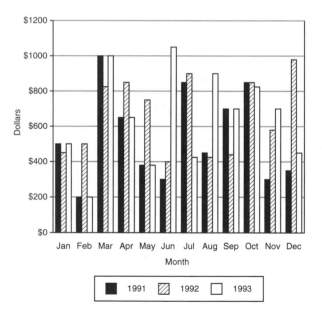

Bar Chart. The problem here is that each slot on the *x* axis contains three sets of figures; this makes it possible to compare June sales figures over three years, but what about trying to gather an impression of first quarter sales for 1992? Though the chart *appears* to be graphing sales figures over time, this really is simply 12 separate bar charts grouped together.

Controlling graphic quality

Finally, remember that, like text, graphics need to be critically reviewed and proofread carefully.

Editors must evaluate graphics for accuracy, relevance, clarity, and appearance. The goal should be to help the reader assimilate the content quickly. Ask these questions when reviewing graphics:

1. Is the information correct and consistent with the text?

2. Can the reader interpret the graphic without referring back to the text?

3. Does the graphic clearly support the writer's points?

4. Can the reader immediately grasp the meaning?

A chart is only as good as its data: If the data are murky or equivocal, the graphic will be too (unless selective data are used to produce a distorted picture, a not uncommon ploy to which editors should be alert). The graphic and the text should match, and the text should refer the reader to illustrations. Graphics should be as close to relevant text as the layout allows. The graphics should be simple—with no excessive or unnecessary elements—and the proportions should be constant. Finally, labels, captions, titles, legends, keys, and footnotes should be clear and accurate.

Publications professionals need to learn to think visually as well as verbally—to think in terms of images as well as words—and develop an eye for graphic elements. Edward Tufte's books *The Visual Display of Quantitative Information* and *Envisioning Information* are filled with several hundred displays of complex data and offer general principles governing excellence in the design, editing, analysis, and critique of information graphics.

Can one picture equal a thousand words?

Probably not. But it's not a contest, after all, and I do not mean to suggest that good writing is obsolete. Graphics, however, can give readers a quicker and more lasting impression of some ideas than many formidable lines of text. Graphics can enhance the appearance of a document and make it likelier that busy professionals will read it. Good graphics can convey substance in a manner that adds to an author's credibility and makes the writing memorable.

Even the Russian novelist Turgenev, a man of more than a few words, admitted, "A picture shows me at a glance what it takes dozens of pages of a book to expound." If you have been putting off thinking about ways your documents could be improved, why not resolve to increase your use of graphics? You'll be more creative, have some fun, and most probably please your readers.

—Claire W. Kincaid

Pull Quotes Enhance Newsletter Layout

These 'teasers' can lighten text-heavy pages and attract readers

Pull quotes (also known as callouts or liftouts) can help advertise a good story and make pages look less gray. Lift a sentence or a direct quote verbatim from a story, or paraphrase a significant or interesting statement. That is, a pull quote can be the story's author speaking or someone else in the story speaking. Here's what pull quotes do:

- Draw attention to an interesting point or to the thesis
- Invite readers to dip into an article
- Make the layout more appealing

Place a pull quote where it will be attractive to browsers but not distracting to serious readers. *Avoid* putting quotes at the very top or bottom of a page—use them as embedded entry points. (Magazines can break this rule but newsletters shouldn't.) Don't shoehorn a long quote into the middle of a short paragraph, and be sure to leave enough white space between body copy and the quote—above and below it.

Pull quotes can be quite simple or play a large graphic role with oversize quotation marks, color, or rules. Pick a consistent style that stands out from body copy (in a different size or type style) yet is consonant with the other layout components—pull quotes shouldn't compete with copy.

Slight edits are often necessary to keep a quote from seeming pedantic, incomplete, or odd, but don't frustrate readers by making them hunt in vain for more about the statement that led them into the article. Keep punctuation and shifts in tense to a minimum, and avoid using ellipsis dots or adding bracketed comments that break the impact of the quote. It's better to use no quote at all than a dull quote.

Pull quotes are a teaser, so keep them fairly short, especially in columned publications. Especially in a scholar's margin, a long, stringy pull quote is a mistake—the lines are uncomfortably short and give the impression someone's afraid of leaving a little white space alone.

One last point: If the quote is a direct statement, it requires attribution. A name and perhaps a brief identification can be set in smaller type, following an em dash, on a separate line.

—Linda B. Jorgensen

Editing a Table

A graphic is only as useful as it is accurate

We took the following table from the *Mini-Digest of Education Statistics 1994* (National Center for Education Statistics, U.S. Department of Education, Washington, DC) and introduced several errors. Try to identify errors and missing or confusing information. A discussion of the problems to be resolved follows.

Table 18—Proficiency of 17-yr.-olds in reading, by selected characteristics: 1971, 1981, and 1992

Selected characteristics of students	1971	1980	1992
Total	285.2	285.5	289.7
Sex:			
Male	278.9	281.86	284.2
Female	291.9	289.2	295.7
Race/ethnicity:	291.4	292.8	297.4
White	238.7	243.1	260.63
Black	—[1]	261.4	271.2
Hispanic			
Control of school			
public	—[1]	284.4	287.8
private	—[1]	298.4	309.6
Parents' Education Level:			
Not graduated high school	261.3	262.1	70.8
Gradauted high school	283	277.5	280.5
Post-high school	302.2	298.9	298.6

* Data not available

Discussion of errors and problems

Tables are very useful in that they present more data than would be digestible in running text and provide visual interest as well. But tables are hard to create. There are so many ways to go wrong—from simple inconsistency of format to puzzling wording. The table presented here has a variety of problems. First we'll discuss the format from top to bottom, then we'll look at the information presented and comment on the effectiveness of the table as a whole.

Format

- At the top is the table number followed by the title. There are as many ways to style the table number and title as there are editors and publications; this one is perfectly acceptable. A possible oddity is the line length: Usually the title is the same width as the whole table. And since yr. is the only abbreviation in the entire table, it would probably be better to spell it out.

- In the "stub" (far left) column are four main divisions that should be similar in punctuation, capitalization, and indention scheme. Note the inconsistencies: The second main stub should be flush left, the third needs a colon, and the third and fourth are inconsistent in cap style. (You'll have to decide between caps and lowercase and sentence-style capitalization. The other main stubs offer no help because they are single words or the equivalent.)

- The indented "substubs" must also be in consistent format; the third group (under Control of school) needs initial capital letters. The group under the last main stub is consistent but hard to read; we'd prefer that the runover lines be indented further, and obviously we'd fix the typo, too.

- The "field" (the actual data) is in three columns nicely aligned on the decimal points, and the em dashes fill the cells for which no data are available—good! (The dashes could be aligned on the right of the column if you prefer, but be sure the superscripts extend past the right side of the column if you choose right alignment.) The individual cells are nearly all three-digit numbers with a single-place decimal; those that are not should be looked at carefully. Near the bottom of the 1971 column, you might be tempted to add a zero so 283 will look like the other numbers, but don't. Adding a zero would falsify the data by saying tabulation of the results (or the experiment) was carried out to that decimal place. Query the lack of the zero instead. Consider rounding off the two numbers that have two-place decimals, and query the 70.8 in the 1992 column—it's just too different from the rest of the data to go unverified.

- Alignment is important in all tables. Note that the 1992 column heading aligns on the right side of its column; the other two align on the left. In this table, it's a subtle difference, but if the numbers in the columns were longer, the inconsistency would be more noticeable. The cells in the "Race/ethnicity" group are misaligned; apparently all nine numbers should move down one line (note that no data follow the other main stubs). In the last group, placement of the data line for a two-line stub is inconsistent. For this table either style would be fine. If the stub or the information in one of the cells ran to several lines, we would insist on first-line alignment.

- The footnote that explains the dashes has an asterisk, but its callouts in the table field are superscript 1. This kind of inconsistency is typical in tables as is having footnotes without callouts and vice versa. We would also expect to find the footnote under the base rule, but its placement here could be the publication's preferred style.

Effectiveness

If you revise the table according to the preceding discussion you will have a table that looks nice and is consistent, but will its meaning be clear? Looking good isn't enough. Does the title reflect the actual information presented in the stubs and column heads? No, the years are not the same. Does the center column present data for 1980 or for 1981 per the title? The column head for the stubs does mirror the table title, although we'd delete "of students" because "Control of school" is not a characteristic of students.

We also wonder if the substubs in the last group could be worded more simply: maybe "Did not graduate from high school," "High school graduate," "Some post-high school" or maybe express these categories in years of education: "Fewer than 12 years," "12 years," "More than 12 years."

The "Total" line is also puzzling: total of what? The columns would obviously not add up to those numbers (although they might be averages). A larger issue is the nature of the numbers themselves. No unit of measure is given: Are they percentages? Scores on a test? According to the table title, they are indicators of proficiency, but it is not clear exactly how. Perhaps they are average scores on a test that has 400 possible points. All we can do is compare the numbers with each other and note the differences or similarities across the three years in the column heads; what the numbers mean outside the context of the table is never explained, and that's essential if the table is to communicate its data clearly.

—*Patricia Caudill*

Editing a Word Table for Less Space and More Sense

Tabular format riddled with errors can't do what it does best:
organize information

Tables can represent details that would require several paragraphs and hundreds of words of text to describe; skillfully handled, they increase the authority and usefulness of any document. Rather than repeating the text, tables are generally used to present full data in a format that invites readers to compare kinds of information. But poorly organized or inconsistent tables may prevent readers from pursuing the details that tabular format is meant to illustrate.

A case in point is the "Before" table on page 262, an editor's challenge if ever there was one because it's all words, no numbers. Specs require it to be a single column, and because space is at a premium, the table must be as short as possible while remaining readable. Try the techniques discussed here next time you're editing a word table so difficult to follow that it leaves you speechless.

Plan your editorial attack

An editor sizing things up might first note the obvious readability problem in the "column of words" on the right, but worse problems come to light quickly: Studies are arranged inconsistently, acronyms aren't explained, and the title and footnotes don't give enough information for the table to stand alone without reference to the accompanying text. There are also the usual editorial inconsistencies like *and* vs. ampersands and comma vs. no comma before the year in the study items.

If you're confronted with these kinds of problems, relax and take on one at a time. Do them in whatever order works best for you. Start with your personal strong suit. If you're primarily a consistency person, tackle the copyediting issues first. If you have an eye for organization, reorder the elements first and then clean them up. However you do them, here are the tasks necessary to salvage this particular table.

Make the citation style for studies consistent. If the references in the text use author/year format, use the same punctuation in the table—this will take care of the comma/no comma and *and*/ampersand inconsistencies. Of course, you'll delete the period after *et*—always a common error.

Decide on a consistent order for the studies. Right now they appear to be in no order at all. The two possibilities are chronological and alphabetical:

- If *when* a study was done is important for the data, or if the data show a *progression* of results (say, from little to considerable benefit after undergoing a procedure), choose chronological order.
- In other cases, choose alphabetical order. Check the reference list for the document; if it's in alphabetical order, arrange the studies having the same first author in the same way in the table. This probably means you'll have the two-author studies before the *et al.* entries.

Check the main stubs ("Area") for consistent capitalization. Choose caps for all important words or only for the initial word (sentence-style caps), but be consistent.

Make sure the footnote style is optimum. Use the footnote style that best matches the content. Numbers are generally used for footnote call-outs in tables that are largely composed of words, letters are used in tables with number data, and asterisks are reserved for the various standard levels of statistical probability. Check the rest of the tables in the document and make this one consistent with them.

Make sure the title is descriptive. "Early Subacute Period (7 to 72 Hours)" leaves the reader asking, Early subacute period of what? 7 to 72 hours before or after what? Although the main text will probably answer these questions, tables should be complete in themselves; the reader shouldn't have to study the accompanying text to figure out what a table means.

Verify that each acronym is explained. The acronyms ECT and WAIS aren't explained. If the text doesn't provide the spelled-out terms, check whatever reference sources you have (an acronym dictionary is a wonderful thing!) or query the author. Even though this table is supposed to be short, it can't take substantive shortcuts. Find a logical place in the table to spell out the acronyms or add a note at the bottom. The revised table shows both solutions.

Try to simplify the wording. Read through all the data for sense. Clarify or query any entry that isn't immediately clear to you. Look for ways to simplify some of the language in the "Effects of ECT" column without changing the meaning. Fewer, well-chosen words would help shorten the table and speed reader comprehension. And while you're cleaning things up, be suspicious of the single "No change" in this column without an asterisk. It's probably a simple typo, but you can't be sure; query the author.

Before:

Table 1. Early Subacute Period (7 to 72 Hours).

Area	Study	Effects of ECT
General Intelligence	Calev et al., 1991*b*	No change*
	Taylor et al., 1985	No change*
	Calev et al., in preparation	No change*
	McKenna & Pratt 1983	Improvement (on Digit Symbol Subtest of the WAIS)
Language	Taylor et al. 1985	Results suggestive that verbal fluency** is adversely affected
	Lerer et al., in press	Verbal fluency** adversely affected
	Taylor & Abrams 1985	No change (on a variety of language tasks)*
	Jones et al., 1988	One of 20 tasks (word fluency, assessing retrieval from semantic memory) affected**
Perceptual and Visuo-Spatial Function	Taylor et al. 1985	No change*
	Taylor and Abrams 1985	No change*
	Calev et al. 1991*b*	No change*
Motor function: Manual dexterity	Taylor & Abrams 1985	No change
Higher cognitive and frontal function	Taylor et al. 1985	No change*
	Lawson et al. 1990	No change*

* No change can be attributed to ECT.
** Calav et al. 1993*b* suggest this may be a memory rather than a language problem.

After:

Table 1. Effects of Electroconvulsive Therapy (ECT) in the Early Subacute Period (7 to 72 Hours After Administration).

Area and Study	Effects[1]
General Intelligence	
Calev et al. 1991*b*	No change
Calev et al. in preparation	No change
McKenna & Pratt 1983	Improvement (on WAIS[2] Digit Symbol subtest)
Taylor et al. 1985	No change
Language	
Jones et al. 1988	One of 20 tasks (word fluency in retrieval from semantic memory) affected[3]
Lerer et al. in press	Verbal fluency adversely affected[3]
Taylor & Abrams 1985	No change (on a variety of language tasks)
Taylor et al. 1985	Results suggest that verbal fluency is adversely affected[3]
Perceptual and Visuo-Spatial Function	
Calev et al. 1991*b*	No change
Taylor & Abrams 1985	No change
Taylor et al. 1985	No change
Motor Function: Manual Dexterity	
Taylor & Abrams 1985	No change
Higher Cognitive and Frontal Function	
Lawson et al. 1990	No change
Taylor et al. 1985	No change

[1] No change = no change that can be attributed to ECT.
[2] WAIS = Wechsler Adult Intelligence Scale.
[3] Calev et al. (1993*b*) suggest this may be a memory rather than a language problem.

Look for ways to improve readability

Now that the largely editorial matters are taken care of, you're ready to deal with the overall look of the table. Narrow columns are no problem with numbers, but this table is all words, and the information is hard to read. In fact, the narrow width of the table is the biggest graphic problem.

Column width. If you spread this material over two columns, the table would be readable. Since the specs require that the table fit into a single column, you have two possible solutions:

• Try a smaller type size, or

• Combine the left and center columns.

Since the type is already pretty small, combining the columns is a better solution. Look at the revised table. We simply changed the column heads to read "Area and Study" and "Effects" and subordinated the items in the column of studies under their appropriate topics. The resulting table has two columns instead of three, and the "Effects" column no longer looks like a column of words but instead offers readable blocks of type.

Runover lines in stubs. Some of the main stubs, the "Area" items, contain a lot of words; the required runover lines will add to the length of the table. Try running these main stubs across the table instead of confining them to their column. Setting in bold or italics will make the divisions of the table data stand out and enhance readability.

Runover lines in columns. What about the runover lines in the "Study" and the "Effects" columns? Your choices are to

• Indent all runovers, or

• Align all lines on the left.

Indented runovers make it clear where one block of type ends and another begins. In this table, space between entries shows the reader where one group of data ends and another begins, so the indented runover lines aren't needed.

We changed the runovers in the studies to align left. If all our efforts at shortening resulted in a table that was still too long, we could go back and close up the spaces between entries and indent the runover lines in both the studies and the effects column. The table would be on the dense side, but the indented runover lines would preserve its readability.

Alignment across columns. Another format inconsistency that affects the readability of this particular table is the alignment of studies with the effects. The recurring effect "No change" is aligned with the end of its study citation, but the first line of each longer effect aligns with the first line of its study citation. This inconsistency is another common error in table formatting—with blocks of type like these, it's better to align first lines across the columns.

Look at the "After" table on page 262. For our trouble we have a table that's well-ordered, understandable as a separate entity, and (maybe most important from a layout perspective) about an inch shorter!

—*Patricia Caudill*

The table was adapted—greatly adapted—from an article in a National Institute of Mental Health journal.

Orphans and Widows

An *Editorial Eye* reader asks: "What is currently considered good publishing practice with regard to orphans and widows? When reviewing page proofs, several of our editors insist that pages ending with the first line of a paragraph be redone. Our production staff feels that each page should have the same number of lines; thus, on pages of text with no blank lines that could be adjusted, they insist the widows or orphans must stay. Since we publish no more than 3,000 copies of any title, it is important that we balance the highest standards with a small budget. Please help us define a moderate position."

The Editorial Eye replies: Regarding widows and orphans, good publishing practice just depends! Generally, an orphan is considered to be a single line that begins a new paragraph at the bottom of the page or column, or a single line that ends a paragraph at the top of a page or column. Most publishers will accept two lines; some insist on three. Some editors *prefer* the single line that falls at the bottom of the page or column because they treat it as a "teaser" or lead-in to the next paragraph, column, or page.

Handling widows amounts to using common sense. With very narrow columns, as in some newsletters or journals, it would be unrealistic to insist on a minimum of five characters on a line by themselves at the end of a paragraph. But if you are using very wide columns, a mere five characters may look lonely indeed. Overall, my suggestion is that, as with almost any style decision, consistent standards should prevail.

—*Connie Moy*

What Editors Need to Know about Desktop Publishing

Simple screening routines can head off manuscript formatting errors

Editors are accustomed to seeing to it that what shows up on paper is a coherent, logical flow of ideas. But how about what's on the disk? The copyediting step—perhaps the last time a manuscript is gone over painstakingly, word by word—is especially significant in the desktop publishing (DTP) environment where the manuscript is formatted in paragraph units. Even editors who do not work online can no longer afford to ignore the mechanics of the electronic production process and the capabilities of word processing and DTP software. Establishing a checklist of details that can be systematically and routinely dealt with in every manuscript is central to the copyediting step and can help editors head off format and style errors early in the process. Adapting to the electronic environment may seem to demand more from editors early on, but the payback is a more effective system that allows them to concentrate on real editing.

Before electronic production: clean up the file

Even in cases where manuscripts are formatted to some degree during the writing and editing process, some "debris" is usually left over and some typographic details will still need to be taken care of. The process of creating a manuscript is messy—false starts, writing and rewriting, adding, deleting, moving, cutting—and its paramount goal is, of course, clear and effective communication. Even editors who are experienced software users may insert erroneous or extraneous codes and characters into the files when they are focusing on tone and content, and borderline users can make some truly admirable messes. Obsolete conventions, such as double paragraph returns and two spaces after periods and colons, are still a reflex for many of us who learned to type BDTP (before desktop publishing). These bad habits can throw a monkey wrench into electronic production or, at the very least, result in a sloppy page layout.

But marking or manually correcting each instance of these and other format glitches is drudgery and (more important) an unnecessary diversion from editing the words. One of the editor's most powerful helpers, search and replace, can streamline the process enormously. (The next step up, macros, can add jet propulsion.)

When preparing a text file to be imported from a word processing program into page layout software, it's a good idea to strip page formatting codes out of the file. Even plain vanilla word processing files may contain some formatting information—for headers and footers and font changes, for example—that may conflict with or corrupt DTP command codes.

Finally, it's a waste of time for editors working in a DTP environment to mark draft copy for things like spacing, indents, and justification. DTP programs work with chunks of text separated by hard paragraph returns and apply typographic and layout formats to these units. The formatting information includes typeface, size, spacing (above, below, and between lines), margins, alignment and justification, indents and outdents, hyphenation, tab settings, and often such special touches as bullets and drop caps.

After electronic production: checking manuscript pages

Once the various typographic and layout treatments are defined, they do not require editorial oversight; the editor need only identify by means of a "tag" or format name the type of treatment that is to be applied to each unit of text. If the DTP layout will be done by someone other than the editor, a short conference can clarify what can be handled consistently by the electronic style sheet or template and what needs to be treated on a case-by-case basis. For example, some programs can set capitalization (all caps, initial caps, or all lowercase) as part of a format; in others, capitalization must be changed and checked each time.

Even in its simplest applications, word processing software provides the full range of characters in a type font, in addition to keyboard characters. But most authors don't incorporate such characters electronically as they write because of the extra time and effort involved. Some coding for these characters can be written into a preliminary formatting program similar to the cleanup already discussed, and some is more efficiently handled during editing. In either case, the editor should see to it that during final production the desktop publisher makes the following translations from conventional typescript to take advantage of full typographic capabilities:

- **Em-dashes and "real" quotation marks.** The double dash (--) and straight quotes (") from the keyboard are not used for anything else in a DTP format, so searching for and replacing them is pretty straightforward. As a matter of fact, most DTP software can now automatically convert double dashes and straight quotes.

- **Single quotes and apostrophes** in typescript are represented by the same straight keyboard apostrophe, so they can't be universally replaced by the proper "real" character. Check quotes carefully after formatting; in cases of complex combinations of punctuation (single quotes beginning or ending within double quotes) or unusual spacing, some marks can slip through uncoded.

- **Replace hyphens** that have been used in word processing to take the place of en-dashes with coding for the special character (–).

- **Nonkeyboard characters.** Some special characters can't be coded automatically because they can appear in different ways in text, thus making an electronic search impractical. Editors should check to see that they are set properly in each case. Besides the obvious examples of **math symbols and Greek, accented, and other foreign-language characters**, the following are non-keyboard characters that contribute to a professionally typeset look:

  - ➤ **Ellipsis points**—they are set as a single character, not just three typed periods.

  - ➤ **Fractions**—again, they are single characters, not two numbers separated by a keyboard slash.

  - ➤ **Trademark, registered trademark, and copyright symbols**—they are more properly rendered as superscripts in a smaller font, not as full-sized letters between parentheses or other workarounds.

- **Italics, boldface, and super- or subscripts** will usually come across from material specified in word processing to DTP software, but you should always check these words or phrases carefully. You might want to mark these treatments on a printout of the original word processed draft (for instance, with a highlighter) as a reminder that they shouldn't be changed but will need to be checked.

Prevent format glitches with global screening

- **Extra spaces** after final punctuation (and anywhere else). Delete them.

- **Double paragraph returns.** Delete them.

- **Manually inserted (or "hard") hyphenation** (use the "search with confirm" option). End-of-line hyphens—unless they are holding together the parts of a compound word or standing in for an en-dash—should always be left alone until the very final tweaking of line breaks in finished pages.

- **Tabs.** Weed multiple tabs in tabular copy down to one, so that the final formatting can take care of how the tabs should be set. And get rid of *paragraph indent tabs* altogether, since a DTP format will usually have indents built in.

- **Convert underscoring to italics.** Writers often do not consistently underscore punctuation following underscored words. The ending punctuation will not be properly translated into italic unless it has been underlined *before* it is translated into italics.

- **Special treatments like italic, boldface, and super- or subscripts.** If your software's conversion process drops word processing codes for these treatments, search and replace them with DTP codes to make sure they come across correctly.

Wish a rote task would disappear?

There's no way around it: Editors need to take some time to learn about the particular strengths of the DTP program used to produce the manuscripts they edit. Software developers are pouring a lot of money and effort into making their products stronger, smarter, and faster, and they are integrating an astounding array of editorial tasks. Just let yourself start thinking about how automated features could free up your time and allow you to focus your attention on real editing rather than on housekeeping.

In essence, the job of copyediting is very much the same as it has always been: to polish a manuscript and prepare it for final form. In the DTP environment, sometimes it seems that we're losing some of the niceties and details as we move from manuscript to final pages. But for those who take the time to harness the electronic workhorse, the potential is there for doing (dare I suggest it?) an even better job of it than in the days BDTP.

—Jayne O. Sutton

It's All in the Links: Readying Publications for the Web

Web publishing may be graphical in nature, but readability is primary

If there were a single door leading to the World Wide Web, someone might hang a giant sign on it reading **EDITORS WANTED**. Adapting existing documents for use on the Web (or on an Intranet, an inhouse-only version of the Web) is a distinctly editorial process that today is often handled by graphic designers or, in some cases, by automation. Web publishing is a temptation to go overboard on graphics at the expense of readable content.

Anyone who wants to work with Web documents should start by learning HTML (hypertext markup language), the code on which the World Wide Web is built. HTML isn't a programming language; it's a system of codes for tagging structural elements in a document. Motivated people can master basic HTML from a book in three or four days—it's no more complex than the editing codes that most newspaper copyeditors are required to learn. HTML codes tag elements, such as headings and paragraphs, according to their purpose in the document. They can also define links between related documents like a set of pamphlets on employee benefits or the five parts of a serial newspaper article.

Readability can be built in

The biggest difference between reading online and reading printed text is that online, the text moves. You're scrolling up and down. As you scroll, you tend to scan the document. The environment urges you to speed-read, so if you don't see anything but plain text, you're likely to lose interest. Two simple practices greatly increase the readability of online texts:

- Use headings and boldface more than you would in print.
- Keep paragraphs short.

Boldface headings enhance the reader's ability to scan text rapidly. In print, too many headings make a page look clunky and disjointed, but online headings disappear off the top of the screen as the reader scrolls down. As a rule of thumb, one heading per screen of text within a document works very well.

Headings aren't window dressing. Each should provide a clear predictor of the content of the paragraphs below it. Try to spare speed-hungry online users from reading anything they aren't absolutely interested in.

Boldface or italics used to highlight key phrases in the text function much as pull-out quotes do in print, but without the redundancy. Boldface can eliminate the need for headings where they would be intrusive or inappropriate, as in brief documents (400 words or less).

Using short paragraphs with a line space between them also facilitates scanning. Just as you would break up a long printed article in which the writer had neglected to use any paragraphs, so in an online article you must break long paragraphs into two or three shorter ones.

Hypertext links are key

Hypertext, the most powerful feature of HTML, is fundamental and also unique to electronic publishing. A word or phrase in the text is underlined or highlighted. When you mouse-click on that word, a new document comes onto your screen. The highlighted text is similar to a footnote numeral—it refers you elsewhere—but it usually links to another large block of text, not a small note.

The text of a hypertext link can be a title (the link goes to a document with that title), a person's name (the link may go to a biographical sketch or résumé), a word (the link may go to a dictionary definition)—or any phrase or clause. Choosing or writing a good phrase or clause to use as a link requires editorial talent.

The cardinal sin of link-making is to use the words "click here." (You'll see those words all over the Web. Many people sin.) A link exists to be clicked, and to say so in the link text is a sorry waste of words.

Writing strong link text

The text used for the link should, first and foremost, produce a reasonable expectation in the user. If the link is a button that reads **HOME**, the user will expect to go to the site's home page (or first page).

If a link said, "Find out more about our product," would you be disappointed if that link went to an e-mail form that provided nothing new but invited you to write for additional information? A better link would say, "Contact us to find out more."

Consider this text:

Find out <u>who we are</u> and let <u>us</u> know what you'd like to see.

Can you guess, without following the two links, how "who we are" and "us" might be different? They actually lead to two different documents: "About This Site" and a page of Web staff bios. This would be a better way to write the links:

Find out <u>about our Web site</u> and let <u>us</u> know...

Link text can't always include active verbs, but a keen editor can often figure out a way to enliven a passive clause or dull phrase: "Our annual report is now online" can become "Read our annual report online," and "Membership form" can become "Apply for membership today."

Avoiding careless links

It's a shame to waste the power of links by creating them randomly. Consider their cumulative effect on your online readers and avoid the following kinds of pitfalls:

Excessive use of links. When links appear in almost every line of a document, users are less likely to follow any link at all (who has the time?). By eliminating links that are irrelevant, extraneous, or redundant, you do a great favor for busy, impatient users. Reference lists and search engines exist for anyone who wants to find every site related to a given topic.

Irrelevant or extraneous links. My favorite example is the word Washington, which appeared as a link in a news article about an action in Congress. Clicking it took me to a page about tourist attractions in the U.S. capital. Yes, it was a page about Washington, but it wasn't directly related to the article where the link appeared. Such links waste users' time and erode their faith in your ability to lead them to something good.

Gratuitous use of external links. You can fill a document with links that go to Web sites all around the world, but keep in mind that a person who leaves your site may never return. The more you send them away, the greater the impression that your own site has little to offer. Provide links to exemplary external sites as appropriate, especially when they add useful information that your site can't provide. But don't send people away without a good reason.

A dearth of link options. If a Web page has only one link, it may as well be printed on paper. Never try to force a single path on the user. Making choices is what interactivity is all about.

Breaking up large articles

In print a reader can flip a few pages and read the last paragraph (or read all the headings, or look at all the photos). A long article formatted as a Web page takes more time to load—to come onscreen—than a shorter one. Because of the linear scrolling path from top to bottom, the user's ability to scan a very long article is reduced.

Careful use of hypertext removes this limitation and makes a longer article more pleasant to read online—and more work for an editor to prepare. The relationship is a direct one: The more effort an editor puts into breaking up a long article and linking the pieces intelligently, the more engaging that article will be.

Basic tasks of hypertext editing

The four basic tasks a hypertext editor undertakes contribute much to the effectiveness and appeal of an online document.

1. Finding appropriate places to break. The writer may have already divided the article into sections, but the editor usually will have to split up the article even further. Base your decisions on content, on presenting a whole idea. Try to make each piece as independent as possible. Sometimes this means you'll delete or rewrite transition sentences.

2. Deciding how long each piece should be. The broken-out pieces don't have to be of equal length, but the goal is to keep them all relatively short (500 words is a good average, although it's too short for some kinds of material). In some cases, one piece will be much longer or shorter than all the others.

3. Creating the link structure. If there are very few pieces (three or four), they might be best handled as sidebars, with the titles of all related pieces listed (as links) at the end of each one. (That structure provides access to any part of the article from any other part, which is good.) A larger number of pieces can be more intricately interwoven. Provide contextual links so that users can skip around, choosing their own paths, but also give them the option to follow a traditional path through the article (using "next" and "previous" as links, if appropriate).

4. Providing an overview. When an article is broken into a dozen or more parts, users appreciate the option of glimpsing the whole cloth before following a thread. The overview may be structured as a table of contents (list), a map (graphics), or an abstract or introduction (text) that has links to all the pieces on one page. Each piece of the article should include a link to the overview.

The online reader is a moving target

Construct your set of documents in such a way that users can easily skip the things they don't care about but won't miss the things they like.

Remember that users are always moving—scrolling up and down and jumping from link to link. They don't like to be still. They don't like to sit with their hands folded in their laps. This doesn't mean they are impossible to grab. They'll stop and read when something catches their eye. The trick is to hang onto them long enough.

—Mindy McAdams

Using Graphics on the Web

Don't lose part of your audience to flashy, slow graphics

One picture may be worth a thousand words, but you can usually download the words a lot faster. While the cable and telephone companies are gearing up to provide high-capacity Internet connections to every household, most people are still accessing the Internet through modems attached to their regular phone lines. At a typical modem speed of 14,400 kilobits per second, a 60-kilobyte graphic takes more than 30 seconds to download—and that's assuming perfect conditions. In the same time, you could download about 10,000 words (the equivalent of 20 single-spaced typewritten pages).

Handle Web graphics with care

If you're putting documents on the Web, it pays to use graphics wisely to avoid annoying your readers or making them miss your message entirely. Here are some of the issues to consider:

- **Screen size versus file size.** All else being equal, a graphic that takes up more space on your screen will also take up more space on your hard drive (and thus take longer to download), but the relationship between screen size, usually measured in pixels (the dots that make up on-screen pictures), and file size, usually measured in bytes, is complicated. Images with more colors produce larger files. Moreover, because most graphics formats use compression algorithms to reduce file size, simple images result in smaller files than complex images. If you have two 150-by-150-pixel images, one a full-color photograph and one a solid blue square, the file for the photo will be many times larger.

- **Appropriate screen size.** Don't make a graphic so wide that it runs off the edge of viewers' screens. This problem occurs most often with banner images at the tops of pages. The Yale Center for Advanced Instructional Media recommends 472 pixels as a maximum width.

- **Minimum file size.** You can reduce the file size of a graphic by reducing its screen size, reducing the number of colors (or shades of gray) in it, or changing to a format that gives better compression. The Bandwidth Conservation Society (**http://www.infohiway.com/way/faster/**) encourages responsible use of graphics and gives tips on how to make them smaller.

- **Thumbnails.** If you have to use a large image (say, a book cover or a work of art), consider displaying a thumbnail—a smaller version that is linked to the full-size image. That's how we handle the pictures of covers in the Web pages for EEI books. For some images, it may look better if the small linked image is some part of the larger image rather than a shrunken version of the whole image.

- **GIF or JPEG?** Most graphics on Web pages are in one of two file formats: GIF (Graphics Interchange Format) or JFIF (JPEG File Interchange Format, based on a standard developed by the Joint Photographic Experts Group). The names of GIF files typically have a **.gif** extension; those of JFIF files (also called JPEG files) typically end in **.jpeg** or **.jpg**.

    Most browsers that support in-line images (including Netscape Navigator and Microsoft Internet Explorer) can display both GIF and JPEG graphics. Which format is better depends on the particular image. Guidelines by Adobe Systems (**http://www.adobe.com/studio/ tipstechniques/GIFJPGchart/**) can help you decide, but the bottom line is that GIF is better for line drawings and images with large blocks of solid color, whereas JPEG is better for photographs and other images with many different shades. When in doubt, save your image in both formats and choose the one that gives a smaller file size. (The JPEG standard allows you to trade off image quality versus file size, so try various settings to get the smallest file that still gives acceptable image quality.)

When designing icons for navigation, include text as part of the image

- **Background images.** It's hard to make a background image that won't render your text illegible for a lot of people. Backgrounds look different on different combinations of hardware and software. I've had the same Web page up on my screen in two windows—one Netscape Navigator and one NCSA Mosaic—and the colors of the background image have looked different. With such variation, finding text colors that stand out enough from the background is next to impossible. But you can't go wrong with plain white.

Text is still important

Remember that not everyone can or chooses to view even carefully designed graphics; words have other advantages over pictures besides downloading speed. Some people have to access the Web without graphics. Visually impaired readers can set the text size larger to make it easier to read. Blind people can use browsers that read the words to them or transliterate them into braille. Search engines can index the words. But pictures are meaningless to a reading machine or an indexing program.

Some people have access only to Lynx or other text-only browsers, and others prefer to use a graphical browser with images turned off for speed and economy. In either case, the browsers display text in place of the graphics—if the coding for your pages includes such alternative text. If not, text-only readers will see nothing, or only the default alternative (generally "[IMAGE]" or "[LINK]").

If you must use image maps (large pictures that link to different pages depending on where you click), provide a text-based way to get the same information. Alan J. Flavell, of Glasgow University, gives guidelines for use of alternative text and image maps, as well as reasons that people read the Web without pictures, at **http://ppewww.ph.gla.ac.uk/~flavell/alt/**.

When designing icons for navigation or other purposes, include text as part of the image. For example, if you use a flashlight to indicate a search function, put the word "search" under the flashlight image in the icon. Otherwise your icons will be like those international symbols used on dashboard controls and in laundering instructions for clothes: They leave everyone equally mystified, regardless of language. There's no point in avoiding language for your icons when the body of your pages must be in English or some other language.

Some Web sites that have versions of their pages in several languages use flags as icons to indicate English, French, German, Spanish, and so on. This scheme is flawed because there is no one-to-one correspondence between languages and countries: Americans must click on a U.K. flag (or Britons on a U.S. flag), Brazilians on a Portuguese flag, Mexicans on a Spanish flag—and what flag would you use for Esperanto or Tamil? It's better to use words (English, Français, Deutsch, Español). Using graphics on the Web doesn't have to mean excluding part of your audience.

—Keith C. Ivey

Publications
Management
and Trends

Estimating Editorial Tasks:
A Five-Step Method

How long should a job take and how much should it cost?

"**H**ow long will it take?" That's a question many publications specialists dread, but they've been hearing it a lot more often lately as managers hold them to tighter schedules than ever.

Accurate time estimates are essential to projecting the costs of doing work, whether it's for external clients or other departments within an organization. In the olden days, it didn't seem to matter how many hours were spent editing, as long as all the errors were caught. Now, managers everywhere are looking for ways to cut costs; they want to know in advance how long things will take so they can monitor their increasingly strained budgets. Publications are often a prime target for cost cuts.

Productivity guidelines help everybody

"But how can we calculate how long it should take?" Managers and editors alike can benefit from a system that makes it possible to estimate costs and set reasonable performance goals. But editors in particular often say that it's difficult for them to look at a stack of pages and come up with a time estimate. There are so many variables, they say, that even a ballpark estimate can be tricky to calculate.

Everyone would agree that publications work is subject to many unknowns, but it's still possible to pin down key aspects of a project, apply educated guesswork, and calculate a relatively accurate time estimate. Here's a five-step method for arriving at that elusive number.

1. Define your process by creating a task list. First, list all the steps in your editorial process. Most projects include more than just editing—you also have to make photocopies, write cover memos to authors, type up query lists and style sheets, make backup copies of disks, and do whatever else comes with the territory in your organization. Even though you may not perform every step on every project (for example, some projects may begin with a meeting with the author, while others may not), you should create a master list of every possible task and use it as a starting point whenever you do an estimate. This list will help ensure that you don't forget a step. Make sure you include on your master task list any administrative tasks that usually take more than 15 minutes.

2. Include levels of edit on your master task list so that you can specify a level of effort and the appropriate productivity rate for each project. At EEI, we have three general levels: proofreading, copyediting, and

substantive editing. You may prefer to call the levels light, medium, and heavy. In most organizations, not all documents receive the same level of scrutiny, and your estimate will depend on how much help the document needs (or how much you're allowed to give). If the person requesting the estimate doesn't specify a level of edit, read through portions of the text and recommend one.

3. Calculate how much material you have to edit. There is really no such thing as a standard "page" of text. These days most authors have access to a wide range of fonts and formatting options, and the number of words on a page can vary greatly.

   For example, a 50-page draft can be anywhere from 10,000 to 30,000 words or more, depending on the format and type size. So you can't simply count pages and get an accurate estimate (unless, of course, every manuscript comes to you in exactly same format and type size).

   Here's the formula for converting the actual page count into "draft-equivalent" pages:

   • First pick a common denominator. That is, set a number of words per page that will become your standard definition of a "draft page." A 250-word page is typical for a double-spaced draft with one-inch margins and 12-point type.

   • Pick a representative page in the document you're estimating and count the number of lines on the page.

   • Then count the number of words in a typical line and multiply by the number of lines to get an average number of words per page.

   • Count the number of pages (count partial pages as half pages), and multiply the total by the number of words per page.

   • Divide the result by 250 words (or your standard draft equivalent), and that's the number of draft-equivalent pages in the document.

   Don't try to be absolutely precise by counting every word in a document. If you get carried away with assessing every last detail, you can easily spend almost as much time estimating a project as it would take to complete it.

4. Establish a productivity rate for each function on your master task list. Start with a standard productivity rate and adjust it up or down, depending on the type of material to be edited. For functions that don't easily lend themselves to hourly rates, establish standard times (for example, 15 minutes to write a cover memo; 30 minutes to type up a style sheet and query list). To keep your estimates from getting too complicated, round all times to the nearest quarter-hour.

5. Put it all on a spreadsheet. Let your computer do the math. Create a spreadsheet with formulas for each function on your master task list so

that all you have to do is select the relevant tasks and type in the number of pages. The formulas can be set to divide the number of pages by the productivity rate for each function and give you total hours for each function as well as a grand total for the project.

Save the spreadsheet while the project is in progress so you can easily recalculate if the specifications change along the way.

Reevaluate your system frequently

The task list and productivity rates should be reviewed at least once a year. It's easy to think of established rates as gospel, but circumstances and processes change. For example, once editors spend a year or so working on documents that deal with a particular subject, they will pick up speed and be able to spot errors in industry-specific terminology more quickly. Hence, their productivity rate will increase.

Likewise, if you add tasks to your editorial process—for example, requiring editors to code text as they edit—their productivity rate will decrease. Keep a record of actual hours spent on individual projects and compare the data with your estimates so you can watch for trends that indicate it's time to rework your estimating system.

Continually educate your customers (or coworkers) about the variables that affect the editorial process. Be sure they understand that if the scope of work changes, the estimate will change as well. If, for example, you're asked to incorporate someone else's revisions to text you've already edited, you'll also have to check to be sure that those revisions didn't introduce any errors or inconsistencies—and that will take additional time.

Even the most experienced estimators still look at each new stack of pages and say to themselves, "I have no idea how long this will take!" Then they go work on their spreadsheets. The more you estimate editorial projects, the easier it becomes.

—*Robin A. Cormier*

Managing Collaborative Writing Projects

Editorial managers shape and support
the work of a commitee of experts

Working with people who are tops in their field to produce a successful print or electronic publication can be stimulating, informative, and gratifying for editorial and publication managers. In this role, one we've often filled, we typically help technical experts who form a writing committee—but who are not professional writers—develop and edit their assigned topics or chapters.

We also serve as copyeditors; writers of ancillary sections such as introductions, author bios, and conclusions; coordinators, supervising the work of specialists such as indexers and proofreaders; and staff assistants to the person appointed to lead the writing committee, whose title is usually *chair* or *editor-in-chief*. (We'll use the latter in this article.)

There are two distinct challenges for editorial managers who work with a panel of subject-matter experts: (1) Their writing styles and abilities vary widely, and (2) their accessibility also varies, because of their professional stature and, in some cases, their egos. After tackling these challenges in developing many publications, including technical procedures manuals and physician self-assessment programs, we offer some ideas on how an editorial manager can work successfully with a committee of experts.

Determine a publication's 'voice' and audience early

Should your final document sound as though it was written by one person, a chorus, or an ensemble? Should sections have separate bylines but be edited to sound alike? Or should each author retain a distinctive tone and style? You can help the editor-in-chief make this decision by offering related examples of other projects and exploring the needs of the audience.

A big part of your job as editorial manager is also to clean up jargon and make the material understandable. Like any good copyeditor, you'll be an advocate for readability. Reading background material is a way to get into the spirit of the project, and if the product is going to the general public, getting a feel for the general readership level is important.

However, every field has language conventions. When we questioned one seemingly odd formulation in a medical project, the editor-in-chief said simply, "It's okay. Doctors talk like that." While you may not want to be quite *that* loose, try to be flexible in working with experts in their "native tongue." If you are not already familiar with the field, reading a few issues of the leading professional journal before you start editing is a big help.

Agreement on the tone and the level of language of the document early on will help prevent discrepancies that can jam a review process and make final edits harrowing. And once these decisions are made, you'll know how to proceed with author guidelines.

Create a master fact sheet

Using project management software or a simple word processing table, create a fact sheet that can be updated as the work progresses. Include the working title of the project, the date, and information about each expert who will be contributing (name, address, phone, fax, and e-mail); the topic each author will be writing about; and dates and places for scheduled meetings.

Distribute the fact sheet and each subsequent update to all participants, with a reminder to toss the one it replaces. Issue updates for changes of address, of authors' assigned topics, or of authors' support staff contacts and revised deadlines and meeting dates.

Become attuned to the team leader

The editor-in-chief may not know at first exactly how valuable a role you can play in smoothing the process. It's up to you to make it clear, or simply to demonstrate your abilities in the following ways:

- Be prepared to advise the editor-in-chief on editorial and administrative matters and to respond flexibly to all requests for help.
- Be sure to keep to yourself any confidences shared with you about group members.
- Be ready to act as a sounding board for ideas.

Suggest meeting with the editor-in-chief before all group sessions to go over the agenda and clarify what sorts of participation will be expected of everyone. Within a few days, review and organize your notes and, with the editor-in-chief's okay, issue a new schedule.

The ideal relationship between the editor-in-chief and the editorial manager is similar to that between a top government official and a chief aide: part confidant, gentle critic, devil's advocate, and, yes, part gofer. You should strive to be regarded as a professional, but never stop acting like the dutiful subordinate.

Give authors guidelines and goals

From the start, the editorial manager has to keep an eye on the projected specs for the finished product and translate them into specific working guidelines for authors. How many pages does each author need to write? How many photos, tables, or figures can each section have? Will authors be asked to create or provide graphics? Is color going to be available? How many footnotes or references may be listed? Is an index required?

Be ready to act as a sounding board for ideas

We served as editorial consultants to a panel of authors who are among the country's leading cardiologists. They were happy to learn that we would handle version control, style consistency, and so forth for the manuscript, but they really perked up when we told them exactly how many pages—including line spacing and margins—they needed to write to yield the overall goal. Successful people get that way by being precise, thorough—and busy! They'll appreciate your taking the guesswork out of their assignments.

If the authors are uncertain about how to divide topics, provide examples of similar publications and suggest organizational schemes. What topic has seen the most recent research or technological development? What topic is the most controversial or troublesome? What topic is of greatest practical concern to the audience? Questions like these can help the committee assign its work effectively.

Maintain document version control

Be sure to ask all authors to submit text in hard copy and on disk (or by modem). Once you've "captured" the text on your hard disk (with backup, of course), make sure that any further changes are submitted as handwritten notes on the printed page. That's the best way to maintain control of the most current edited draft. Authors who are computer-literate will understand why you reject additional disks.

But some authors still want to provide disks in order to "make things easier for you." No sooner had we completed our editorial work on one author's document than we received another disk from him with "minor changes" throughout. That left us with two choices: redo our work on the new document or compare the two documents side by side. (The comparison features in recent wordprocessing programs can help, but you're still left with a lot of work.) We chose to start over, as if the resubmission were his first draft. It went faster than we'd expected because the editing we'd done earlier was surprisingly fresh in our minds.

More version control basics: Add a header that prints on every page and provides the section title, author's name, draft number and date, and anything else that will help you keep track of sections and revisions. Update the header on each version. Be sure to use line numbering; this seemingly minor enhancement allows immediate and precise identification of passages as they're discussed in review meetings.

Clarify the system of peer review

Make sure that a system of peer review is in place and that you're aware of all its parts and players. You'll need answers to these questions so you can build the various stages of review into the schedule—and determine how you'll keep track of reviews and changes:

- Will all authors review all sections?
- Will some authors exchange sections?
- Will the editor-in-chief make final decisions?
- Will any reviewers outside the committee be involved?

On some of our projects, the system has been for several reviewers to comment on a document and the editor-in-chief to have the final say. For cases like those, we follow this procedure:

- From each reviewer's marked-up copy, pull out only those pages with comments and discard the rest. Keep one copy of pages with no comments for continuity and possible future reference.
- On each page with a comment, write the reviewer's initials.
- Put all the marked page 1s together, all the marked page 2s, and so forth.

If you have time or if the comments are not lengthy, you can transfer them plus initials to a master copy of each page. The editor-in-chief can then see what each reviewer has to say about each page. This will also clearly indicate "dueling comments"—mutually exclusive remarks by two or more reviewers. If you use this method, double-check the master copy to make sure you included *all* the comments.

Keep 'flexible control' of the schedule

Just as all authors appreciate *guidelines* on how much to write, most want help keeping on schedule. The members of your committee will appreciate tactful reminders when deadlines are approaching.

But staying flexible about deadlines can pay off. Authors for two recent projects asked to make last-minute additions of study findings. Making these changes required some weekend work, but the resulting product was clearly more current and valuable to the audience.

However, just about every committee has its laggard—the author who, because of overcommitment, self-importance, or plain laziness, is always late. You can't shackle authors to their PCs and give them only bread and water until they produce the document, but you can tell them how far behind the schedule they really are—and try to make them understand the consequences for the project.

Make life easier for authors

Perform personal services that are easy for you and can be burdensome for authors. For example, when you send out material that must be returned to you, provide self-addressed, stamped envelopes or self-addressed, bill-to-recipient express delivery airbills.

Include a cover sheet that lists possible responses ("I approve these page proofs for printing," "I approve printing with the indicated changes") so the author can simply check off the appropriate choice. Recently, when we sent out page proofs for author approval, we enclosed a packet of red tape flags that the authors could use to mark any changes. We told them that this was the only kind of "red tape" they could actually send back to us in Washington—and they loved it.

Offer to convert disks, obtain original artwork, seek reprint permissions, and handle other supportive tasks. The authors will welcome your help, and performing these tasks yourself will also give you more control over continuity and the project schedule.

A few words on deportment

Call us old-fashioned, but we advocate showing the utmost respect for the experts, particularly if they have achieved some recognition in their field. Always dress as well as the best-dressed committee member. Use first names in conversation only when invited and never in formal sessions. Such professional regard will be reciprocated.

We've barely mentioned the significant pluses of this role. With luck, you'll have the great satisfaction that comes with playing a key role in shaping a product that breaks new ground, becomes a best-seller, or answers an urgent need.

—David Stauffer and Susan Bury

How to Prioritize
When Everything Is Urgent

Something's got to give—but not your sanity

Question: I'm a one-person graphics department at a small research firm. I design, lay out, and create graphics for reports. I usually have many projects going at once, each with different requirements and deadlines. My boss expects me to prioritize my own work. When I tell him that every project is presented to me as "urgent," he just says, "Do the best you can." How can I set priorities when everything seems equally important? How do I let people know what my workload is without sounding like I'm whining?

Answer: You're obviously aware of one of the biggest "don'ts" when it comes to juggling multiple priorities: Don't whine to your coworkers about how much you have to do. They have their own problems; even if they're sympathetic, they probably can't help you. Yet they do need to know that there's a valid reason why you can't always turn things around as quickly as they'd hoped. Here are some ways to cope with your heavy workload and make good decisions about what comes first.

Keep a running list of all the projects you're working on, and post it in a prominent place. This list serves two purposes. First, it lets everyone know how many projects you have (much more clearly than whining would) and gives them some idea of the challenges you're facing. Second, it lets them see that their project is in the queue and hasn't been forgotten.

Get as many specifics as you can about each project when it's given to you. When someone says her document is due next Thursday, what exactly does that mean? Is it due back to her so she can review it and make revisions? Is it due to an in-house review committee? Or is it due, polished and perfect, to an external client? Once you establish the true status of each project, you can schedule your work more accurately. There's often some room for negotiation.

When you need to negotiate deadlines, be prepared to offer compromises. Can you provide a first layout by Thursday without the graphics, and then continue to work on them while the text is being reviewed? Can you hold off on incorporating any revisions until all the review copies are in? If you can get some part of the document in the requestor's hands, you can often get extra time for other projects.

When discussing deadlines and project requirements, be diplomatic. Remember that though a document is just one of many on your list, it may be the culmination of a year's work for your coworkers. Acknowledge the importance of the project and stress your commitment to making it a document they'll be proud of. People are much more cooperative about negotiating deadlines when they feel that you are on their team and are doing your best to meet their needs.

Give people updates so they know that progress is being made. Let them know where things stand—ideally, before they ask. Even a simple "I haven't started that yet, but I wanted you to know it's next on my list" can go a long way toward calming an impatient coworker.

Pin down vague requirements. Beware of people who say, "I don't need this any time soon; just do it whenever you can." If someone doesn't give you a deadline, assign one yourself. If you don't, the project can end up at the bottom of your pile, forgotten until the day it becomes an emergency. Also, the requestor's definition of "no time soon" might be next week, whereas yours might be next month. Setting deadlines helps prevent misunderstandings.

Be honest about the status of your projects. Never attempt to give the impression that you are further along on a project than you really are. Some people think they'll make the requestor happy temporarily and buy time to get caught up before anyone finds out the truth. When this approach backfires—and it usually does—you lose credibility.

Once you've established priorities, stick to them. Don't abandon your list and cater to the person who screams the loudest. People have different ways of expressing the urgency of their needs. If you drop everything for the screamers, others may catch on to the fact that screaming works and approach you that way, too. Likewise, don't play favorites. If you fit in special projects for your pals, the others will have good reason to complain.

Treat everyone fairly and objectively, maintain a well-organized system of tracking your deadlines, and learn as much as you can about the actual requirements of each project. As they say, you can't please all of the people all of the time, but you can manage your workload in a way that minimizes conflicts.

—*Robin A. Cormier*

Taking a Team Approach to Publishing

A case study of interlinked editorial, graphics, and production efforts

In the business environment, people are constantly looking for ways to save time and money. At The Johns Hopkins University Applied Physics Laboratory (APL), the Technical Publications Group, of which I am a member, has worked hard to improve the editing and production process, and our success has resulted in considerable savings in time and money and significantly better products. Vital to this process has been a team approach.

Setting up publishing teams

The APL Technical Publications Group comprises 37 people with expertise in editing, writing, illustration, and graphic design. When a client brings a job to our scheduling office, a team is immediately assigned to work on it. The schedulers make a concerted effort to form a team whose skills match the requirements of the job.

In general, each team is composed of at least one editor/writer, one publication specialist (who creates layout), and one artist/illustrator. Before work begins, the team members meet with the client to assess the job and discuss its requirements. The team then chooses a leader—usually the person who will be doing the lion's share of the work. In addition to his or her own responsibilities, the team leader usually oversees the entire editing and production process, serves as the primary contact for the client, and ensures that the deadline is met.

Input from all team members is strongly encouraged, and members take full responsibility for their contributions to the job. Because of the many documents edited and produced each year, at any given time each staff member is assigned to several different teams and must juggle priorities accordingly.

Good communication within the group is fundamental to ensuring that the workload is distributed as evenly as possible and that deadlines are met. We have discovered that frequent group meetings, usually twice a month, are very useful in keeping the lines of communication open. We also have a team that prepares and distributes a monthly summary of activities, and everyone has voice mail and e-mail.

A team approach brings tracking problems

In adopting a team approach, we have had to face several challenges. One of the most difficult was job tracking: How could we keep the schedulers informed of the status of each job? Currently, each person is given a weekly printout of the jobs for which he or she is the team leader. The status of those jobs during the previous week is indicated on the printout. The team leader is responsible for updating the printout and returning it to the schedulers. The team leader alone provides this update to prevent the schedulers from receiving duplicates for each job.

In addition, each person is provided a printout of all the jobs to which he or she is assigned. We are still working on how to distribute responsibilities among the members of a team, and particularly how to determine the team leader's overall responsibilities. Several people in the group volunteered to serve on a task force that is investigating these issues.

Comparing team and traditional approaches

We adopted the team approach more than a year ago to replace the more traditional division of the group into editorial and graphics sections that operated somewhat independently of each other. There were no formal means of communication, such as team meetings, among the various people assigned to a particular job. Often clients would bring manuscripts for editing to the editorial section supervisor and take the accompanying figures to the graphics section supervisor to be redone, and no one in the group would know that the two parts went together.

Our team approach, however, allows us to work closely together and complement each other's skills. We have become more productive because better communication has resulted in less duplication. Our increased efficiency allows us to produce review copies that are essentially page proofs with all text and graphics in place. Yet if an author needs to make changes, they can usually be incorporated without substantially reworking the layout. An added bonus in showing authors a "final," laid-out copy for review is that they tend to make fewer changes, thereby saving production time. The authors are happy to see beforehand what their documents will look like, and if the copy reads well and looks good, they are less likely to make further changes. Further, by empowering us with the responsibility for our own work, teaming has resulted in more creativity and fewer errors, thereby improving the quality of our products.

—*Karen M. Belton*

The Editor's Authority

How can editors do their job if their decisions are undercut?

Problem: As the editing manager at a large software company, I supervise two editors and two illustrators. I report to the publications manager, who also supervises six technical writers. My problem involves the writers. They frequently overrule or disregard our editing decisions and say things like, "We don't have time to incorporate that change," or "I know it's wrong grammatically, but I like it that way." Some of our debates are about grammar problems; others involve overall writing style. For instance, one writer insists on starting every paragraph with an "if" clause, such as "If you want to..." or "If this situation occurs...." My boss, who is herself a writer by training, supports the writers, even though their choices sometimes go against basic principles of good grammar or good writing style. To put it mildly, this situation has created an adversarial relationship between the editors and the writers.

Currently the writers are in another building, but they will soon move to our floor. I'm afraid that the friction will get worse when we are closer together. How can I establish some authority for my staff and persuade our boss to support us?

Solution: Although the upcoming move seems like it will make the problem worse, it might actually be the first step toward a solution. Sometimes physical distance makes teamwork more difficult. You can use this move as an opportunity to propose some changes in the ways the two groups work together.

Some editors believe that in an ideal world they would be the ultimate authority on all matters pertaining to grammar, style, and usage. However, anyone who has worked in the editorial field for very long has learned how and when to compromise. In the words of Arthur Plotnik, "A good editor has the confidence to say no to any author who would compromise the medium's standards, and the humility to recognize when those standards are transcended."

Ask for your boss' support

First, you'll have to convince her that your primary goal is for the division to produce high-quality work—not for you and your editors to have the final say. To make your problems clear to her, show her examples of two kinds of editing changes that have been rejected by the writers: Objective changes that are not open to interpretation and subjective changes that involve preferences or judgment calls. Show her authoritative references that support your position in each case.

For changes that involve the finer points of style, accept the fact that you may have to give in. For example, starting every paragraph with an "if" clause isn't really a sin; a repetitious writing style is not necessarily a drawback for technical manuals. For the changes that are objectively necessary and supported by references, hold your ground. Tell your boss that you and your staff are prepared to be flexible on the subjective changes, but that you need her to uphold your decisions on the other kind—your division's reputation and morale depend on it.

Use a lighter touch with the writers

To establish a better relationship with the writers, you will have to make some concessions. They need to view your editing as a valuable contribution to their products, not as a bottleneck in getting their work published. Whether what they say is true—that there isn't always time to make editing changes—or just an excuse, you can propose a way to prevent time crunches.

Give in on the finer points;
hold your ground on necessary changes

Start by demonstrating your willingness to use a light touch when a heavy edit isn't necessary. Drafts of documents that need a quick cleanup before they go through your in-house review process probably don't need the thorough scrub you would give to something that goes to your clients. If the text will undergo substantial revision, you don't want to spend time polishing it unnecessarily. You may find that your editors have been digging in their heels even on drafts as a defensive reflex; this is a good place to ease up.

Define editing responsibilities

You can clarify everyone's expectations and ensure that the products get the attention they deserve if you categorize each project before you begin editing. Define each category and include productivity rates so writers can plan ahead and allow enough time for editing. Here are some suggestions.

- **Level A: Initial drafts.** The Level A edit takes place before a document goes to the content reviewers. The editor's purpose is to clean up the document so that reviewers don't get bogged down in typos and grammatical errors. The editor doesn't do any major reorganizing or restructuring at this stage, since the document will likely go through more changes. The editor's pace should be about six to eight pages per hour.

- **Level B: Final drafts.** Once the content reviewers sign off on the document, the editor does a Level B edit. This edit is the heaviest of the three categories. Unless the document is extremely technical, very poorly written, or very well written, the editor's pace should be two to four pages per hour.

- **Level C: Client deliverables.** At the Level C stage, the document has already been seen by both content reviewers and an editor. The editor then does a final check to ensure that no errors were introduced or missed when the Level B changes were incorporated. The editor's pace should be about 10 to 15 pages per hour.

Use these levels of edit as negotiating points

Suggest to your boss that she meet with both groups right after the move; perhaps you could arrange a cheerful fruit, coffee, and pastry breakfast to welcome your new neighbors. Undoubtedly there will be other matters to discuss, and this fresh start will give you a chance to begin working face-to-face with the writers.

Ask your boss to offer these levels to the writers as negotiating points. Realistically, not every document will go through all three levels. For example, if a writer is behind schedule, editors might be asked to skip the Level A edit, but subsequent reviews may then take longer. To allow the editors to do a proper job, writers might have to build a couple of extra days into the schedule for the Level B edit.

As the editing manager, you should keep track of each document. Note when it comes to you, how long you have to work on it, and when it is due back for another look. If you continue to have problems, you'll have some documentation to support your position.

As long as you present your case in a positive manner, and highlight the mutual benefits, you may be surprised to discover that it is well received.

—Robin A. Cormier

Defending Your Staff When Things Go Wrong

Publications specialists may need a bit of public relations help

Problem: One of my least favorite tasks as publications manager is defending my staff when things go wrong—and I seem to spend too much time responding to complaints about the work we do. It just happened again: A major research report went to press with an error on the first page. My boss, the vice president for administration, wanted me to fire the editor assigned to the project—until I explained what had happened.

When the director of research reported the problem to my boss, he left out a few important details. The editor had been given less than half the time she needed to work on the document, and the tight schedule didn't give her the opportunity to review the final pages after her changes were incorporated. There was plenty of blame to go around in this case, and I felt the editor did the best she could under less than ideal circumstances.

I'm certain that the problem isn't my staff. I've reviewed their work closely, and I believe them to be well trained, experienced, highly skilled, and dedicated to producing quality publications. The problem is one of perception—people in other departments don't understand publications work and don't realize how much time should be allowed for editing and proofreading. They also don't realize that quality is certain to suffer when we're forced to work under unrealistic time constraints.

I don't want to sound like I'm always making excuses, but I need to convince my boss and our in-house customers of two things: that our editors are competent and that they must be given the opportunity to do their best.

Solution: If it's any consolation, publications specialists everywhere have felt the way you do at one time or another—misunderstood and unappreciated. One of your important tasks as manager, however, is to serve as a public relations agent for your staff. It's essential that you address problems as they occur so that your staff doesn't develop an undeserved bad reputation within the company. Correcting misunderstandings on a case-by-case basis is one step; another is educating your customers and your boss about the editorial process in general.

Even though you may find it unpleasant, you must investigate the complaints you receive, evaluate your findings, and respond appropriately. Here are some steps that will help you ensure that your staff gets a fair shake.

Find out what happened. Meet with the person who complained about the work. Listen carefully to the complainer and take detailed notes. Most important of all—and this is a common mistake—don't offer any preliminary opinions about what happened. Comments like "I know Sue would never have missed that error—she must not have reviewed the final page proofs" will only make you look foolish if in fact she did.

Talk to everyone involved to get a balanced picture

Find out what *really* happened. Keep in mind as you're listening to the complainer that this is only one interpretation of what happened. Talk to everyone involved to get a balanced picture. Your investigation should be positive and low-key; don't make the people you're talking to feel like someone's fate lies in their hands. Emphasize that you want to find solutions, not place blame.

Set the record straight. Talk with your boss and present a summary—not every little detail—of what you discovered. Present your conclusions about the problem, but be sure to back up your opinions with industry-standard statistics. Here are a few for your arsenal:

- An experienced, well-trained editor can copyedit six to eight double-spaced (250-word) pages per hour. (Poorly written, error-ridden manuscripts take longer.)
- For a 200-page double-spaced draft manuscript, an editor would need three to four days to do a thorough job.

With only half that time, your editor couldn't be expected to detect and fix every last error. It's important that you correct any inaccurate perceptions your boss may have as a result of hearing only one side of the story. (See the "Estimating Editorial Tasks" on page 279.)

Focus on prevention rather than on blame. You won't sound like you're just making excuses if you also offer ideas to prevent problems in the future. You may not be able to prevent tight deadlines, but maybe you can set up procedures that will enable your staff to respond to emergency requirements more effectively. For example, you could design a checklist for rush editing jobs. When there isn't time to fix everything and the deadline can't be moved, customers should prioritize the areas they want editors to focus on.

Educate your customers *before* problems occur. Meet with your customers before their projects begin so they'll know what to expect, and give them guidelines that will help them develop accurate project schedules so quality won't have to be compromised at the end. Make it clear that you and your staff are there to help, not to slow things down. Comments like "I know you've been working on this project for months, and I realize how important it is that the final report be perfect" and "We're here to help you" can go a long way toward establishing a good working relationship before the deadline pressure hits.

Publicize your staff's achievements. When your editors receive letters of appreciation, post the letters in a prominent place. (If they haven't received any lately, drop some hints to your customers.) Encourage those who are pleased with your services to let your boss know. You may even consider developing a feedback form for people to fill out after their projects are complete—asking for comments will also show your customers that you value their opinions. You may get negative as well as positive comments, but that's good: They'll help you build on strengths and identify problems.

It can be difficult to keep your cool when you feel that your staff aren't being treated fairly, but a defensive response will only diminish your credibility and antagonize your customers. If you focus on productive solutions and continuing education instead, you'll spend less time playing defense attorney.

—*Robin A. Cormier*

Testing for Editorial Skills

Hiring the right person may be the most important part
of a manager's job

Most publications managers have found out the hard way that a new employee's real skill level often doesn't reveal itself until *after* he or she has been hired. Many of us have been impressed by résumés that show just the right experience, only to find out—too late—that time in a job doesn't necessarily mean a job well done.

Interviews and reference checks can tell you a lot about a person, but the only sure way to determine skill level before hiring is to test your applicants. Copyediting and proofreading skills are relatively easy to test for, as is proficiency in desktop publishing and wordprocessing programs. Writing and substantive editing are a little trickier, however, because grading becomes more difficult. (More on that later.)

Before you begin any testing program, you should be aware of the legal aspects of this part of the hiring process. First, check with your personnel or human resources department. Many companies, aware of the fact that discrimination complaints can arise from unfair tests, shy away from any kind of testing. Other companies allow only very straightforward tests, such as typing tests, or commercially available tests that screen for aptitude and psychological factors.

The reason for their caution is that the federal government's EEOC (Equal Employment Opportunity Commission) guidelines warn employers to be sure their tests do not in any way result in discrimination against minority groups. The EEOC's Uniform Guidelines on Employee Selection Procedures refer to this type of discrimination as "disparate impact on a protected class," and a job applicant who feels that he or she was unfairly tested must show that the test "selects applicants by religion, race, national origin, or sex in a pattern that significantly differs from the pattern of groups in the applicant pool" (*Employment Law Deskbook*, Matthew Bender, 1993).

If someone does file a complaint against you, you must be able to prove that your test is fair and job-related. A good test has the following characteristics:

- **The test must be a fair reflection of the skills required for successful job performance.** The process for ensuring fairness is referred to as *validation*, and it's a somewhat gray area; few formal guidelines exist for employers to follow. Basically, you must be able to show that the content of the test represents the type of work the applicant will be required to do and that passing test scores are a valid indicator of success on the job. Construct tests that contain the kinds of problems you expect your editorial and production employees to deal with. It's a good idea to administer new or revised tests to current employees first, to determine that the content is sound and to establish pass/fail scores.

- **The test must be given consistently over time, and it must be graded consistently.** You can of course change a test as job requirements change, but if substantial changes have been made, you should revalidate the test with your current employees. You should not adjust test scores or allow different cut-offs for different purposes.

- **The test should be as objective as possible.** Stick to errors that have undeniably right and wrong answers (that's why it's difficult to develop a writing test). In a copyediting test, for example, stay away from material that leaves room for different style and usage choices (unless you ask the applicant to follow a particular style guide). Your grading scheme should include factors like "Are all the necessary facts present?" and "Did the writer use the active voice?" Make sure you develop a grading key that establishes point values for various factors, and grade all applicants the same way.

- **The test should be given in a controlled setting.** To guard against copying of your materials, give the test only at your office. It's also a good idea to set time limits. Limits provide a level playing field, and they're a useful (if less than foolproof) way to assess a potential employee's speed and efficiency. Keep in mind that tests unnerve some people more than others.

Make it clear to all applicants that, in addition to test results, you will be looking at how well the person will work with others in the organization, suitability and enthusiasm for the job, and a host of other traits that a personal interview should attempt to reveal. Finally, keep records, including the actual tests, of all applicants tested for at least five years in case you are ever challenged.

If your human resources department balks at your request to give tests, assure them that you will seek their advice in developing and administering tests. The knowledge you want to test for is concrete and easily assessed, but some human resources managers may need to be convinced that much of an editor's or desktop publisher's job requires certain learned skills—which are easily and objectively tested for.

Hiring the right person may be the single most important part of your job as a manager. The wrong person will cause you untold losses in terms of productivity and quality of work and will ultimately reflect poorly on you and your department. Hiring the right person is well worth the extra time and effort it takes.

—Andrea J. Sutcliffe

How One Company
Handles Editorial Testing

Even highly skilled persons will fail your test—if they're not for you

When I interviewed for my first writing/editing position, an internship at a midsize newspaper, the editor-in-chief greeted me in a friendly enough manner, invited me to sit down, and immediately asked me to spell *rhinoceros*. I know now that he was testing my nerves as much as my ability to spell, but even today, several lifetimes later, the unfairness of that test still rankles. Oh, I spelled the word right (and got the job), but that editor learned nothing about my abilities. A thorough proofreading or copyediting test would have been more revealing—and fairer.

Since then, I've tested a number of editors myself. It's an illuminating experience. We have interviewed extremely talented people with incredible credentials—so skilled they gave us cause to fear for our own jobs—on paper, at least. But if they score poorly on our tests, they're not for us. We've constructed a test that plants "land mines" that people who edit for us need to be able to dodge. We feel more confident about offering employment to a candidate who can recognize and handle the subtleties of correct usage. Here is a partial list of errors that I expect someone to catch.

- Italics or boldface that is used improperly
- Indents, tabs, leaders, dashes (em and en) that vary in length
- Verb tense that changes in midstream
- Words that are improperly hyphenated at the ends of lines
- A new typeface or font size that creeps in for no particular reason
- Triple *l*'s (as in *willling*), especially in italic copy
- Repeated words, especially articles (as in "It isn't the the universe, but it is a fair representation")
- Errors that cluster (as in "It seamed as thought the party was over")
- Words that are misspelled in headlines
- French spacing (that is, two spaces after a period or colon)
- Perennial spelling goofs such as *flourescent*

It's also useful to see how applicants react to the terminology peculiar to your publications. Our audience consists of graphic designers and illustrators, so my tests include words like *gouache, bristol board, PostScript*, and *cropping*. It's important to test the professional vocabulary of editors who would be working with technical publications. Another way to do this is to seed the test with "correct but wrong" spelling of terms (as in "He used a simple palate in designing the stationary").

We have a test that plants "land mines" for editors to dodge

Finally, I introduce factual errors to see whether applicants are comprehending and analyzing what they are reading (as in "Twenty-seven of the 114 participants, nearly 35 percent, returned their surveys").

I never expect perfect scores, nor do I grade on a curve. That is, we don't hire the person who did least poorly, and we give extra points for intelligent queries or edits. We decide which "misses" could be rectified by training and which are unacceptable. Unfamiliarity with techno-jargon could be corrected by consulting a style guide or specialized dictionary, for example, but a shaky grasp of grammar should send up a red flag.

That's why I advise discussing the graded test with applicants so they can explain their edits. Perhaps there are mitigating factors or other employers' preferences at work that could be overcome by on-the-job training. What you're looking for is a sense that good judgment is being exercised.

I've often thought that the perfect editing or proofreading test would be a "princess and the pea" scenario: one very subtle and completely telling error buried in a dense 20-page document. The best candidate, the "real" editor, would sense the problem easily and not be paranoid about the piles of words that surround it. Of course, such a test would be as unfair as my *rhinoceros* episode. Instead, we settle for laying traps like the ones I've outlined here.

—*Catharine Fishel*

What's in a Name?
Plenty, if It's a Job Title

Your title should reflect your level of responsibility

Problem: I work in the publications department of an association. My problem is my job title: It doesn't adequately reflect what I do. I'm called the assistant editor, but my job duties go far beyond those of the typical assistant. I'm responsible for the production of two magazines, and although I don't determine the content of the articles, I set deadlines and work directly with the authors to ensure that their submissions are consistent with our association's standards. I coordinate all aspects of production, from design to printing, plus I handle a variety of other details.

My boss—not an editor—doesn't come from a publishing background, doesn't understand the distinctions between the many titles in the editorial field, and doesn't see why these distinctions are important. My concern has nothing to do with status or prestige (okay, maybe it does just a little); it has more to do with how I am perceived by the editorial and production staff I deal with. When I try to enforce deadlines, I can't help thinking that authors would be more responsive if they thought I was higher on the totem pole. How can I convince my boss that she should change my job title?

Solution: To describe the typical editor's job accurately, you would have to add so many modifiers that the title wouldn't fit on a business card. Although it can't spell out *all* of a person's duties, a job title certainly should reflect the level of responsibility that person carries. There are several steps you can take to help your boss understand why yours doesn't work.

First, write your own job description. Be as concrete as you can to give your boss a clear understanding of everything you do. Her management style may keep her from being aware of the full scope of your job, particularly if you keep things running smoothly and she doesn't have to get involved with the details. List every task you perform—even the most routine—and estimate how many hours of your workweek you spend on each. That will help you and your boss see which tasks take up most of your time.

Next, choose the title you believe best matches your duties. If no one title is a perfect match, choose the one that best reflects the *majority* of your responsibilities. Here are some titles and the duties commonly associated with them:

- *Managing Editor*—Is responsible for the publication's content. Often has subject-matter expertise; works with authors to help refine their articles.
- *Production Editor*—Oversees design, layout, composition, proofreading, and printing. Sets up schedules; coordinates and monitors costs and the performance of freelancers and vendors.
- *Copyeditor*—Reviews the text and corrects grammar, spelling, and punctuation errors; ensures consistency and conformance to the publication's style.
- *Editorial Assistant*—Performs administrative functions. Does fact-checking, secures copyright permissions, and researches. May proofread text or check bluelines.

Not all editorial positions fall neatly into one of these categories, and there are many more. Professional groups and associations, such as the American Society of Magazine Editors, the Association of American Publishers, Inc., and Women in Communications, Inc., often publish job descriptions and salary data specific to the various kinds of publications. Another good source is the *Dictionary of Occupational Titles*, published by the U.S. Department of Labor's Employment and Training Administration. Although it doesn't list salary data, this guide gives detailed descriptions of tasks and required education for thousands of positions.

Show your boss the job description you've written and a summary of your research. Explain to her that although publications job descriptions vary from one organization to another, certain basic definitions usually apply. List for her the specific areas where you feel your duties go beyond the usual definition of your current title, and explain why you want a new one: chiefly, to make your job go more smoothly. Be sure she understands that you aren't asking for a promotion.

A job title can be a very sensitive issue. Some organizations give people important-sounding titles in an attempt to make up for low salaries. For some people, this tactic works—their title is almost as important to them as their paycheck. Others don't care what they are called as long as they are compensated fairly. In your case, your title affects your dealings with others in your organization and may be interfering with your ability to keep the magazines on schedule. A new title may not make all of your authors meet their deadlines, but at least they'll have a better idea of whom they'll have to answer to when they don't.

—*Robin A. Cormier*

Many libraries have the Dictionary of Occupational Titles, *which is published by the North Carolina Occupational Analysis Field Center.*

Working with Vendors

They can be an economical alternative to handling work in-house

Problem: Until recently, I worked for a company that had a full-service, in-house publications department. The company I just joined uses outside vendors for all the services I am accustomed to having right down the hall. I've heard horror stories about the things that can go wrong—missed deadlines, unacceptable quality, skyrocketing costs, etc. How can I avoid unpleasant surprises and be confident that my publications projects will go smoothly when I work with vendors?

Solution: Working with outside vendors can be tricky if you don't establish good working relationships. Whether you are dealing with a printer, typesetter, designer, or editorial consultant, these basic guidelines will ensure that your project stays on schedule and within budget.

Before starting a project

- **Find out each vendor's specialty.** For example, not all designers specialize in four-color work, not all typesetters can handle complex mathematical equations, and not all printers can guarantee quick turnaround. However, not all vendors will turn away a job that falls beyond their capabilities. And almost all vendors will promise the optimal combination of price, quality, and service. Once you know each vendor's specialty, you are better equipped to choose the best one for the job.

- **Check references.** Before using a vendor, ask for the names of at least three clients who have used them for projects similar to yours. Ask to see samples of the work. Call each reference and ask detailed questions. Did the vendor meet the deadline? Were the actual costs close to the estimate? How well did the vendor accommodate changing requirements? Did the quality measure up to what was promised?

- **Clarify the mechanics of doing business.** Does the vendor require a deposit or purchase order to start the job? Will the invoice contain a breakdown of costs incurred? Is there a separate charge for pickup and delivery? How long does it typically take to get estimates? Will the vendor provide one point of contact for the job?

- **Find out how mistakes will be handled.** Even the best vendors experience occasional glitches. Pose a few "what if" scenarios. What if you mark an error on the blueline but it isn't corrected? Responsible vendors never charge for correcting their mistakes, and they should offer a significant price break if redoing the job isn't possible.

Getting bids

- **Put your requirements in writing, and get written bids as well.** Give vendors a deadline for submitting bids. Allow at least 24 hours; more time may be necessary depending upon the size and complexity of the job. Be available to answer questions; if you must designate someone else to answer questions, ask that person to document vendors' questions and the answers given.

- **Compare apples with apples.** If you want bids on the same job from several different vendors, be sure to give them all exactly the same information. If one vendor raises a question that changes the specifications, tell the other bidders about the change.

- **If someone else in your company will be handling the job and working with the vendor, have that person get the bids.** Most vendors report problems when an intermediary who knows very little about the project is in charge of getting bids. Explaining the job as completely and accurately as possible and clarifying all your expectations up front can help ensure that the bids you receive will be accurate.

- **Find out how much changes to the original specifications will cost and at what stage they will cost the most.** Most vendors of publications services will confirm that changes are the most common cause of escalating costs, no matter what the service. Knowing the cost implications of a change may influence your decision about whether or not to make it. Don't wait until you get the bill to find out that adding a paragraph at the last minute doubled your costs—it may not have been that important!

- **Don't choose a vendor on the basis of price alone.** Once you have worked with all the bidders and become familiar with the quality of their work, you can make a more informed decision. Consider responsiveness as well. Did the vendors meet your deadline for bids? Were they able to answer questions clearly and completely? Remember that the lowest bid is not necessarily the best choice.

During a project

- **Stay in touch.** Know the name of the representative handling your job as well as that person's backup. If you don't hear from anyone, don't assume that everything is on track—check in. It doesn't hurt to reiterate critical instructions, particularly if the specifications changed while the job was in progress.

- **Give the vendor a "heads up" whenever possible.** Even if the job isn't a rush, the advance notice will be greatly appreciated. Furthermore, be sure to let vendors know when a project *won't* be arriving on schedule after you have put them on standby.

- **Establish the sequence of interim steps in the process.** For example, will your designer show you comprehensive layouts and then page proofs? At what point will you see the material for the last time before no further changes can be incorporated? If you make changes to the blueline, will you get another one? If so, will you be charged for it? Get dates for your review steps and find out how long you can take for each one without disrupting the schedule.

Establish a relationship

- **Be loyal to a vendor.** Although it's advisable to develop a pool of vendors, there are some benefits in using only one resource for certain jobs. It takes time for you to establish a good working relationship and for a vendor to determine the best way to respond to your needs. You can make the most of this investment in time by continuing to use the vendor routinely. Most vendors offer price breaks for quantity, but they don't always advertise this fact—ask about it. Most vendors will ensure that you get superior service if there's a possibility of more work.

- **Discuss your budget.** Once you work with vendors and understand their pricing, be open about your budget constraints. Vendors may be able to make some money-saving suggestions once they know your priorities.

- **Know each vendor's full range of capabilities.** Most vendors welcome the chance to give you a tour of their facilities. Take advantage of this free education. Talk to the vendor about your work in general, not just a particular project, to see whether there are other ways you could work together. For example, you may be surprised to discover that your editorial firm also offers design services.

- **Ask for feedback from vendors after the job is complete.** Find out whether you conveyed your instructions in the best way. For example, a desktop publisher may prefer a summary sheet of changes rather than Post-its on each page. Ask for ideas on how to cut costs. Is it more cost-effective to submit the entire job at once rather than one section at a time? Could you have saved money by adding a week to the turnaround time? Once you know a vendor's procedures, you can set up your own schedule in the most cost-effective way.

Working with vendors can be an economical alternative to handling some kinds of work in-house, if you make informed choices, keep close tabs on the project, and convey your expectations clearly.

—Robin A. Cormier

Delegating without Getting Burned

'Every time I hand off part of a project, something goes wrong'

Problem: As a communications manager, my biggest priority is getting things done under tight time constraints without sacrificing quality. I generally achieve this goal, but during performance reviews, every supervisor I've ever had has marked me down in one area: They've all said I don't delegate enough.

It's not that I don't want to delegate; I'd love some help. But every time I try to hand off part of a project, something goes wrong and I have to spend time cleaning things up—usually more time than if I'd done it myself to begin with. I've been burned so many times that I'm hesitant to try again, even though my boss has expressed concern that I'm working so many hours. What am I doing wrong?

Solution: Effective delegating is one of the hardest things for managers to learn. Typically the more dedicated and conscientious people are, the less likely they are to want to hand off work. That's good in some ways, but in the long run it can be detrimental to both the person and the organization. It won't be possible for you to take on new responsibilities and grow professionally if you can't delegate some of your current duties.

How not to delegate

Almost everyone who has ever managed a project has a horror story to tell about an assistant who did more harm than good. Although it's true that the problem is sometimes the delegatee, more often the problem is that the delegator used one of these faulty methods:

- **Not enough supervision: the "sink or swim" method.** Some people's idea of delegating is to drop a project in somebody else's lap, walk away, and hope for the best. Unless you're very lucky, this method won't work. There's a big difference between delegating and dumping.

- **Too much supervision: the "don't make a move without checking with me" method.** You aren't really delegating if you're working with your assistant much the same way a ventriloquist works with a dummy. If you dictate every move a person makes without letting him or her exercise any judgment, you aren't saving yourself much time, and your assistant won't acquire the skills to work independently.

How to delegate effectively

The more time you invest in the initial stages of the project, the better your results will be. These steps will help ensure that things don't go off track:

- **Give clear, complete instructions.** Put as much as you can in writing. This forces you to really think through what you're asking your assistant to do, and it gives him or her something to refer to while working. Have someone else—preferably someone not familiar with the project—review your written instructions before you go over them with your assistant to be sure everything is clear. Sometimes when you're intimately familiar with a project, it's easy to forget to mention an important detail.

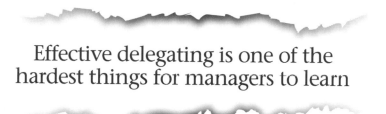

Effective delegating is one of the hardest things for managers to learn

- **Explain the big picture.** Don't just explain the tasks at hand; explain the goals of the project as a whole. Your assistant probably won't be very inspired if you just say, "Check this list of names against the database printout." Explain why it's important: "We think this mailing will be our most successful yet, but we have to be sure our lists are accurate."

- **Set up checkpoints and give clear feedback.** Don't wait until your assistant is almost finished with the project to check on it, but don't pop into the office doorway every five minutes to see how things are going, either. Agree on a checkpoint up front: "Once you've edited the first 10 pages, bring them to me so I can be sure you're on the right track." Then give clear, meaningful feedback. Comments like "You aren't doing enough" won't help; be specific: "You caught a lot of typographical errors, but you missed these grammatical errors. Slow down a little, and read the manuscript a second time."

- **Maintain a healthy mix of trust, patience, and common sense.** Try to forget about your bad experiences and assume that this time delegating will work. An assistant who senses your lack of faith will be more likely to fail. Reassure him or her that asking questions won't be an unwelcome interruption. Of course, there's always the chance that things won't work out, and this is where common sense comes in: Be sure you've given the arrangement a fair chance before you pull the plug. The most common mistake in delegating is deeming the effort a failure without giving the person a chance to learn from mistakes. If you "clean up" after things go wrong, you haven't gained anything. An assistant who gets a chance to fix his or her own mistakes will learn from the experience (we hope).

- **Give thanks and credit.** It's natural that you'll get better results from people when they know you'll be appreciative and give them credit for their efforts. Letting your boss know what a good job your assistant did will serve two purposes: Your assistant will get well-deserved credit, and your boss will see that you're delegating as requested. One of the most important aspects of delegating is acknowledging the contributions of others while still taking full responsibility for the end product.

Although delegating may not seem worth the risk at first, it can be very rewarding when it goes well. You'll be able to meet your deadlines without spending day and night at the office, and your assistant will learn valuable new skills.

—Robin A. Cormier

Managerial Burnout—Is There a Cure?

Do you need a vacation or are you ready for a job change?

Problem: I've been managing a busy proposal production department for about four years. We produce 100 proposals yearly—all on a quick-turnaround basis. Because I coordinate all production schedules for the department, my day is a steady stream of phone calls, meetings, questions, and problems. Until recently, I enjoyed the fast pace and the challenge of problem solving. Lately, though, it is all I can do to drag myself to the office in the morning. I'm afraid that if one more person dumps a problem in my lap, I'll become violent. My job hasn't really changed; I just seem to have lost my ability to cope with it. Is there any cure for burnout? How can I tell if the time has come for me to look for another position?

Solution: The most frustrating thing about your job as a proposal manager is that most of your good work is invisible. If you are doing your job well, people see only that your department meets deadlines and produces high-quality work. They don't see the juggling you do to maintain that reputation. Few people realize that to meet those daily deadlines, you probably had to deal with malfunctioning equipment, a chronically absent employee or a demanding client, or inevitable last-minute rush jobs. You don't get too many pats on the back just for getting through the day, and sometimes that's the toughest job of all. Under these circumstances, it takes effort to stay motivated. People in almost every line of work come to a point where the daily problems seem to outweigh the satisfactions of the job. That can be a hard point to get past.

There are two kinds of burnout: temporary and permanent. Maybe all you need is a relaxing vacation, but you could be ready for a job change. You have to figure out which kind of burnout you are experiencing before you can determine the best course of action to take.

Face the situation squarely

The most important thing to do when burnout sets in is to take some kind of action. At your level of frustration, it's unlikely that you'll be able to conceal your dissatisfaction from your coworkers for long. Burnout is highly contagious. As a manager, you set the tone for your entire department: If you have a negative attitude, a lack of energy, and a short temper, you will probably start to see those symptoms in the people who report to you. And a departmentwide case of burnout will only make your problems worse.

The worst thing you can do is try to keep your feelings to yourself. Before they have a noticeable effect on your job performance, have a heart-to-heart talk with your boss. Before you meet, though, take time to gather your thoughts. If you ask for a consultation without first trying to identify the sources of your frustration, your boss may feel that you are just whining and won't take your problems seriously.

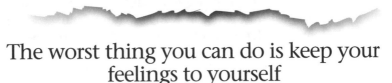

The worst thing you can do is keep your feelings to yourself

Make a list of everything you *like* about your job. Include what's important to you, like having talented coworkers and earning a good salary, as well as superficial pluses, like a nice office and a short commute. If you have trouble coming up with more than one or two items, think back to when you first accepted the job—what was it that made the position seem appealing? Then make a list of all the things you *dislike* (this list should come quickly, given your current state of mind). Try to list the drawbacks in order of importance to you.

When you meet with your boss, you must explain that you have some serious concerns but want to do whatever you can to help straighten things out. Go over the items on your list, and ask your boss to help you see which of the problems can be corrected and which can't. For example, you probably can't fire your entire staff, but maybe you can purchase some new computer equipment.

Weigh your options

Chances are, your boss won't be able to give you a cure for every problem. In the end, you'll have to decide whether the good things on your list outweigh the bad. Here are some other steps that can help clarify your thinking:

- **Take a few days off.** It's almost impossible to take an objective look at your job while the phone is ringing and people are lined up outside your door. Try to escape to a calmer setting and give yourself a chance to relax before making big decisions about your future.

- **Update your résumé.** Even if you don't intend to send it out, documenting your strengths and accomplishments can be invigorating. Maybe you don't give yourself enough credit for the load you juggle every day.

- **Go on a few job interviews.** Even if you haven't decided for sure that it's time to change jobs, take a realistic look at your options. Checking into other positions can make your own job seem not quite so bad—and remember, *no* job is perfect.

- **Take on a new project.** Even though taking on *more* work can seem like a ridiculous step to take under the circumstances, doing so can actually give you a shot of adrenaline. One editor I know volunteered to write her company's annual report, a task that was usually handled by a freelancer. She didn't get to do much writing in her editorial position, so the annual report was a refreshing change of pace. She had to work long hours for a few weeks to meet the deadline; although she enjoyed the project, it gave her a new appreciation for her regular job.

In today's economy, few of us have the luxury of holding out for the perfect job and accepting nothing less. Certain frustrations are just part of the territory with almost any job. But you shouldn't be afraid to move on if your situation becomes truly intolerable. The trick is figuring out whether your expectations are realistic; don't run away just because you had a bad week or even a bad month. To make a sensible decision, assess the situation carefully, take an active role in trying to make things better, and, meanwhile, research your options thoroughly.

—*Robin A. Cormier*

Making Sure That Big, Important Rush Project Gets Done Poorly

It's easier than you may think!

When you're in charge of a publications project, your entire attention and energy should be focused on making it as difficult as possible for the players on your team to accomplish their mission. Here is a distillation of my 15 years of experience in impeding the production process.

- **Don't make a plan.** After all, if you take the time to figure out all the steps involved, the order in which they should be done, and how long they're going to take, you might be able to anticipate potential problems and have the staff available to complete the project on time.

- **Don't write a schedule.** Instead, continually rant about how difficult the final deadline will be to meet, thus increasing the anxiety level while ensuring that nothing can be done to relieve the tension. An important part of this strategy is to see to it that team members have no idea ahead of time what might be expected of them or when. When you give someone a task, don't give a real deadline—just say ASAP.

- **Micromanage design.** If the project requires creative design work, be sure to require a justification and explanation of each layout detail, type choice, and color specification every step of the way; don't evaluate design in terms of overall effectiveness. The degree to which you employ this strategy should be in inverse proportion to your understanding of the craft of design—the less you know, the more you pick!

- **Change the task several times.** Preferably, adjust the specs with each review cycle. The best way to accomplish this is not to tell anyone what you expect to be done or how you expect them to do it—until they've gone ahead and done it another way. Another good strategy is to rewrite text during the production process; this can be employed at any stage, but increases in effectiveness the later it is used. The very best time is after your job has gone to the printer—at blueline or (preferably) on press.

There are, of course, volumes that can be written on this topic, but if you follow just the pointers given here, you will be well on your way to becoming a complete roadblock to any publications project you may undertake. It takes practice and discipline, but you can do it. And, as an added bonus, half of your production staff might just quit in the middle of the job.

—Jayne O. Sutton

Taming the Beast:
Lessons for Managing Large Projects

Take a deep breath—and create a schedule. It may just work

A few years ago the writers and editors at EEI embarked on their most ambitious publishing project to date—writing an 800-page reference book for writers and editors. As we began to plan our efforts, one thought kept haunting me as lead editor: "If we only knew now the lessons we will have learned when this is over, we could save ourselves a lot of time and agony." When we finished three years later, we had learned those lessons, and perhaps not surprisingly they are similar to the lessons learned at the end of any large editorial project.

Although every large job has its own special set of challenges, knowing the common pitfalls can help you avoid trouble. Here are a few observations, drawn from 15 years spent managing a variety of large projects, from coordinating the editing and production of research reports, to managing the quick-turnaround production of 2,000-page proposals, to planning and writing a reference book.

Don't let the size of the task get you down

Soon after you've accepted your assignment, you will wake up one morning convinced that you are facing an impossible task. To overcome this paralyzing feeling (which, by the way, may recur at fairly regular intervals), remind yourself that all large projects are really just many small projects and that all small projects can be completed. Taking one step at a time, without stopping to agonize over the magnitude of it all, can help you get through the days and weeks ahead. Set small goals for yourself and then singlemindedly do whatever it takes to meet them. The sense of control that results from even the smallest achievement will give you the momentum to carry on.

Make a detailed schedule

Creating a written schedule for every detail of the project will restore your feelings of competence and control. Step 1 is to assign people to as many of the tasks as possible. Step 2 is to estimate how long each task will take; give yourself plenty of cushion. (But be careful not to set unrealistic—or worse, false—deadlines for your staff and reviewers; once they find out that you're not playing fair, you'll lose their cooperation.) Step 3 is to map out those tasks in pencil on a calendar, thinking about how you can organize things so that several tasks can be done concurrently (the more people you have helping, the easier it is to do this).

By starting with final due dates and working backward to the present, you can begin to get a concrete picture of the realities facing you. You'll no doubt adjust these milestones as the project moves along, but at least you can determine up front whether a job is physically possible given the time and resources available. A word of advice: The best way to get others to adhere to the deadlines you set is to ask them to help you draw up the schedule. If you listen to their concerns and invite their suggestions, you'll increase the odds that they will work with you, not against you.

It's a good idea to set up a calendar, either on paper or on the computer (using one of the many project management programs available), so that you can monitor progress day by day.

If you have any leeway in deciding task order or priorities, consider tackling the toughest parts first. This approach has two benefits: You know the worst is over relatively early on, and if the task is really as tough as you think it will be, you'll have time to recover. In the case of the book project I mentioned earlier, we first tackled the six chapters that explained grammar, and, yes, we had to rewrite the entire first draft. But at least we had time to recover, and we learned some valuable lessons that helped us when we wrote less demanding chapters.

Getting results from staff and reviewers

Assigning the right person to the right task is obviously important; you try to find that perfect match of skills, experience, and availability. Once you're ready to make assignments, take the time to put in writing exactly what you expect each person to do. To prevent misunderstandings and possibly the need to redo work, meet with each person to go over the assignment in detail; time spent here almost always pays off later. Brainstorm ideas, try to predict areas of difficulty, and decide on an approach. Then agree on the time needed to do each task and on the interim and final deadlines. The result is that everyone starts out feeling that the project is doable, manageable, and perhaps even enjoyable. Be aware, however, that this will be the last time anyone will have those feelings.

After a few days or a few weeks, all the details that you somehow overlooked will come to light; they range from overly sanguine estimates of time and money to difficulties encountered by your staff. On our book project, I assumed that all editors were really frustrated writers at heart and that this book would give our staff editors a chance to write on topics near and dear to their hearts. What I later discovered was that most editors become editors because they find writing to be extremely painful. They also find it painful to be edited! Here, a dose of encouragement and a few suggestions helped put them back on track. If that approach doesn't work, you may have to start over with new people; this is one of the times you'll be glad you added a little cushion to your original schedule.

Regular team meetings—once a day or once a week, depending on the pace of your project—are a good way to encourage communication and head off problems. Try to keep these meetings short; some managers feel

Regular team meetings are a good way to encourage communication

that a 15-minute status meeting first thing every morning is essential to holding together a large project with an approaching deadline.

Another factor that can wreak havoc with your plans is surprises from the people who are reviewing or evaluating your work—your "clients," whoever they might be: your boss, your publisher, or other managers in your company. The impact of their involvement can take many forms, including objections to your tone, approach, writing style, or design; failure to meet the review deadlines you so carefully established; or a switch in the direction or scope of the project as a whole. The words you hope you don't hear are "Start over."

Get organized

Early on, you'll need to figure out the best way to organize the paper that will begin flowing across your desk. Create file folders for each section, chapter, or other logical division of the job. If writers and editors will be working on computers, draw up a list of file names for them to use so that it will be easy to find everything later on. Also, to save time later, give everyone a style sheet that gives formatting instructions, including head levels, fonts, margins, and spacing, and that also specifies the preferred editorial style—points such as capitalization, abbreviations, and treatment of numbers.

To keep track of revisions, get in the habit of putting a date on every version (and every photocopy) of the manuscript. Some offices find that photocopying review copies on different-colored paper helps reduce confusion; if the latest version is on blue paper, for example, and someone turns in revisions on pink paper, you'll be able to spot the problem immediately. The pitfall here occurs when reviewers turn in photocopies—on white paper—of their changes. Also, never throw away any early drafts or review copies until after the project is printed. Your work area may begin to look like a fire hazard, but if something gets lost or overlooked, you'll have a paper trail (or paper highway, as the case may be).

Keep it moving

If you've come this far, you have realized that persistence, patience, and a sense of humor are the qualities you've needed most. You may find inspiration in Winston Churchill's famous remark, "Never give in, never give in, never, never, never, never..." because there will surely be days when you will want to. Churchill, obviously an experienced manager of large projects, also said, "Now this is not the end. It is not even the beginning of the end. But it is, perhaps, the end of the beginning," which may be all you can say about your progress at this point.

It is also at this point that you become the project cheerleader. It's time to empathize with, soothe, motivate, and encourage your team. Try to help them over the rough spots and nudge them gently toward their deadlines. Be willing and available to roll up your sleeves and help in any way you can. (This is more important to morale than you will ever know.) Speak optimistically about how great things will be when everything is finished, and talk about the celebration party to come.

The light at the end of the tunnel

There is a magic—if fleeting—moment in every project when you know that everything will turn out fine: Your reviewers have run out of time or gone on to other projects, your writers have finished, editing and production are well under way, and except for the occasional minor crisis (at the last minute, someone decides to delete figure 2 on page 9 of a 300-page document with 75 figures), the worst is probably over.

At this point you may start to feel a sense of relief (and perhaps a twinge of regret) that the project that has taken over your life is about to end. Enjoy this moment while you can: With one large successful project behind you, it won't be long before news of your accomplishment reaches others who will need your help.

—Andrea J. Sutcliffe

Steps for Reviewing an Index

An index should be a reliable map to your publication

If you use in-house or freelance editors or indexers, you'll need to review their work. Just as a writer isn't usually the best proofreader for his or her own work, even the most careful indexer may make a mistake and not see it. No index should be considered final until someone other than the indexer has reviewed it thoroughly. If that ends up being you, here's a step-by-step guide.

Style and format. These are the first things to check. Use the checklist you provided the indexer to make sure these items have been properly taken care of:

* Has the index been alphabetized to your specifications?
* Has the preferred indented or paragraph style been followed?
* Has the indexer placed the cross-references properly?
* Are the page references given in the style you requested?

Main headings. Next, read all the main headings for general coverage and content as well as wording. Check them against the table of contents, introduction, and executive summary to make sure all major topics have been covered. Ask yourself the following questions:

* Are key words given first?
* Will the headings make sense to the reader?

Subheadings. Read the subheadings for conciseness, wording, and logic.

* If you feel that a subheading is too long, inaccurate, or misleading, now's the time to correct it. For example, the heading *Cooperative apartments* with the subheading *documentation* means something quite different from *Cooperative apartments* with the subheading *documents to study before buying.*
* Try to eliminate single subheadings. Consider either doing away with a single subheading completely or else join it to the main heading with a comma. For example, if *Annual percentage rate* is a heading with the single subhead *manufactured homes*, make the heading *Annual percentage rate, for manufactured homes.*
* Make sure subheadings are grammatically parallel. For example, if *Mortgages* is a heading with the subheadings *prepayment* and *refinancing*, change them to *prepaying* and *refinancing.*

Cross-references. Check all cross-references for accuracy. If you've made changes in the headings in text, make sure these changes haven't affected any cross-references in the index. Watch out for

- differences in wording between a cross-reference and the heading it refers to, and
- a cross-reference to a heading that has been deleted.

Page references. As you go through the index, spot check the page references for accuracy. It's easy to mistype a number, particularly if the page references are complicated. If you find many errors, you may want to go back through the index more thoroughly. Otherwise, a final random check of about 10 percent of the page references should be enough.

Spell checking. If the indexer hasn't done so, or if you've made extensive changes to the index, you'll need to spell check it. For very technical text, consider using a spell checker that is specifically geared toward your field. For example, the online version of *Stedman's Medical Dictionary* has a spell checker that is invaluable for indexes to medical books. You may want to have the index proofread one last time for spelling errors an electronic checker won't catch.

Last and most important. Put yourself in the shoes of a reader:

- Will this index help me understand the kinds of information I can find in this publication?
- Will the wording and cross-references make that information easy for me to find even if I don't know everything about the subject?

If the answer to both questions is yes, your job is done. If not, go back to the headings, subheadings, and cross-references and look for ways to improve them.

Like any other essential piece of a publication, an index needs careful reviewing—despite its last-place position in the publication process.

—Catherine Dettmar

Crossing a Bridge of Shyness: Public Speaking for Communicators

You don't have to be a silver-tongued devil to hold your own

Americans in general are more afraid of speaking in front of others than they are of snakes, heights, or death itself. That's the finding of one widely cited survey and, asked to step outside the written word, many writers, editors, and publications managers certainly would say they share that fear.

Communication expert Nusa Maal Gelb says there is a "culture of fear" surrounding public speaking. It's almost as if we believe we're *supposed* to be afraid. Yet it's clear that effective interpersonal communication—and that mostly means speaking—correlates highly with personal and professional success.

Speaking ability says a lot about you

Oral skills count in a wide range of situations and audiences: personal interviews, casual staff meetings, formal presentations before hundreds. As with any other human behavior, success in public speaking depends on two factors: confidence and competence, both of which tend to improve with practice. How do you acquire them? Becoming a good speaker requires an ongoing mediation between personal and public selves. The mediation involves two interrelated processes:

- Recognizing and managing the internal (personal) component—feelings—that can get in the way or help.

- Constructing and delivering the external (public) component—a message—that can miss an audience or reach it.

Start by building your self-confidence

Facing an audience will be less threatening if you acknowledge and work through the natural shyness that we all feel to some degree.

Recognize how your fear affects you. Maal Gelb says that it's "a deep psychological truth" that speaking before others is asking your true self "to cross a bridge of shyness." Barbara Daly, a management trainer in Rochester, NY, asks her students to examine their fears about speaking. Are they fears of failure? Of exposure? Of judgment? Does the fear "save" you from having to put yourself out there? Focusing on the personal and professional benefits of speaking can help put fear in its place.

Some experienced speakers admit that their fear hasn't ever completely disappeared, but they've learned to manage it. Others say that their fear gives them an edge that helps them succeed—assuming, of course, that they manage to speak in spite of it. *Editorial Eye* readers who are would-be speakers might try listing the Top 10 Most Humiliating Bloopers Anyone Could Conceivably Make, and imagine living through them. For word people, articulating fear in writing can help defuse it, and there's good news: The worse that *can* happen almost never does.

Look for chances to practice. In a study of fear conducted at the University of Wisconsin, researchers checked physiological signs of stress such as pulse rate and blood pressure in students who were taking a public speaking course. Results showed that the students were uniformly less fearful at the end of the course than at the beginning, and they remained less fearful even when they spoke later before an unfamiliar audience. Each speaking experience makes it likelier that the next one will be less stressful.

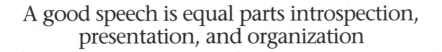

A good speech is equal parts introspection, presentation, and organization

But if you're leery of plunging in, restrict your first efforts to somewhere other than your workplace. Take a class at a community college, join a group like Toastmasters, or make a point of speaking up at meetings of your civic association. If these seem too risky, videotape yourself; then, if you must cringe at your obvious verbal tics (*like, uh, um, I mean, you know*) and distracting mannerisms, at least you can do so in the privacy of your living room.

Then work at increasing your competence

It's a truism that we enjoy what we're good at, so we do more of it; and as we practice, we get better at an activity and therefore feel more confident. Though intangible, confidence correlates in the real world with competence. But aren't some people just "naturally" gifted at speaking?

Perhaps so. But again, exercises can help everyone—even the Churchills of the world had to do what the rest of us have to do: practice, pay attention to how audiences respond, and keep the goal of effective speaking before us. These points are pivotal:

Express your message in human terms. Use quotations, anecdotes, humor, and vivid verbs to anchor the message in emotions the audience can empathize with. Maal Gelb says, "People are attracted to humanity. Much of the analytical information people hear, they simply filter out. Instead, we must communicate authentically if we are to reach an emotionally receptive place [in the listener]." In other words, speak about what matters to you and go on the faith that it will make a difference to your listeners.

According to Maal Gelb, physical and emotional delivery are the elements that "convey the multisensorial reality." In other words, a speech that conveys genuine emotions resonates with listeners. This resonance strengthens your rapport with them, and that's essential for getting an audience to pay attention. Given a choice, people resist a humorless, didactic presentation.

Remember the promise that competence keeps. An effective speaker goes beyond introspection and presentation that set the stage. The content of a speech must show deliberate, direct, and transparent organization.

For most speakers, just thinking about what to say ahead of time isn't enough. When speaking is extemporaneous—just thinking out loud—it's common to be "all over the place," says psychologist and writer/editor Bonnie Becker. She says that when we're preparing to speak, "The next step is to put our good ideas into a form that will reach another person." The structure of a speech *is* its content for an audience, which is why it can't be subtle. Listeners usually get only one chance to absorb a spoken message, so it's essential to articulate your structure and reinforce it with clear transitions throughout.

Continually refine your speaking skills

The goal is a speech that leaves both speaker and listeners feeling energized, encouraged, and, perhaps motivated for future action. As Jeff Scott Cook says in his book, *The Elements of Speechwriting and Public Speaking,*

> The ability to speak confidently and well is a talent universally admired and envied. But it is more than just a novelty, like juggling. The ability to hold an audience—to be heard by those who matter—is a crucial skill at any age.... [G]athering the courage to speak and the skill to do it well, we flex the mightiest muscle of civilization. Speaking up on what matters can be the proudest (and possibly the most important) moment of one's life....

Build on your strengths. When it comes to formulating ideas for speaking effectively to an audience, writers and editors have some real advantages. They are accustomed to using words carefully, emphasizing significant points, and organizing thoughts in meaningful patterns for an attentive audience. These skills are as applicable to speaking as they are to writing. A speech is just a vehicle for communicating ideas and information. Your skill with the written word can be transferred to a new dimension; you don't have to build it from scratch.

From the best writers you can continue learning the secrets of lead paragraphs, texture, tone, logical transitions, and conclusions and apply these elements to your speeches.*

Learn how to 'read' your audience. Make a commitment to speak whenever you can—especially in situations that will give you feedback. Volunteer to talk about your field to students at job fairs or local schools. Conduct an in-house training session, or join a professional group and give a presentation on your specialty. Ask the event organizer to let you hand out evaluation forms afterward. You can learn from all the comments you receive, negative or positive, as long as you keep an open mind.

Here's the magic of mediation. Over time, the focus on your own fears shifts toward an interest in the reactions of people listening to you. And you'll learn how to adjust for them. If you notice your voice has gotten stuck in rapid-fire fortissimo, for example, you'll take a deep breath and slow it down.

The turning point, then, for publications professionals determined to cross the bridge of shyness is accepting opportunities to speak instead of avoiding them. Transformation into a silver-tongued devil may not be your goal, and it can't be guaranteed anyway, but you *can* learn to give a comfortable and credible speaking performance—no small feat. You may never speak effortlessly in public, but you'll enjoy knowing you can reach the other side if you need to.

—Diane Ullius

---

*Ed. note: I found that serving as a volunteer judge for local high school debate competitions sharpened my ear for *contentions* ("This is what I'm going to say"), *signposting* of evidence ("This is why you can believe me"), and strong *conclusions* ("You heard it here and you love it!"). It's a worthwhile activity for novice would-be speakers, and the kids are quite wonderful.

Proofreading in the Computer Age

This quality control step matters more than ever

An *Editorial Eye* reader wrote: As lead editorial assistant (EA) in charge of quality control for our manuscript unit, I find more machine-made mistakes than ever before. Our EAs are great, but they trust their machines too much. I'm convinced that although we can turn out beautiful, professional-looking reports, it takes more proofreading than ever to ensure a nearly error-free product because we need to watch for mistakes made by both humans and machines. How do your editors feel about this?

The Editorial Eye **replies:** Thank you, thank you, thank you! It's with great distress that I hear people say that proofreaders are going the way of the dinosaurs—first of all, because if proofreaders disappear from the face of the earth I'm out of a job, and second, because I agree with you that with electronic publishing the proofreading step is more important than ever. Certainly there are companies and people who consider proofreading a simple matter of running the spell checker. We all know the pitfalls that can lead to: from/form, bored/board, United States/Untied States. But in most cases, proofreaders today are relied on to take more, not less, responsibility for content and sense. What is happening is that proofreading is changing. It's being done by different people and called by different names. Desktop publishing may rearrange roles and bring new demands, but the need for a thorough proofreading continues.

For example, a beautifully formatted page of text includes a reference, "The chart on page 42 illustrates the percentage of voters in favor of Ross Perot by state." The reader turns to page 42, and (lo and behold!) there is no chart. It's parked in all its graphic glory on someone's hard drive. Proofreaders are expected to alert someone to the fact that the chart is missing and to ask if it is still to be included and, if so, where? Human beings make these kinds of errors, and software cannot replace this kind of checking.

Proofreaders are also counted on to point out the fact that the dateline on a newsletter reads *volume 4, number 12, December 1996*, but that the running footer says *January 1997*. Software has been known to "automatically" adjust such information as a by-product of making (or correcting) another error. It has happened to *The Editorial Eye*. Boilerplate material is ripe for errors because it doesn't get scrutinized beforehand as closely as new material, and designers and desktop operators don't always read what's being placed on the page.

Proofreaders are still relied on to look at overall page makeup: Are ragged-right margins *too* ragged? Are lines *too* spacey or *too* tight? Have ellipses been treated differently in the same document? Electronic tools are only as good as the style sheets that have been set up and the people who use them. In short, nothing's guaranteed to be consistent or correct just because it has been coded and printed in an elegant font.

In the quality control classes I've taught, desktop operators and designers have *insisted* that these things never happen. At the risk of offending those who believe that their machines can do no wrong, I insist that these errors do happen. Desktop makes it easy to incorporate changes, small and large, and there tends to be more tweaking of documents. If it's a small change, like adding a sentence or word, the desktop operator may just type it in and forget to run spell check (or worse, presume that he or she couldn't possibly make a mistake). The result may be a line like this in a training manual: "Don't assume you know how to spell 'paraphenalia.' Look it up in the dictionery." If there is no proofreader to review such sentences, who will catch the errors?

Careless, last-minute changes can also result in contradictions of fact. Perhaps text has been added to update some demographic information. Did someone also think to update the accompanying graphic? Some reader somewhere will be chortling at your carelessness or writing you off as less than knowledgeable: Never underestimate the power of a foolish error to undercut the message. Only a final proofreading step can catch such a discrepancy.

Consider, too, this communication problem. I recently marked (ROM) in the margin of a document. The document I received back looked like this: TIMES ROMAN, from that point on. What happened was that the operator understood (ROM) to mean "Use Times Roman font." As a result, half the text ended up Times Roman and half Helvetica. If no proofreading is allowed for, who's expected to catch such an error?

You may not think of these tasks as proofreading. And, in fact, maybe in your organization it's the editor's job to review a document in its entirety before it goes to a client or the printer—or the project manager's job, or the desktop person's job, but proofreading by *somebody* is always going to be necessary, because errors will always be made.

—*Connie Moy*

'Endurance Training' for Electronic Publishing Specialists

Keep your career moving forward

Problem: During our recent search for an art director, we were surprised to discover that, regardless of experience or portfolio, most applicants could not pass a desktop publishing test in the software package they said they knew best. They simply didn't have the range of skills we needed: a talent for creative design accompanied by an understanding of electronic execution.

We're sending most jobs to the printer on disks, not mechanicals, and the art that goes with these jobs is usually part of the electronic file. Such files must be carefully prepared for output to avoid last-minute glitches that require expensive and time-consuming "fixes," color proofs, extra bluelines, and so on.

Our scenario isn't unique; many creative or production groups are looking for graphics professionals with strong software and prepress skills. What advice can I give applicants and aspiring staff members about how to prepare for this exciting but demanding and rapidly changing field?

Solution: Now that desktop technology has spread to the smallest offices and throughout the federal government, clients everywhere expect fast-turnaround electronic design and production, as well as the freedom to make changes at any point in the process. Most production groups can't afford the mistakes that result from putting someone with borderline technical skills on a key job or in charge of the technical performance of others.

Get an idea of what publishers need

An easy place to start your career endurance training is to scan the want ads in your local paper to see what publication design and production software experience employers are looking for. If you have the good fortune to have picked up working skills in QuarkXPress or PageMaker, highlight that fact in your résumé. If not, plan to learn. More newsletters, reports, brochures, and magazines are produced using these softwares than any others.

If you've already acquired strong design skills based on years of experience, consider learning to work with Adobe Illustrator or Macromedia FreeHand, which will give you more flexibility in executing your sketches and concepts for smaller publications like brochures, CD covers, and posters. For desktop publishers, speed and flexibility are of the essence.

Quark or PageMaker skills together with proficiency in a wordprocessing software such as Microsoft Word or WordPerfect will make you very marketable. Experience with all four will open most doors for you.

Target specialized skills others may lack

Some positions require familiarity with scanning photographs and using an image manipulation software such as Adobe Photoshop to crop and size or touch up digital photos. Employers may also require experience with a graphics software package—Adobe Illustrator, CorelDRAW!, or Macromedia FreeHand, for example. More specialized desktop production software, such as FrameMaker, Interleaf, and Ventura Publisher, is used to produce large, templated publications: directories, manuals, and textbooks. Potential employers with a need for these skills may have a harder time finding available candidates. If you know these types of software, you may qualify for a small group of higher-paying jobs.

Get real: get training

The advanced technical and creative skills that publications designers have are generally acquired over time through experience and exposure to a variety of publishing projects. EEI's art director, Sharon Rogers,* recommends what she calls "active looking": always keeping an eye out for page and type designs that work. But training in the desktop software of your choice at an authorized training center is also a professional necessity. A recognized program of study leading to a certificate or degree

For desktop publishers, speed and flexibility are essential

can introduce you to the creative concerns associated with design for print. Critiques from knowledgeable instructors or art directors will help you translate your creative concepts into working options and give you problem-solving ideas. Rogers recommends that people who are thinking about undertaking formal study research the instructors first. Do they have strong backgrounds in publishing or publication design? Will they give you a good foundation in the history of typography? If in doubt, talk to former students.

To master FrameMaker, Interleaf, or Ventura will probably require training and at least two years of professional application. If you take a class in

QuarkXPress and use it in a publications environment every day for a year, you will probably be able to pass a basic software test. You'll need to understand how to execute design specifications, create a style sheet, work with templates and master pages, format tables, import graphics, and use the automated features of each program.

Look for jobs that let you learn as you work

What if through your workplace or home business you don't get exposure to the software you need to learn? This can be a particularly difficult problem when you want to move into electronic publishing from another computer-related job. Consider making a lateral move into an organization that provides opportunities to advance to projects that will challenge you, while giving you a chance to get up to speed with a greater variety of software.

Too often, I receive résumés from wordprocessing specialists who want to be desktop publishers but who lack the professional skills needed to obtain an entry-level desktop position. If your software skills are limited to WordPerfect, Lotus, dBASE, and MS Mail, you fall into this category. Consider taking a wordprocessing job with an organization that does a variety of publications and work into new projects slowly while learning from others. In short, figure out the kinds of projects you want to be involved with, find out what tools come with the territory, and learn them. The rewards will be worth your effort.

—Amy Lenihan

---

*Sharon Rogers, who died unexpectedly in December 1995, believed that every creative project gives designers a chance to put a little something of themselves into it—even bread-and-butter work.

Surviving the Transition to a New Electronic Publishing System

Computer training comes in many packages these days

Problem: I'm the graphics manager at a branch office of a large equipment manufacturing company. Most of my office's publications are heavily formatted catalogs and training manuals; the desktop publishing software we've been using is fairly basic. Until recently, the branch offices selected their own software and chose their own production methods. The only companywide requirement was that all publications follow some general style guidelines.

Corporate headquarters has now decided to standardize the production process and unify the look of company publications. A high-end electronic publishing system has been selected and will be installed at all branch offices next month. Each branch must produce all its publications on the new system within a month. That gives us only a month to train. We have two options: We can purchase a set of books and videos and use them to train ourselves, or we can attend outside classes. The costs of either option, including our learning time, are deducted from our training budget for this year.

Fortunately, my six graphic artists are already computer-literate and are familiar with at least one or two different types of software, but none of us has any experience with the new system. We're working against tight deadlines as it is, and I'm not sure how we'll be able to switch over smoothly. I want to choose the most cost-effective option that keeps everybody's stress level to a minimum.

Solution: Because your learning time counts against your budget and you only have a month to get everyone up to speed, you'll have to look beyond the immediate, definable costs and think about the big picture. Don't assume that books and videos are cost-effective because they cost much less than tuition for outside classes; self-instruction is likely to take more time, which is money in the long run. Books and videos are good resources, but your staff can't ask them questions—and people have questions when they're learning.

With formal training, your staff will get instant feedback and learn the most efficient techniques from the very beginning. For example, most software programs offer users several choices for performing a single function. An instructor can guide your staff through the options and help them solve problems as they go along. Also, formal classes enable your staff to block off learning time. They won't progress nearly as quickly if they try to work through a book between deadlines and interruptions. It is almost impossible to learn a complicated software program this way.

One mistake many managers make when trying to save training dollars is sending their quickest, most productive staff member to class and expecting that person to come back and train the others. Even under ideal circumstances, very few people retain everything well enough to teach it. Also, because of the time spent helping others, the personal productivity of this "teacher" will be reduced just when it's needed most.

Since no one at your branch has any experience with the system and time is so short, your best bet is to opt for formal training instead of expecting your staff to train themselves. But there are many choices for computer training these days. Here are some ways to get the most for your training dollars.

- **Weigh the training options.** Training companies, individual consultants, community colleges, retail stores—these are just some of the resources available. If your corporate headquarters doesn't give you a list of preferred programs, ask the company that developed the electronic publishing system for referrals. Even better, the vendor may have a certification program for trainers, which means they have been screened to ensure that they meet a set of requirements and merit recommendation.

  Investigate several pricing options. The more customized the classes, the more quickly your staff will become productive on the new system. The ideal training experience would be to have the instructor tailor the course around your publications and teach it in your office. This option would be more expensive than sending your staff to a more general open-enrollment class, but the instruction they receive would be more relevant to their work.

  If deadlines won't allow your entire staff to be in class at the same time during the day, consider evening or weekend training. Because you have six people to train (seven, if you include yourself), you should also inquire about group rates. Even if the companies you are considering don't advertise group discounts, be sure to ask whether special rates are available.

- **Lay the groundwork for training.** Once you have decided on a source, meet with the person who will teach the classes. Telling the trainer your priorities in advance will help ensure that your objectives are met. Explain what you and your staff liked and didn't like about your old system. Review samples of the documents you will be producing on the new system. Give the trainer some background on your staff—their job duties, their software experience, their degree of computer literacy, and their reservations about the new system.

Good trainers know how to deal with the fear of the unknown and can highlight the benefits of the new system as well as its similarities to the old. It's very important that the trainer be an advocate of the system—so be wary of someone who has a strong bias toward some other program.

Before they attend class, meet with your staff to ensure that they all know what will be expected of them when they get back. Discuss your plan for the transition and how it will affect project schedules. Be sure they all understand that they'll have to hit the ground running. If your new system comes with a tutorial, have them work through it before class to become familiar with the system's features. They should also review the documentation that comes with the system to get an overview of how it works.

- **Minimize threats to newly acquired skills.** Once your staff has attended classes, the new system should be in place and ready to use when they get back. Be sure your hardware and software are set up correctly and that all settings have been tweaked before your staff begins using the system. Problems with the setup can cause instant frustration and get everyone off on the wrong foot. Don't give staff any reason to use the old system as a crutch. They'll be tempted to think "I'll use our old software for this project one last time because it will be quicker, and *next time* I'll figure out how to do it on the new system."

  To get you through the transition between the old and new systems, consider hiring temporaries to help you meet your deadlines. Bring in someone who is already well-acquainted with the system and who can help your staff solve problems rather than doing the work for them. If temporaries aren't an option, you may be able to enlist help from your company's other branch offices.

One of the simplest ways to minimize the problems associated with any transition is to maintain a positive attitude. Your staff take their cues from you. If you present the new system to them as a nightmare, that's exactly what it will be. If you emphasize the merits of the system, rather than the problems it will create, the adjustment period is bound to be smoother. And finally, express confidence in your staff. Their adaptability may surprise you.

—Robin A. Cormier

Electronic Copyright: We'll Be Spending the Next 10 Years Figuring It Out

Here are the issues writers and editors need to watch

The track record for fair use of copyrighted printed materials is mediocre; $5 billion is lost in this country each year from improper photocopying alone. Now we're faced with trying to define fair use of electronic text. Most publishers are rewriting their contracts to include electronic rights, often without additional compensation to authors. In fact, every time I wrote a contract for an author or a publisher this summer, I was writing new language.

The issues are so complex that we'll be spending the next 10 years figuring them out. (After all, we're just getting a handle on sales of copyrighted T-shirts.) The important thing to keep in mind is that the basic principles of copyright apply to electronic documents. Here's a refresher course in what they are.

What are 'rights'?

Upon completing a work, a creator becomes more than the owner of a new creation; that person becomes the owner of a valuable property, the copyright. One can do with a copyright whatever one might do with any other property—sell it, lease it, or leave it to someone in a will. The owner can restrict others from using it and sue to protect it.

It's important to remember that owning the copyright in a work and owning the work itself are two very different things. For example, when a photographer develops a picture, he or she owns both but is free to sell or license all or a part of the copyright interest to a publisher client and to sell or give away the original print to a fan.

What is fair use?

Original material, electronic or not, must pass two tests to qualify for copyright protection: It must show a minimal amount of creativity, and it must exist in a fixed form. The alphabetical order of a phone book represents hard work, but not originality of coordination, selection, and arrangement.

If both conditions are met, a work is automatically protected. But only the expression created by the author is protected: facts and ideas are freely available for others to copy, and the incorporation of materials created by others does not count toward meeting the author's creativity requirements.

The copyright scheme balances the rights of creators and users. Under the fair use doctrine, uses of copyrighted material without the owner's permission are favored for criticism, comment, news reporting, teaching, scholarship, or research—uses that facilitate the dissemination of knowledge. Courts consider the purpose and character of the use, the nature of the copyrighted work, the amount and substantiality of the portion used in relation to the entire copyrighted work, and the effect of the use on the potential market for or value of the work.

What do owners own?

The copyright law provides protection to the authors of original works of authorship, both published and unpublished. The copyright owner has the exclusive right to do and to authorize others to do these things:

- Reproduce the copyrighted work in copies or phonorecords.
- Prepare derivative works based on the copyrighted works.
- Distribute copies or recordings of the copyrighted works to the public by sale or other transfer of ownership or by rental, lease, or lending.
- Perform the copyrighted work publicly, in the case of literary, musical, dramatic, and choreographic works, pantomimes, and pictorial, graphic, or sculptural works, including the individual images of a motion picture or other audiovisual work.

How about other owners?

Ownership of copyright belongs to the creator unless a work is a joint work or a "work made for hire," created by two or more people "with the intention that their contributions be merged." The Copyright Act states that the authors of a joint work are co-owners of the copyright in the work. Each owns an undivided percentage interest in the whole and is free to exploit all of it as long as the others receive their respective share of income. In fact, each joint author can grant a nonexclusive license in the whole work without obtaining the permission of co-creators.

With a work made for hire, however—the employer or the commissioning party owns the copyright. Section 101 defines a work made for hire as meeting one of these requirements:

- It was prepared by an employee within the scope of his or her employment.
- It was specially ordered or commissioned for use as a contribution to a collective work, as a part of a motion picture or other audiovisual work,

as a compilation, as an instructional text, as a test, as answer material for a test, or as an atlas, if the parties expressly agree in a written instrument signed by them that the work shall be considered a work made for hire.

What works are covered?

Copyright protects "original works of authorship" that are fixed in a tangible form of expression. To be fixed the work need not be directly perceptible in three-dimensional form, so long as it can be communicated with the aid of a machine or device. For example, copyrightable works include the following:

- Literary works
- Musical works, including any accompanying words
- Dramatic works, including any accompanying music
- Pantomimes and choreographic works
- Pictorial, graphic, and sculptural works
- Motion pictures and other audiovisual works
- Sound recordings
- Architectural works

What about registration?

The fact is that you get copyright from the moment you take your hands off the keyboard. But there are some good reasons for demonstrating your claim. Litigation can be expensive and the loser may end up paying all costs. If you register within three months of creation, you become legally eligible for recouping attorney's fees and receiving statutory damages in the event of infringement.

Putting the copyright symbol on World Wide Web pages is also a good idea. Be very specific about the rights you're licensing, transferring, or retaining. Electronic publishing blurs the line between authors and publishers. For example, some publishers are claiming the right to include an author's print articles in an online database without express permission because it's just a storage medium—the equivalent of putting them on microfiche.

Sometimes, of course, copyright violation is a matter of innocent infringement. Many people don't realize that material "put up" in an electronic environment is not free for the taking.

Placing copyright notice

Although a published piece is copyrighted whether registered or not, placing notice is strongly recommended for electronic works because they are so easily copied and manipulated. The printed notice for visually perceptible copies (that is, other than recordings) should contain the following three elements:

- The symbol ©, or the word **Copyright**, or the abbreviation **Copr.**
- The first year of publication of the work. (For compilations or derivative works incorporating previously published material, the year of first publication of the compilation or derivative work is sufficient.)
- The name of the owner of the copyright, or an abbreviation by which the name can be recognized, or a generally known alternative designation; for example

© 1995 Gail E. Ross

For works reproduced in machine-readable copies (such as magnetic tapes or disks) from which the work cannot ordinarily be visually perceived without the aid of a machine or device, here are examples of acceptable notice:

- A notice embodied in copies in machine-readable form so as to appear on visually perceptible printouts either with or near the title or at the end of the work.
- A notice displayed at the user's terminal at sign on.
- A notice continuously displayed at the user's terminal.
- A legible notice reproduced durably so as to withstand normal use, on a gummed or other label securely affixed to the copies or to a box, reel, cartridge, cassette, or other container used as a permanent receptacle for the copies.

How long does copyright last?

Protection for works created after January 1, 1978, lasts from the date of creation until 50 years after the death of the creator. For works made for hire and anonymous or pseudonymous works, copyright lasts 75 years from publication or 100 years from creation, whichever is shorter.

What's not protected?

It's just as important for anyone concerned with protecting intellectual property to know about significant categories of material that are generally not eligible for protection:

- Works that have not been fixed in a tangible form of expression; for example, choreographic works that have not been notated or recorded or improvisational speeches or performances that have not been written or recorded.

- Names, titles, slogans, short phrases, familiar symbols or designs; mere variations of typographical ornamentation, lettering, or coloring; mere listings of ingredients or contents.

- Ideas, procedures, methods, systems, processes, concepts, principles, discoveries, or devices, as distinguished from a description, explanation, or illustration.

- Works consisting solely of information that is common property and containing no original authorship; for example, standard calendars, height and weight charts, tape measures and rulers, and lists or tables taken from public documents or other common sources.

- Works in the public domain; that is, after the term of copyright expires or, for a pre-1978 work, if it was published without proper notice. Anyone can use all or part of such work without getting permission or rendering payment.

- Works of the U.S. government. Copyright is not available for such work.

Keep your eyes open

Writers and editors have a responsibility to educate publishers and others, as well as a vested interest in following landmark legislation. Comprehensive new laws have yet to be written, but several recent court decisions concerning unauthorized electronic use of text and of scanned, derivative, computer-generated photographic images have confirmed the rights of the original creators. The Copyright Act is probably adequate for the transition, as long as it is interpreted correctly—and paid attention to.

—Gail E. Ross

Will Web Publishing Change the Way We Edit?

Publications people will have to learn new things, but the new media won't make them obsolete

Atechnical writer and editor asked *The Editorial Eye* about the future of editing, given the revolutionary changes that publishing on the World Wide Web has brought to the traditional process:

> We have established an internal Web where many departments publish individual home pages. The process for publishing on the Web has been an informal one so far, and there are no aesthetic, stylistic, or technical standards or guidelines in place.

> I am writing to you to inquire if you or any of your readers have experience in establishing standards and guidelines for Web or Internet publishing....

> I believe it would require a small army of editors to edit the volume of text now on the Web combined with future publications. My feeling is that editing as we know it must change to fit Web publishing. I would welcome feedback on this subject and greatly appreciate any guidance, information, and stories you can share with me.

The Editorial Eye **replies:** Editing must change for the Web, but perhaps not so much as you think. In paper publishing, different documents require different rules and procedures: An annual report requires more editing and more attention to detail than an office memo. Similarly, not all Web documents are equal.

Formal or informal?

Consider the purpose of your document. Is it permanent or temporary? Internal or public? The answers will determine how formal the editing and review process should be. When you say that some of your documents are for an internal Web, I assume that means they are inaccessible to people outside your organization. If so, you can treat them like internal paper documents. Memos and internal reports don't usually need an army of editors.

The sheer number of pages that you're putting up isn't the only consideration. For the kinds of documents you're publishing on the Internet, you'll have to determine the level of editing that's appropriate, just as you do for paper documents.

Part of the difficulty is that the word "publishing" brings to mind books, journals, annual reports, and other formal publications of an organization. But everything that comes out of your laser printer and is seen by someone else is in a sense a publication. Just as you trust your employees to correspond on your letterhead without subjecting every letter to editorial scrutiny, you may want to have places on your Web site for posting informal documents that won't need strict quality control. Whether that's appropriate depends on your corporate culture and the purpose of your Web site.

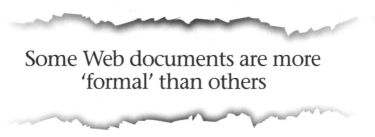

Some Web documents are more 'formal' than others

All "formal" documents will need to be routed for evaluation through a central quality control point—whether a publishing committee or a lone editor—before being posted online. What you don't want is people independently putting formal stuff on the Internet without regard to style (the way they're doing now on your internal Web).

Online style guides

For your home page and other formal Web documents, you'll need a style guide to help editors maintain consistency and correctness online. You'll have to add guidelines on standard headers and footers, electronic images, colors, use of tables and lists, file names and directory organization, and other Web-specific issues.

Several organizations have put together style guides for their Web documents. One of the most comprehensive is that of the Yale Center for Advanced Instructional Media. The address is **http://info.med.yale.edu/caim/StyleManual_Top.HTML**. Look at it and others to get ideas for making your own guide. You can find a list of Web style guides in the Yahoo index; the address is **http://www.yahoo.com/Computers_and_Internet/Software/Data_Formats/HTML/Guides_and_Tutorials/**.

Informal documents have a place on the Web, too. Just be sure to add disclaimers or other notices indicating how official they are or are not. In his "Style Guide for Online Hypertext," Tim Berners-Lee, director of the W3 Consortium (an industry consortium based at the Massachusetts Institute of Technology that coordinates the development of the Web), says,

> Some information is definitive, some is hastily put together and incomplete. Both are useful to readers, so do not be shy to put information up which is incomplete or out of date—it may be the best there is.

The address is **http://www.w3.org/hypertext/WWW/Provider/Style/.**

How will editing change?

One difference between the Web and paper is important in editing: Web documents can be changed after publication. That eases the pressure of the quest for perfection (but don't get too sloppy). When you find a typo on your home page, you can fix it immediately. With a book, you have to wait until the next printing.

Ease of revision can also make an editor's job harder. Because Web pages are so easy to change, readers expect frequent updates. A publication that was revised every year when it was on paper might need to have smaller revisions every month if it moves to the Web.

Part of the editor's job (on paper or online) is to be an advocate for readers. But on the Internet it can be hard to know who your readers are and how they're using your pages. Knowing more about the way people use the Internet itself will help you serve the readers you're publishing for. Editors are going to be living in interesting times.

—Keith C. Ivey

Multimedia Storyboarding for Technical Writers

The credits for the better projects include technical communicators

Multimedia—there's that word again. When it's covered in the popular press, the expert source is often some hotshot multimedia producer or virtual reality guru. But in real life, developing multimedia projects involves steps and processes similar to those used to develop traditional media. Is there a place in multimedia development for writers? The answer is a resounding yes. In fact, it's a symbiotic relationship: The medium needs talented messengers.

Who's who in multimedia?

At present, most multimedia development is being done by technically sophisticated programmers with a creative streak and the ability to string a few sentences together. Writers are in the same situation they were in with respect to the software industry during the 1960s and 1970s. At that time, much of the computer documentation was written by programmers after the code was complete. This functionally oriented documentation, generally written in a software-centric way, wasn't geared to the typical user.

Today, many multimedia projects are being developed the same way. However, when you review the better (and sometimes more popular) multimedia products on the market, the credits often include not only programmers, graphic designers, and technicians, but also technical communicators. Why are the producers of these CDs using tech writers? They've discovered that writers can transfer not only their unique skills and attention to detail and consistency, but also their willingness to work as part of a creative team.

Writers can join the multimedia team

Like other forms of electronic communication, multimedia products require specialized skills and experience. But possibly more than in other areas, multimedia development is truly a team effort. By definition, projects that include several media call for a cast of specialists.

Most teams consist of video and audio specialists, multimedia programmers, instructional designers, artists—and technical communicators. Before beginning their respective tasks, team members all need to understand the scope of the project and how the content will be presented. One way to provide structure for a complex project is to create a *storyboard*—a kind of game plan for the process.

True storyboarding isn't a tool all technical communicators are familiar with, but tech writers (working with graphic artists) can set up a *storyboard script* that in essence is an outline of the content in both textual *and* visual form—the structure is needed to begin development. Tech writers know how to write procedural information as steps in an overall task structure, so the storyboards they create can steer other team members who are developing individual multimedia elements. Most important, storyboarding needs writers with the ability to say more with less.

Project storyboarding precedes the script

The term *storyboard*, originally used in the motion picture industry, refers to a set of drawings that document the progression of a story from beginning to end. Containing the visual elements of a comic book, the storyboard also depicts the angles from which the film will be viewed. It's a way to visualize the final product without the expense of shooting any film. Generally, a motion picture storyboard is created after the screen writer has completed the script.

In multimedia, this process is often reversed: A project storyboard may be one of the first things developed, with scripting added later. *Project storyboards* may be as simple as a diagram sketched on a luncheon napkin or a white board, or notes grouped on 3-by-5-inch cards, or components organized as a flowchart. A rough schematic guide to the elements of a project helps team members agree on the overall scope and the order in which elements will be presented.

The storyboard script is a diagram

After the project storyboard is reviewed and modified, it's expanded to include more detailed information. The resulting *storyboard script* is organized sequentially and the information about each screen it contains may include

- a *thumbnail* sketch (a small drawing) of all images,
- an identification of the source of any sounds,
- an identification and description of any animation or video, and
- all the text that will appear on the screen.

Storyboard scripts may look like a table or a printed form, with categories for listing important information about how the project will work, including navigation, all the user actions that can take place from each screen, and the responses that each user action will evoke. For example, correct and incorrect answers to questions, additional feedback, and comments are listed and clearly explained.

Some storyboard scripts are developed by creative staff in such detail that they can be turned over to programmers or multimedia *authors* (a slightly misleading name for the people who integrate the segments) to assemble into the final product.

Multimedia content is more visual to begin with than even other online communication systems, such as online help, and the *media* in multimedia sometimes compete with one another. Graphic elements include simple pictures, animations, and video, not to mention navigational features (menus and buttons), all candidates for valuable screen real estate. It's the writer's job to make sure that text is clear, concise, and powerful enough to hold its own and deliver information.

The verities of clear communication apply

At its best, multimedia uses the computer to inform, teach, and entertain people with text, pictures, animation, video, or sound. An electronic press kit that hypes a rock star's latest CD, the multimedia kiosk that directs you to a new bookstore in an unfamiliar mall, the online quick demo that comes with that new piece of software you're learning, the touchscreen that locates the newest exhibit in your favorite museum—all of them use multimedia.

Impressive technology and marketing hype aside, the success of these and other multimedia tools is measured by how logically and reliably they help people find out what they want or need to know. And that success begins with anticipating how people will follow directions, respond to cues, use search options, and build on a given set of data to create new connections.

At its heart, multimedia is just a sophisticated form of communication that relies on the clear and simple organization and explanation of complex information. That's a job description for a technical writer, but the lessons that technical communicators have learned from traditional publishing are not just marketable in the game plan of multimedia but essential to its future: The quality of the content of multimedia products and publications is what makes the difference to users once the novelty has worn off.

—John Zuchero

Contributors

Ellie Abrams, owner of ESA Editorial and Training Services, is a freelance editor and trainer. She was an associate editor for *The New York Public Library Writer's Guide to Style and Usage.*

Malcolm E. Barker is the author and publisher of *Book Design & Production for the Small Publisher*, as well as a series of California travel guides, available directly from Londonborn Publications, P.O. Box 77246, San Francisco, CA 94107.

Karen M. Belton has a B.S. degree in chemistry from St. Mary's College of Maryland and an M.A.S. degree in business from The Johns Hopkins University. She is the managing editor of the *Johns Hopkins APL Technical Digest,* which is published quarterly by The Johns Hopkins University Applied Physics Laboratory.

Bruce O. Boston has been president of Wordsmith, Inc., a writing and editorial firm in the Washington, DC, area, since 1976. He was editor of *The Editorial Eye* from 1984 to 1988 and a contributing columnist from 1984 to 1992.

Susan Bury is chair, since 1983, of Stauffer Bury Inc., a Washington, DC, corporate writing and project management company that provides speeches, annual reports, marketing material, and management news and information. She is president of the Washington Humane Society.

Patricia Caudill is a quality control specialist for EEI and trains all of EEI's new proofreaders. A former secondary school English teacher, she has been doing editorial work for 25 years.

Judy Cleary is a senior editor and project manager at EEI. She previously worked as a magazine and book editor in California and Colorado.

Robin A. Cormier is EEI's vice president for design, editorial, and production services. She is the author of *Error-Free Writing: A Lifetime Guide to Flawless Business Writing* and was an associate editor for *The New York Public Library Writer's Guide to Style and Usage.*

Mia Cunningham, an EEI editor since 1988, developed a training workshop on substantive editing for EEI and taught it until spring 1996. Her biography of Anna Eikenhout Hubbard—wife of Harlan Hubbard, a well-known Kentucky painter and writer—will be published in 1998.

Elisabeth Dahl is an editorial specialist and writer at EEI. She has taught English for Georgetown University.

Rick Darby, a senior editor at the Flight Safety Foundation, worked as a writer and project manager for EEI and as an advertising copywriter and radio announcer.

Catherine Dettmar has been indexing for EEI since 1988. She has taught aerobic dance since 1980 and enjoys traveling with her husband.

Karen Feinberg, a resident of Cincinnati, has worked as a freelance writer and editor since 1982.

Catharine Fishel, former editor of *Step-By-Step Graphics* magazine, runs Catharine & Sons, an editorial services firm that improves the communication value of corporate products.

Judith Goode is president of a consulting firm that offers corporate information analysis and design to companies, Online Editor, Inc., based in Boulder, Colorado.

Gerald Gross has been an editor for over 40 years. He is the editor of *Editors on Editing: What Writers Need to Know About What Editors Do* and lectures at writers' conferences. A partner in Gross Associates, he lives in Croton-on-Hudson, New York.

Kathryn Hall is EEI's production manager. Her work in the publishing industry includes a stint in Costa Rica, where she wrote and translated training manuals.

Keith C. Ivey is a technical editor and the webmaster for EEI. He writes a monthly column, "Untangling the Web," for *The Editorial Eye.*

Edward D. Johnson, a longtime book editor, is author of *The Handbook of Good English,* published in paperback by Washington Square Press and in hardcover by Facts On File.

Linda B. Jorgensen is editor of *The Editorial Eye* and was an associate editor of *The New York Public Library Writer's Guide to Style and Usage.*

Claire W. Kincaid has been president of EEI since 1983. She previously worked in other positions at the firm and was a technical writer and editor at the Office of Naval Research in London.

Amy Lenihan, a senior project manager at EEI, was EEI's production manager from 1994 to 1996.

Mindy McAdams, an independent consultant on information design based in Toronto and Washington, DC, was part of the small team that created the *Washington Post*'s first online edition in 1994. She worked as a copy editor for 11 years. Her home page may be found at http://www.well.com/~mmcadams/.

Lee Mickle is a senior project manager at EEI. She has also served as a proofreader, editor, and production manager for the firm.

Mark R. Miller is the publications director for the Corporation for National Service, which oversees AmeriCorps and other service programs. For the first two years of the Clinton administration, he was senior editor for the Presidential Letters and Messages office.

Ann R. Molpus was editor of *The Editorial Eye* from 1988 to 1992. She is an events and publications manager for the Development Office of the Duke University Medical Center in Durham, North Carolina.

Connie Moy is an account executive for EEI. She previously managed the firm's proofreading/quality control division and was an associate editor of *The New York Public Library Writer's Guide to Style and Usage.*

Catherine Petrini is the author of 14 pseudonymous novels for young adults and the co-author of *Opportunities in Training and Development Careers.* Formerly managing editor of *Training and Development* magazine, she is a national officer for the National Federation of Press Women.

Arthur Plotnik's books include *The Elements of Expression* (Henry Holt), a fall 1996 offering of the Book-of-the-Month and Quality Paperback Book Clubs, and *The Elements of Editing* (Macmillan). He is editorial director of the American Library Association Editions in Chicago.

James Rada, Jr. has been a freelance writer for six years. His first two novels were published this year: *Beast,* an Internet horror novel (Renlow Publishing), and *Logan's Fire,* an adventure book for young adults (Covenant Communications). He has done marketing and technical writing for national and international corporations.

Jane Rea, manager of EEI's editorial services, has been a proofreader, editor, and quality control expert for 20 years. Before coming to EEI she was a project manager for the Department of Health and Human Services.

Gail E. Ross is a media lawyer, literary agent, and publishing consultant in Washington, DC. She is a popular speaker on the topics of electronic publishing, evolving copyright law, and fair use.

Mary J. Scroggins, a past president of the Board of Directors of Washington Independent Writers, is a writer, editor, instructor, and publications consultant with more than 20 years of experience, She is the owner and president of Nekima, Inc., a small publications firm, and a volunteer storyteller and public school writing mentor.

Dianne Snyder has been a freelance editor, writer, and trainer for many years in the Washington, DC, area. She is the author of a children's book, *The Boy of The Three-Year Nap.*

Anne H. Soukhanov writes the column "Word Watch" for the *Atlantic Monthly.* The author of *Word Watch: The Stories Behind the Words of Our Lives* (Holt, 1995), she was executive editor of *The American Heritage Dictionary of the English Language,* 3d ed.

David Stauffer is president, since 1983, of Stauffer Bury Inc., a Washington, DC, corporate writing company that provides speeches, annual reports, marketing material, management news and information, and writing committee management. He currently holds the volunteer position of board member and services chair of the National Capital Chapter of the American Red Cross.

Mary Stoughton is senior editor at EEI and the author of *Substance and Style: Instruction and Practice in Copyediting.* She is also an associate editor of *The New York Public Library Writer's Guide to Style and Usage.*

Andrea J. Sutcliffe, a freelance book editor in Basye, VA, was the lead editor of *The New York Public Library Writer's Guide to Style and Usage* and EEI's vice president for publications from 1992 to 1996. She has worked as an editor for 20 years.

Jayne O. Sutton is a senior publications project manager and trainer with EEI. She has worked in print production since 1980 on projects ranging from direct mail to government publications. She is a frequent contributor to *The Editorial Eye* on print production and management topics.

Priscilla S. Taylor is a senior EEI editor and the editor of Phi Beta Kappa's quarterly newsletter, *The Key Reporter.* She is also a former editor of *The Editorial Eye.*

Craig Tyler has been writing advertising and promotional copy for industrial and high-tech clients since 1979 in New York, Philadelphia, and Washington, DC.

Diane Ullius runs Word Tamers, a training/consulting firm that focuses on improving written and oral communications. She bases her training on some 20 years' experience in publishing.

Bill Walsh, copy desk chief at *The Washington Times,* runs "The Slot: A Spot for Copy Editors" on the World Wide Web (http://www.theslot.com).

Maron L. Waxman, associate director of special publishing at the American Museum of Natural History, was editorial director of Harper Reference and executive director of book development at Book-of-the-Month. She has taught at the Publishing Institute at City University of New York and The Center for Publishing at New York University.

Elizabeth Whalen is a medical writer for Alliance Pharmaceutical Corp. (San Diego, CA). In a 20-year editorial career, she has run her own consulting business, worked in academic, medical journal, and computer industry settings, and taught medical editing in Beijing. She coordinates and teaches in the Copyediting Certificate program at the University of California and teaches biomedical writing to Chinese researchers via the Internet.

Alex White is a visual communication consultant and professor of graphic design at the Hartford Art School of the University of Hartford, Connecticut. He is the author of *Type in Use: Effective Typography for Electronic Publishing.*

John Zuchero develops multimedia computer-based training for Unisys Corporation and is a freelance writer covering topics about the impact of technology on technical writers and editors. His column "Eye on Change" appears every other month in *The Editorial Eye.*

Index

The Editorial Eye

66 Canal Center Plaza, Suite 200
Alexandria, VA 22314-5507
phone: 703-683-0683
fax: 703-683-4915
e-mail: eye@eei-alex.com
web: http://www.eei-alex.com/eye/

Start my subscription to *The Editorial Eye!*

☐ **2 Years**—24 Issues for $168/Canadian $188/Foreign $208
☐ **1 Year**—12 Issues for $99/Canadian $109/Foreign $119

Multiple copy and group subscription discounts available on request.
For fastest service, phone in or fax your order.

Send to

Name, Title _____

Company _____

Address _____

City, State _____ ZIP _____

Payment options

☐ Check enclosed (*make payable to EEI*).
   D.C. residents add 5.75% tax

☐ Charge my ☐ Visa ☐ MasterCard ☐ American Express

Account # _____ Exp. Date _____

Signature _____ Date _____

Daytime Phone: _____

☐ Bill me (companies only). Purchase order attached.

Bill to (if different)

Name, Title _____

Company _____

Address _____

City, State _____ ZIP _____

Guarantee: If *The Editorial Eye* doesn't meet your needs,
the balance of your subscription will be refunded for the asking.